SPORTS ETHICS

A Reference Handbook

SPORTS ETHICS

A Reference Handbook

Lawrence H. Berlow

CONTEMPORARY WORLD ISSUES

ABC-CLIO

Santa Barbara, California
Denver, Colorado
Oxford, England

Library of Congress Cataloging-in-Publication Data

Berlow, Lawrence H., 1945–.
    Sports ethics : a reference handbook / Lawrence H. Berlow.
      p. cm. — (Contemporary world issues)
    Includes bibliographical references and index.
    1. Sports—Moral and ethical aspects—Handbooks, manuals, etc.
  I. Title. II. Series
  GV706.3.B47 1994   796′.01—dc20   94-34467

ISBN 0-87436-769-7 (alk. paper)

00 99 98 97 96 95 94   10 9 8 7 6 5 4 3 2 1

ABC-CLIO, Inc.
130 Cremona Drive, P.O. Box 1911
Santa Barbara, California 93116-1911

For Barbara, Amy, and Corey

Contents

Preface

This book attempts to provide a guide to sports ethics by presenting some of the major questions in sports, and then by providing varied resources and documents for further examination. Chapter 1 discusses various questions concerning ethics in sports. Chapter 2 is a chronology of sports-related events that have touched on ethical issues. Chapter 3 provides brief biographies of individuals that have had an impact on ethical issues in sports. Chapter 4 examines documents related to sports ethics, while chapters 5 and 6 provide a directory of organizations and print and nonprint resources.

Acknowledgments

Many people helped with this book. I'm thankful for the many people who helped me navigate in the universe of sports studies, and those who encouraged my efforts.

Paul Turner suggested several fruitful lines of inquiry in the early stages of the book, and Bob Baird helped clarify many important threads in the book. Both tolerated endless questions about people, places, and bits of sports trivia and always responded helpfully with the utmost patience and grace.

I'm grateful for the assistance and friendship provided by Michelle Zmajkovic who helped with several essential steps in my research, and calmly withstood outbursts of frustration, delight, anxiety, and obsessive excitement as the book progressed.

George Yansik of the Suffern Library Reference Department was a tremendous help in locating sources, suggesting methods for research and fact checking, and calmly assisting me with research requests for obscure but necessary information. Carol Cutler, also of the Suffern Library Reference Department, provided many useful suggestions in the early research stage.

The organizations and experts I contacted for information or assistance were almost uniformly helpful and friendly. Professor David Gough and Dr. Charles Yesalis responded to requests for assistance with information and suggestions that went far beyond what was asked. Gayle Bodin at the USOC went to exceptional lengths to assist me and to see that I received needed material on time.

David W. Montgomery deserves special thanks for his assistance. When I first contacted David, I was seeking someone who could render a window into the academic worlds of ethics, sociology, and philosophy. He provided all of that, and also made many valuable suggestions which helped me focus and clarify my work.

In addition, he freely offered me access to his own research files and book collection, which aided me immensely. Most importantly, his ongoing encouragement and interest was a major source of strength to me. Of the experiences I went through in writing the book, the most important to me is having found a new friend in David.

Special recognition goes to my family, which found the strength to bear with me as I worked. My wife, Barbara, assisted in much of the research and in the final preparation of the manuscript, and patiently accepted all of the problems that accompany a major project. Amy was a continual source of encouragement and optimism, and provided quick response to last-minute fact-checking problems. Corey calmly tolerated and accepted my unusual and disruptive work schedule, and made it his business to see that I didn't wander too far from the computer and the library. This book is dedicated to them, with gratitude.

1

Introduction

SPORT, IN ALL OF ITS ASPECTS—amateur, professional, individual, team, and even as a form of self-competition—is an integral part of our world.

Millions of us compete in one sport or another, and millions of us compete against ourselves. We jog, run, swim, organize pickup games, and more. Many of us assiduously watch the activities and antics of our favorite teams and players, making the activity of being a fan an important, if not consuming, part of our lives. The extent of the relationship between sport and society is not easy to delineate, though its importance cannot be doubted. Thomas Kean, former governor of New Jersey, has observed that it is unclear whether sport is a mirror of society, or society a mirror of sport:

> The sports world is in crisis. Even as professional leagues continue to set attendance records, even as the NCAA basketball tournament kitty fattens with each mad March, the X's and O's of athletic competition must themselves compete with scandals, rumors, and revelations for space on the news pages and programs that expose and exploit sports controversies. At times it is difficult to know whether these incidents set or follow the mood of society.[1]

Why is sport so important to us? Perhaps because the sports universe is so large and visible, it is natural to assume that there is a back and forth flow between our everyday lives and what happens on the field. In many ways, the sports universe can seem better and easier to understand than our everyday lives. Sports seem to operate according to well-defined rules. The seeming decisiveness with which sports operate appeals to a natural pleasure in seeing things resolved in black and white. Even an insider such as a baseball umpire, who knows that his calls are not always clear-cut, wants it to be so and will rarely if ever change a decision.

We frequently use sport as a way of viewing the world. National Basketball Association (NBA) Commissioner David Stern noted that "sports has become a place where more people get more information than any other place. . . . AIDS, with Magic [Johnson]. Due process, with Pete Rose. If you want to engage people in dialogue, it's almost easier to do it in sports, as if it's a safe place."[2]

Many people believe that sports, especially college sports, are important contributors to the development of the adult man and woman. Russell W. Gough, an assistant professor of philosophy at Pepperdine University, says that "sports build character. . . . People inside and outside college sports must recognize that so we can treat athletics programs as they should be treated—as playing a significant role in higher education and moral development."[3]

How do we relate aggressiveness and violence in sports with the rest of our lives? Are they acceptable on the playing field and not off of it? Should aggression and violence in sport be curbed in one way or another to make sport a reflection of our desires for an ideal world?

Don Atyeo notes that, following the publication of Konrad Lorenz's *On Aggression,* there was some imaginable justification for violent sports. Lorenz proposed, and some psychologists and sociologists agreed, that "the main function of sports today lies in the cathartic discharge of aggressive urge. . . . "[4] Lorenz's view of the social usefulness of sport is disproved in many ways, including the violence and aggression that takes place off the field and after sporting events (i.e., the effect of observing violence in sport has increased and not decreased violence elsewhere).

Nor is it at all clear that sports aggression and violence are an inevitable reflection of ourselves. If there is a link between aggressive behavior and our taste for aggressive sports, it is far from being a hopelessly deterministic one. Felicity Huntingford and Angela Turner point out that "the probability that people will show aggression . . . increases if such behavior is condoned or justified by peers or society at large. . . ." Human behavior, even behavior dictated by biology, can be mediated by society: "The means of preventing and controlling human aggression are available to us, but they are sociological and political rather than biological in nature."[5]

Our children are constantly encouraged to join in sports. In school systems throughout the country, sports and athletics are considered essential parts of the curriculum. Few if any school districts would dare to announce that, in pursuit of academic goals, the physical education staff would be fired and the gyms and playgrounds replaced with additional classrooms. Outside of the schools, we enroll our children in a dazzling array of sport activities, typified by Little League baseball and Pop Warner football. Children's leagues for almost every conceivable sport exist wherever a sport is played—on local, regional, statewide, and national levels.

Sports (or at least games) have worked themselves into our everyday lives. In 1963, for example, most readers understood the topic, if not the contents, of Eric Berne's *Games People Play;* the analogy was to sport. Berne presented relationships and problems among people as game-playing situations; the actions of individuals and of groups were comparable, though sometimes unconsciously so, to the goal-oriented tactics and strategies of sport. Relationships, in Berne's view, were healthier when the motivations and goals of those involved were clearly focused on the goal or goals to be achieved. Today, the word *player* is in common usage to refer to anyone competing in a particular field. A radio commentator, for example, said in early 1994, "Because of the snow, not many *players* were on Wall Street today." Though it would be simplistic to consider sport and games as a complete metaphor for our lives, there can be no doubt that we often want our lives to have the same decisiveness and rule-based clarity that we find in sport. Even if close examination shows it is not always so, sports *seem* to have a beginning, middle, and end, a standard of achievement (a score), clear limits on what is acceptable behavior and what is not, and the opportunity for individual glory as well as the chance to contribute to the success of the group.

It is important to try to understand the values that we bring to and demand of sports. The study of these values, of our desires and impressions of sports and of sports' relationship to society, comprises sports ethics. While a scientifically rigorous definition may be difficult, it may be worthwhile to take a look at one definition provided by David Gough. Gough says, "Ethics is not merely a manual of do and don't rules. . . . Ethics is also an established way of doing things, a shared sense of values, goals, and significance. And it is above all a matter of *character*, which very often cannot be measured in terms of obedience to rules."[6] Because sports are so important to us, the relationship between sport and society is symbiotic. Professional football, for example, would simply not exist if there were no public to watch and appreciate the game. Society, on the other hand, draws inspiration from watching the progress of sports, believing that sports are played according to a higher and more worthy set of rules.

Sports rules and ethics involved in the play of the game are ideals; unlike social ethics, which have evolved over long periods of time, organized sports are more of an attempted utopia created over a short period of time. Organizers begin with certain principles that they want their sport to observe (no tackling after the flag falls, for example). If a question arises, either a quick decision is issued by a high authority or a conference is held to resolve the issue. Penalties are also clearly defined; in basketball, for example, a player with five personal fouls must leave the game, and cannot be replaced. The players who have *been* fouled are allowed retribution via free throws.

Like society itself, different sports embody different constellations of attitudes and beliefs. The message of ice hockey's penalty box, for example, is that rule violations most certainly will occur, and are perfectly acceptable if the player and/or the team are willing to accept the penalty of temporary removal from the game. Similarly, there are many who feel that society should teach that "if you can't do the time, don't do the crime." A logician would point out that this is the same as "do the crime if you can do the time." In comparison to ice hockey, some other sports will not tolerate "crime" regardless of the player's willingness to accept a penalty. The tennis world's emphasis on "appropriate" individual conduct is an exemplar—too many brusque words directed at a linesman or opponent, or even an excessive display of pique at one's own failings is not acceptable. If sports reflect the ethics of society, they also reflect the confusion of society's ethics.

Ethics are not only about crimes (or fouls), but about how we deal with one another in everyday situations, how we attempt to resolve an endless string of questions about what is an appropriate way to live. What is the relationship of the individual, and of his or her goals, to the goals of society or of a particular group? What methods of advancement or achievement are acceptable, and what are not? What are our responsibilities to others? What is the group's responsibility to the individual? What do we want our children to learn when they are outside the home? The same questions and dilemmas have their equivalents in sports. What is fair play? What is unfair? Should a team depend upon a few chosen "star" players, or should all members of the team be encouraged to do their best? How should team owners treat their players? How should players relate to team owners? What should an athlete's relationship and responsibilities to fans be? Should sports be ahead of the rest of society or just keep up with it in dealing with social issues such as discrimination? Is achievement in sport sufficient to make one a luminary elsewhere? What values should be taught to youngsters participating in youth sports?

At least in post-Victorian Western society, play had been looked upon as something that only children do; hobbies and sport activities for adults were pastimes that had little or nothing to do with the way our essential, everyday lives were structured. Nineteenth and early twentieth century American newspapers dealt only with what we would today call "hard news." The addition of sports news to the pages of the popular press was usually considered by the publishers to be a way of increasing circulation, rather than a reflection of an area of genuine news interest.

For many years, the serious study of sports as a social phenomenon, as a reflection of our cultural ethos, did not exist. One part of the American experience involved taking sports and play seriously, but the common belief was that, underneath it all, sports and games did not really matter. Attitudes began to change after World War II, perhaps because of the increased leisure time available to many of us in the postwar economic boom. The recognition of the importance of sports in our lives began to be acknowledged in the academic world with the publication of Johann Huizinga's *Homo Ludens* (1950). Among a slew of important observations and conclusions, Huizinga, a philosopher and a sociologist, correctly characterized those of us who make up society, both male and female, as "game-playing."

Within a few years of Huizinga's work, the study of sport had become a legitimate academic activity, with studies appearing in all of the social sciences, especially philosophy, sociology, psychology, and anthropology. At the same time, newspapers and magazines, which had focused on sports as a matter of reporting, began to also cover ethical issues (though few would have put it so baldly).

Both popular and academic books began to appear which tried to understand and evaluate the place of sports in our world, including Paul Weiss' *Sport: A Philosophical Inquiry* (1969) and Robert Lipsyte's *SportsWorld* (1975).

Today, in the first half of the 1990s, there are few sports magazines or newspapers that do not regularly publish "conscience stories," articles that challenge our ideas about sports and morality or disclose the seamier side of sports.

A Review of the Problems

When our children are young, we are likely to enroll them in some form of organized sport such as Little League baseball, Pop Warner football, Police Athletic League basketball, or some other locally or nationally organized sport.

Though the experience is frequently a satisfying one for both the parent and the child, there are often times when the reality of children's sports differs greatly from the ideal. Most of us know one or two children or adults who have withdrawn from a league or sport program because an activity that should have been enjoyable and healthy had turned onerous or ugly.

College athletes, particularly those few chosen to participate in National Collegiate Athletic Association (NCAA) Division I programs, find themselves in a world where they are pulled in many directions. Their athletic programs may not be designed with education as the main goal. Though most coaches are committed to their athletes' education, there are enough instances where the athlete can have legitimate questions about the role that college sports should and does play in his or her life.

While we would like to idolize or make role models of sports professionals, we sometimes find that, like some entertainment stars off stage, and like people in the world around us, not all professional sports-persons are the nicest people around. What do we expect of athletes, especially professional athletes, in terms of being role models? Are our expectations legitimate, or are we burdening athletes with an unfair responsibility? Does rape become a more serious crime when it is committed by a heavyweight boxing champion? Is it right to expect star athletes who earn far more than they could ever need for a lavish lifestyle to "give something back?"

Discrimination against women, homosexuals, and racial minorities, though far from the exaggerated separatism of only a few years ago, still exists in sport, both amateur and professional. Drug abuse, which is a national social problem, is found in sports as well as everywhere else. Does the treatment of these issues in sports reflect the way our society treats these issues, or is the world of sports behind, or even ahead of, the rest of us in resolving these important problems?

The relationships between professional players and team owners has never been as pleasant or relaxed as team owners would wish for us to think. Professional players, both black and white, have not failed to make the occasional comparison between themselves and slaves on a pre–Civil War plantation.

Professional athletes, white as well as black, female as well as male, and golfers and tennis players along with baseball and basketball players, know that many of the people who own their contracts, manage their venues, and broker their deals, even the people who cheer at their games, often think of them as expensive, but fungible, subhuman pets who can do wonderful tricks but little else.[7]

Relationships between owners and players, especially when it comes time to write bargaining agreements, have sometimes come to resemble the acrimonious strife that is more commonly seen in some industrial labor-management difficulties. While fans are distressed by the idea of athletes actually striking, there may be valid reasons for professionals to deal with economic issues in the same way that workers in other industries deal with theirs.

It is clear that both American and international sports are far from the ideal worlds that fans would like to imagine. Because we expect sport to be special—an ideal world populated by people who *achieve* by following the rules that lead directly to success—we also expect those involved in sports to hew to higher ethical standards than we see around us in other areas. The challenge both for the observer and the participant is to first understand what the ethical problems of sports are, to determine what, if anything, can and should be done to solve those problems, and, finally, to consider if those problems can be solved in sports without solving them within the society at large. The ultimate questions that each of us must answer are: To what extent is sport a reflection of society, and to what extent should sport be expected to reflect the best in our society?

Degrees of Play

Children in Sports

The problems of tennis star Mary Pierce combine, in an extreme case, all of the heart-rending difficulties that a concerned parent has with his talented child's career with the further problem of including a father who is, at minimum, verbally abusive, and who seems likely to allow his abuse to become physical.

Mary Pierce began her professional tennis career at the age of 12 and as she rapidly acquired a reputation as an up-and-coming professional star, her father, just as rapidly, acquired a reputation as a verbally abusive parent. From time to time, Jim Pierce, a several-times convicted criminal and former Marine (reportedly dishonorably discharged) was banned or removed from various tournaments in which his daughter was playing. Almost invariably, Mary's play was steadier and better when her father was not in the stands.

By 1993, when Mary was 18, her mother had separated from Jim. Mary now makes it a practice to seek a court order of protection from her father in whatever locality she is playing. Jim's picture is posted in ticket booths in an effort to prevent him from even buying a general-admission ticket.

Even without the verbal abuse and the possibility of physical abuse, it is likely that tennis has taken some psychological toll on the former child star. Mary told *Sports Illustrated* in 1993: "I would like to have stayed in school, gone to a prom."[8] Mary's 1994 performances at tournaments, including the French Open, fortunately seem to reflect an admirable resilience. Without her father around, she plays an intense game on court, coupled with a relaxed and happy attitude toward herself off the court.

Tennis is the professional sport that most visibly stresses its young stars. Though the reasons are not clear, Jennifer Capriati withdrew from tennis in early 1994, announcing that she was going to finish high school. Many other young players besides Capriati and Pierce seem to have been subjected to the demands of professionalism without benefit of teen-hood. In some cases, perhaps most, there is no visible damage in the long run; on the other hand, it is hard to believe that leading an abnormal life, a grownup's life when only in one's teens, doesn't have some detrimental effect.

Cindy Hahn, in her articles, has made several suggestions for improving the stressful life of youngsters on the tennis circuit. Among her suggestions are limiting the number of tournaments, depending on age, in which young players can participate; limiting participation in the Grand Slams (International) to players 16 or over; requiring a minimum educational level of a high school diploma or equivalent for anyone in "the tour" or for membership in the Association of Tennis Professionals (ATP) or the World Tennis Association (WTA); hiring multilingual tutors at the tournaments; having players' unions hire psychologists to help deal with the stress of professional tennis; requiring annual physical exams from specialists in sports medicine; and establishing and enforcing physical fitness standards.

Tennis is not the only sport that can seriously impinge on young athletes. Sports where youth is a prerequisite to high achievement, such as gymnastics, figure skating, and swimming, can demand such concentration and commitment that there is little room for a normal childhood. Oksana Baiul, the 1994 Olympic figure-skating star, is frequently portrayed as someone who spends all of her time practicing, and little of her time being a teenager. That Baiul and others do not seem to protest is beside the point; their lives are radically different than those of other young people. In deciding to encourage their commitment, the adults in charge are deciding that athletic achievement is adequate recompense for the different life. Some of Hahn's suggestions for youths playing professional tennis could well be applied in other sports.

Even in local school and league amateur sports, there is always the opportunity for a youngster to be pushed too far, too fast. Most medical doctors would firmly recommend against any type of a special diet for a teenager except in extreme cases. Despite this, it is common practice for high school and college wrestlers and boxers to struggle to "make weight" in a short period of time by dieting to lose weight, or bingeing to gain weight. Weight classifications are extremely narrow, and it is not uncommon for a young athlete to compete in several different categories in a season, depending on where he and the coach feel he is needed. In *Sportswise: An Essential Guide for Young Athletes, Parents, and Coaches*, Dr. Lyle J. Micheli says this about the problem:

> At this very moment, as many as a quarter million young American males may be deliberately starving themselves in order to make

weight in wrestling. Undernourishment, dehydration, anorexia, and bulimia are just a few of the unnecessary occupational hazards of sports such as wrestling, gymnastics, figure skating, and ballet, in which athletes try to control their weight. In the short term, these practices may interfere with normal growth and development. In the long term they may impair basic health.

Bulking up is a practice almost exclusively of high-school or junior-high football players. . . . Without proper nutritional counseling, the practice of bulking up is not only useless but dangerous.[9]

In many youth football leagues, weight as well as age determine the group in which a youngster competes. If a returning player wants to continue with his peers for another season, he or she must sometimes diet or binge to reach the required weight category.

Physical safety can and should be the primary concern of youth sports organizations. There is, however, an alarming number of injuries each year, and it is uncertain if the national rule-making organizations have propagated the most forward-looking safety rules. In baseball, for example, it seems likely that a double-eared batting helmet, if not a full face mask, should be the protection that batters are required to wear, though there is no national rule as of 1993 to that effect.

In youth ice hockey, the practice of "checking," as close to the professional assaultive behavior as possible, is often the reason for significant injuries among children. In youth football, the inclination is undoubtedly to let children play their games on a full-sized field, utilizing all of the forceful plays used by the pros. While this may make the sport seem more "real life" than other games, it is clear that children should be playing on a modified field, scaled down to match their size and age; and, while certain notoriously dangerous plays *may* be acceptable in the professional ranks, they have no place in what should be an amiable activity for younger children.

In an excellent 1992 article, Curt Brown reviewed some of the causes of the large number of injuries each year in youth sports that could have been prevented—or at least mitigated. Large numbers of injuries come from a variety of causes, including lack of appropriate safety equipment, improper activities (Brown's best example is illegal "checking" in ice hockey), and "overuse microtraumas," resulting from young athletes working far beyond the capabilities of their bodies. The overuse injuries are important to understand because they appear even in sports where physical contact does not occur, such as in gymnastics.

Brown also surveys some of the protective equipment available for various sports. Though equipment may help prevent injuries (the clearest example is breakaway bases in youth baseball), other equipment designed to prevent injury needs to be examined carefully. A softer ball in youth baseball, for example, *might* be more dangerous than a conventional hard ball, because a softball might stay in contact with a player's chest longer and exert a pressure over a larger area. Face masks in such sports as hockey and football might well protect the face, but may give the young athlete a feeling of invincibility leading him or her to attempt other dangerous activities such as "spearing" in football games.

In addition to injuries, Brown suggests that the physical strain of athletics as it is currently practiced is preventing many youngsters from benefitting from sports. He cites a survey of 26,000 athletes showing that three-fourths of them had quit playing sports for a variety of reasons, including the quite reasonable conclusion that playing hurt or taking the chance of being hurt is just not fun.

Preventive strategies and hardnosed questions about attitudes toward winning and playing hurt might well help evaluate if a child should be playing in a particular locality's organized sports program.[10]

Apart from physical injury, the most common question in dealing with children's organized sports is whether they are exposed to or initiated into a world of competition which is too psychologically stressful for them. Although most children playing organized youth sports such as Little League have a positive experience, the possibilities for difficulties still exist, and occur often enough for an observer to ask if the experience is truly worthwhile.

Part of this problem is the stereotypical, screaming sideline parent, complemented by the angry, aggressive coach who teaches his charges that "winning isn't everything—it's the only thing." With such a coach or sideline parent encouraging unhealthy competition and displeasure in athletics, children are being taught highly inappropriate values that can be carried over into both adult play areas and other social interactions. Competition is certainly within the range of activities from which children can benefit. The obvious danger, of course, is that the competition can become unwholesome, with the child trying to live out a parent's or coach's unfulfilled dreams by struggling to imitate the overly aggressive adult world, consequently failing to enjoy the competition and the sport as only one part of his or her life. One experienced observer of children's sports noted that the most common parent problems at youth sports events come from unfulfilled parent "wannabes." Rick Wolff, a concerned parent and coach, believes that parents must act to restore appropriate behavior to youth sports. In *Good Sports: A Concerned Parent's Guide to Little League and Other Competitive Youth Sports,* Wolff asserts that

> there are a lot of uneasy signals coming out of our kids' sports leagues in the 1990s. These worrisome signals are early warning signs that the leagues in which our kids play are either flat out of sync with our educational priorities or just not emphasizing fun enough. . . . if you care about your kids' development in sports, it's time to get involved."[11]

In *With the Boys,* sociologist Gary Alan Fine concludes that the possible social damages of too-aggressive league play, along with other potential drawbacks, are not as great as they might seem on first consideration. On the other hand, Fine also believes that many of the touted benefits of organized play are not very real either. He concludes that most organized youth sports, from a sociological point of view, provide a pleasurable experience for those involved—a benefit of childhood that many who are now parents may not have had themselves.[12]

As every youth league coach, manager, umpire-referee, or other official knows, problems with overly aggressive children and overly aggressive parents do occur and must be dealt with occasionally. How well the league and the on-field officials handle that problem is an ongoing, central concern for every local organization. In some localities, the manager of the youth team is held responsible for the behavior of his fans. A team can forfeit a game if a fan becomes too unruly or too vocally aggressive against the opposing team, other players on his child's team, or even his own child.

The NCAA and the College Athlete

College sports in four-year colleges and universities are organized and sanctioned under the umbrella of the National Collegiate Athletic Association (NCAA). NCAA schools are organized into three divisions, according to how much effort a college puts into recruiting and how much it subsidizes the athletes' sports effort in return for admission to the school.

Division I schools are those that invest the most—athletic scholarships, room and board, etc.—and that make a vigorous effort to recruit athletes who will most benefit their athletic programs. Division I schools have national followings, television contracts, and extensive media coverage. Division II schools also offer athletic scholarships, but on a much more modest basis than Division I schools; a significant proportion of students playing Division II sports do not necessarily receive athletic scholarships. Division III schools make use of the NCAA's tournament-organizing ability and other services, but offer student-athletes no special treatment simply because they are athletes.

In return for its imprimatur, the NCAA, in theory, is protecting both the school and the athlete. NCAA regulations dealing with the treatment of athletes seem designed to keep them away from any possible hint of special under-the-table treatment. No athlete at a Division I school, for example, can be given money for transportation to home, and back to school, more than once a year. Athletes may not receive goods and services from "boosters" or fans of the schools who, with sad regularity, seem to think they are helping a school's athletic program by "lending" a car to a sports star, employing him or her for a no-show job, or even distributing cash to favored athletes.

The NCAA's origins trace back to 1906 when, under pressure from President Teddy Roosevelt, collegiate intramural football was organized in an effort to control the large number of football injuries that occurred each year. Through the years, the NCAA grew to encompass other sports besides football, and in 1982 it absorbed the organization that had been formed to handle women's sports. Over the years, the NCAA has grown to the point where, for all practical purposes, it *is* four-year college athletics. (The National Junior College Athletic Association [NJCAA] regulates many intramural sport activities at two-year colleges.)

There are few indeed who feel that the NCAA is doing its job properly. Those who endorse the regulations of the NCAA believe that the organization has hampered its enforcement efforts by not allotting enough money for investigations into numerous serious violations. On the other side, there are many who believe that the NCAA's enforcement efforts are little more than a joke, aimed only at the most grievous and obvious cases, while really acting in a way that seems to countenance an unethical approach to college sports. Still another group of critics has severely criticized the NCAA's investigative techniques as being unfair and dictatorial.

The investigation budget of the NCAA is determined by its membership, primarily coaches, athletic directors, and college presidents. As a rule, the budget for investigation rarely surpasses more than 6 or 7 percent of the organization's budget; this pays for perhaps twenty or thirty investigators. Investigations are begun when obvious signs of improper behavior (such as a local paper's exposé) or other information are brought to the attention of the investigators. Regardless of the integrity of the investigation staff (which is itself rarely the target of scandal), it may be truly impossible to police the American college sport scene adequately.

The NCAA is most vulnerable to criticism of its enforcement efforts when it deals with seemingly minor violations as if they were major ones. The case of Joe Castiglie illustrates many of the problems engendered by current NCAA enforcement practices.

Castiglie was the newly appointed head coach at State University of New York, Stony Brook, a Division III school, in June 1990. He had worked as a part-time coach at Stony Point for six years previously. He resigned after the 1990–1991 basketball season following an NCAA investigation for loaning money to a player. According to Kostya Kennedy, a freelance writer, Castiglie had loaned $118 to a varsity basketball player for a plane ticket home to Buffalo. On the player's return, Castiglie withheld the player's meal money until the loan was paid off.

The NCAA investigation found Castiglie guilty of advancing money to a player in the 1988–1989 season, a violation of NCAA rules. Castiglie, who now says that he was "confused and ... scared," originally denied the loan, both to the school's athletic director and to an NCAA investigator. (There might be some cynics who believe that the denial of wrongdoing to the NCAA was the major sin of the two violations.)

Although Castiglie may not have been the most saintly coach who ever ran a team (there had been a complaint that Castiglie "used harsh and sexually suggestive motivational tactics," which was resolved with a warning to Castiglie from school authorities, *without* determination of guilt or innocence), he certainly seemed to do well for his players. Nineteen of the twenty players that Castiglie coached graduated, a higher percentage than is common in many colleges.

The investigation concluded that, in addition to the denial of wrongdoing which constituted misleading investigators, only the $118 loan was in violation. In contrast, investigation expenses mounted up, including the $906 it cost to fly Castiglie and two other sports department members to North Carolina for a disciplinary hearing. Castiglie resigned, partly in order to prevent penalties from being assessed against the school, and was put under a three-year "show cause" restraint by the NCAA.[13]

Castiglie's situation is not very unusual; most college sports fans (and certainly many coaches) can cite chapter and verse about colleagues (or themselves) being disciplined for bringing an athlete home for a meal, lending a few dollars to a student in need, or even driving a hitchhiking athlete to a game (i.e., improper payment of services with a financial value). In fairness, it should be said that coaches guilty of violations sometimes cite minor violations of which they have been found guilty as examples of NCAA heavy-handedness, but ignore major ones.

The problems raised by the Castiglie incident, and others like it, bring into question the NCAA's effectiveness in distinguishing major from minor violations, and in dealing with situations that are against regulations but which are nonetheless quite likely to occur.

A serious case can and has been made (by Murray Sperber, among others) that the NCAA is not willing to truly police college athletics.[14] In this view, the NCAA is an organization devoted to assisting its members to make money in a variety of ways—developing lucrative television contracts, running highly publicized events, and encouraging a benevolent public view of the sports establishment. Economists Fleisher, Goff, and Tollison, in fact, have suggested in a very persuasive manner that the behavior of the NCAA mirrors the classical model of a cartel that seeks to control market behavior for the benefit of its members.

Cartels are not necessarily bad or evil by design. Organizations are formed, after all, for the purpose of benefiting their members. However, at some point, the groups that are not benefiting from the cartel go from being ignored minorities to being harmed minorities. Understanding the NCAA as a cartel has important benefits for someone interested in understanding the ethical situation in college athletics.[15] NCAA engendered problems, and the NCAA's reactions to these and other problems, are satisfactorily understood (but not excused) when its behavior is seen as a classical reaction of a cartel to a threat against its existence or power. Admittedly, cartel behavior does not explain everything about the NCAA and the collegiate sports world. Although some of the news media is openly hostile to the NCAA, the NCAA's behavior is generally accepted or glossed over—a response that is not explainable by cartel theory.

Certainly NCAA regulation is better than no regulation at all, but the NCAA is composed of representatives of member colleges. And, though the NCAA has, from time to time, alienated certain colleges (as mentioned, it has been criticized for both too-rigorous and too-negligent enforcement), it is, ultimately, an organization created and paid for by the colleges it supervises.

NCAA regulations prohibit the granting of scholarships to athletes who do not meet minimum admission standards of the association, and who do not maintain minimum standard grade levels. These regulations, most recently codified as Article 14.3 (after extensive and heated debate among the members), still allow a college to recruit, grant a scholarship to, and graduate a student who would otherwise be ineligible for admission to that college.

It is understandable why colleges would want to field successful athletic teams—money. A successful football or basketball team in one of the Division I colleges can earn millions of dollars for the school, although the number of schools that actually profit from a successful team may be smaller than is generally thought.[16] Is the scholarship structure of Division I schools appropriate for any institution of higher learning, or is it inimical to the educational purpose of colleges and universities? In 1994, the NCAA was the focus of objections by black college coaches to the NCAA's refusal to restore a higher number of scholarship awards than in 1993, when the limit had been lowered. The coaches argued that athletic scholarships allow minority youths more opportunity for higher education. While some might have the NCAA forbid athletic scholarships totally, others would have the number of scholarships increased.

Having paid athletes with scholarship money to attend, colleges then have a stake in how well their athletes perform. Again the NCAA has some definite regulations about what can and cannot be demanded of a student-athlete in terms of practice hours, schedules, and participation in intramural tournaments. Clearly, though, Division I athletes live in a different world than other students on their campuses.

Though many colleges observe the NCAA regulations, there are always some that do not, and the NCAA frequently turns up instances where athletes have been abused by excessive practice or other sports requirements. Similarly, it is in the interest of colleges to see that athletes stay eligible by passing the courses they are registered for, and there are several schools whose athletic departments operate tutoring and academic referral systems that are the envy of other remedial efforts.

It is against NCAA regulations to offer tutoring to athletes that is not available to other students. If, however, the athletic department is more aggressive than other departments in checking on a student's status in his or her coursework, and in pressing the student in trouble to get assistance, there is no violation. Sometimes doing the right thing can look bad! In reality, of course, aggressively checking on student progress and aggressively helping a student to seek remediation can come close to asking for special favors for an athlete from a teacher.

At the least, then, athletes sometimes get a much larger share of the remedial pie than other students; in return for the dollars earned by these athletes, other students at the college are being shortchanged. In many cases, the money earned by the athletes is not put into the college's regular operating budget, but is jealously guarded by the athletic department and used to build the "department of the future"—bigger, better, more powerful, stronger, and capable of earning even more.

Not only is the student-athlete watched over and cared for excessively, but there are other ways in which he or she comes to realize that the athlete's world is not the world of the everyday student. To begin with, the athletic director and coaches at Division I schools are paid star salaries; while a full professor at a typical campus might earn $50,000 to $60,000 on average, a successful Division I coach or athletic director might well earn a few hundred-thousand dollars. In addition to his or her pay from the college, a coach also has other visible benefits that members of the faculty do not, including being given a regular number of quality seats to athletic events which he or she is free to distribute or sell.

Among other obvious benefits that coaches had up until 1993 was the right to sign contracts with athletic footwear companies. In exchange for requiring students to wear a particular brand of sporting shoe, the coach was usually paid large amounts of money by the shoe company, and the athlete had no choice in the brand of footwear that was seen on the field and court. A single photograph of an endorsed pair of brand-name sneakers on the feet of a player doing something sensational during a sports event can be gold to the shoe companies.

In a 1991 *Washington Post* article which included excerpts from a shoe contract, Bill Brubaker noted that in exchange for the contracts, coaches were generally expected "to make themselves available for promotional efforts, wear the company's symbol during sporting events, and comment favorably about the company's product."[17] Along with cash payments, the companies usually provided a large number of shoes and other equipment to coaches: Unless he or she had an extremely large family, it was more than likely that the clothes would be pressed upon the coaches' players.

Sneaker and apparel contracts had long been an issue among some observers of college sports. Former NCAA Executive Director Dick Schultz had noted that he believes that shoe contracts should be with a college or university, rather than with a coach. "[I]f a university wants to pay a coach $500,000 or $600,000 . . . that's their business." Others believed that there was nothing wro ig with the contracts. John Thompson of Georgetown University, remarked "So all of a sudden it's sinful in this society for a person to be capitalistic? . . . But as long as I live in America, that's exactly what I'm going to be."[18]

With an NCAA rule revision in 1993, the contracts for shoes and other apparel are handled not by the coaches but by the schools themselves; coaches may now receive some of the money that the school receives, according to their contracts or any other legal agreements that they reach. The revision may seem like reform to some, but in the eyes of others, it simply means that it puts colleges rather than apparel companies in the business of paying exorbitant sums to coaches. Problems remain. One potential problem area is in dealing with student athletes who do not want to wear the shoes (or clothing) of the contracted manufacturer. If a student-athlete were to tape over a logo, would he be in violation of the contract which the university signed, and in which he had no voice? In at least one contract that John Weistart knows about, the university indeed commits to not permitting taping-over of a company logo, and to insuring that the free products associated with the contract "remain unaltered." Apart from the contract issue, there is also a clear freedom of speech issue raised. As Weistart, a well-known expert in sports law notes, "The message is unmistakable. Students cannot dissent from a deal that earns their school millions. One can almost hear the A.C.L.U. lawyers opening their law books."[19]

While much of college athletics is still a matter of earnest competition between skilled amateur athletes, there are sufficient reasons to consider deeply the structure of college sports. Do college athletics, especially in "money sports" (basketball, football) at the most powerful schools, fulfill the goals we wish to set for our young athletes? For that matter, do college sports exist for the educational benefit of the young athlete at all, or do they serve the disparate interests of the institutions?

The dangers to athletes and the educational system are clear. Youths are hired as athletes, via scholarships, to attend a school and take part in college activities that can gross large amounts of money for the school and for the coaches. If they are in college to be athletes, and not to be students, they are there for the wrong reason.

Schools exist in order to help their consumers, the students, advance themselves. To have students whose primary purpose at a particular school is to advance the fame and fortune of the college or the university seems a perversion of the principles of education. E. Gordon Gee, president of the University of Colorado, addressed this issue in a 1990 op-ed article appearing on the day that the Colorado team was playing in the Orange Bowl. Gee noted that, in addition to bowl games, there were even calls for a "super bowl" of college football. He stated that "it is clear that calls for a national playoff game are marked by disregard for academic identity and values, and by an unseemly commercialism. We seem to have forgotten that college teams represent colleges, and that student athletes are students first."[20]

Certainly not every coach and college manipulates students solely for the financial benefit of the college and themselves. Yet, the incredibly high salary figures of coaches, the large number of shoe endorsement contracts, and the literally millions of dollars that colleges stand to make or lose by virtue of the strength of their athletic programs, mean that the college athletic system does not exist solely for the physical education of the majority of a school's students.

The effects of the current system of dealing with college athletes are that athletes may find themselves in an academic environment for which they may not be fit, in which their athletic skills are devoted to making money for the school and its coaches, and in which they even give up the right to choose their own shoes.

Additionally, the scholarship terms of NCAA regulations prohibit them from getting almost any other benefit from their efforts than tuition, room and board, and books. Usually required to be in practice 20 hours a week in addition to following a full academic schedule, the college athlete, even the star, may have no choice but to bend NCAA regulations just to have enough money for a date or a trip to the movies. In the view of many, there is more than a passing resemblance here to contractual bondage, if not indentured servitude. The professional though underpaid student athlete, paid only with tuition, room and board, books, and little else, and committed to spending four years performing for the pecuniary benefit of coaches and schools, is not having the typical (and important) college student experience.

When and if the college athlete graduates, even the star finds that his options for a future in sports are extremely limited. According to one tabulation, for example, of approximately 948,000 high school football players, only 150 make it to the National Football League; of approximately 517,000 high-school basketball players, only 50 will make it to the National Basketball Association. Retention rates in both leagues after one year are less than 2.5 percent.[21] Various calculations of the chances of an athlete successfully becoming a professional yield varying results, some even lower than the preceding ones; some are marginally more optimistic, but none suggest that a professional sports career is more than a pipe dream for all but a very, very few.

The Olympic Games

Few major sporting events are so respected, well known, and misunderstood as the Olympic Games. An examination of the Games and its governing organizations discloses several interesting ethical issues with which the generally well-intentioned organizers have to deal. The most misunderstood aspect of the Games, at least in the United States, is the question of amateurism.

A revival of the ancient Greek Olympics, the goal of the modern Olympics, founded by the Baron de Coubertin at the turn of the century (the first modern Olympics were held in Athens, Greece in 1896), is to bring together the world's best athletes in the best possible spirit of healthy competition. Those who compete should ostensibly be those who compete for the pleasure of the sport. Though this definition of the Olympic competitor might resemble our current ideals of "the amateur," it is really quite troublesome. At the least, there is no reason why professional athletes can not enjoy what they do as well as the amateurs. More importantly, if the goal of the Olympics is to show the best that can be done, there is no reason to ban the professional. What the professional has going for him or her are the benefits of constant practice and, theoretically, the best off-field assistance possible (coaches, trainers, etc.).

Certain Olympic sports, notably those traditionally engaged in by the upper classes, never made distinctions about who would or would not be admitted to competition. In these sports (such as shooting or rowing), the only available competitors did not need to compete for money, which they earned outside of their sport, or received from their monied backgrounds. Just as clearly, there were sports in which certain athletes competed solely to make money for themselves, and these professional athletes were not, by late nineteenth-century sensibilities, attuned to the Olympic spirit. That the broad strokes which originally defined the Olympic competitor smack of nineteenth-century classism cannot be denied. To their credit, however, the Games have moved with the times, their organizers aware of and responding to more democratic social currents.

As the Olympics grew, it became obvious that easy distinctions between amateur and professional athletes could not be drawn. Is the college athlete who is sustained by a scholarship a professional? Is the former Olympic contender who tours in an exhibition of his specialty (commercial ice-skating tours are, perhaps, the best example) a professional? Olympic rules began to change, and by 1988 the United States team included the basketball "Dream Team," primarily made up of professional basketball players who, not incidentally, were the best players in the world. These changes are reflected in the International Olympic Committee (IOC) rules in effect today.

Today's Olympic star may well be a professional. If he or she is not, then there is more than a good possibility that he will not be "starving for his art." The United States Olympic Committee (USOC) has an extensive program of financial support and educational services for Olympic winners, and winners of other competitions, which goes far to guarantee that the best athletes get to compete. (For a description of the support program, see chapter 4, page 116.) Eligibility is determined by the athlete's own sport, and though there are differences between amateur and professional, they are nowhere near as severe as they were only a few years ago.

The Olympic movement has other problems besides the question of "amateurism" with which to deal, although generally it has responded well to challenges and difficulties both from within and without the organization.

Like most sports, the Olympic organization has had to face up to the worldwide problem of drug abuse, especially steroid abuse. In the early 1980s, charges of steroid abuse were easily thrust aside, and the uncomfortable dilemma of how to deal with steroids was not one relished by the IOC. The 1988 Olympics, which saw the revered track star Ben Johnson revealed as a steroid user, made it clear the problem could not be wished away.

Although the IOC had banned steroid use, and had installed a program of testing, there were legitimate concerns that the testing was not as efficient as it could be, and that the IOC, as well as the USOC, were not pursuing the matter as strongly as they should. The testing was good enough, however, to catch Johnson, and the revelation that he had used steroids sparked an effort to stamp out steroid and other drug abuse.

The program, though rigorous, seems not to have convinced all of the athletes that steroid abuse would not be tolerated. Regular testing catches drug users regularly, though one would be hard pressed to claim a decrease in usage. In addition to steroid abuse, the IOC also had to deal with such exotic related matters as "blood doping," in which an athlete transfuses some of his blood several weeks before a competition. The blood is then transfused back before the competition, giving the athlete an increased number of oxygen-carrying red blood cells. The increased number of red blood cells might give him or her an advantage, since red blood cells carry oxygen and thus might extend an athlete's stamina. Though forbidden, like steroids, there is, as of mid-1994, no test that will demonstrate that blood doping has occurred (short of careful inspection of each athlete for needle marks in the skin, clearly an impossible task). In addition to the possible advantages blood doping might give an athlete, there are serious dangers arising from such problems as dirty needles or harm from improperly stored blood.

Still another issue that the IOC must deal with on a continual basis is the relationship between sports and politics. The IOC has always insisted that the Games are conducted without reference to international politics. This doesn't mean that the IOC has buried its head in the sand and is refusing to face the constant fire-storms that are impinging on it. Rather, the IOC clearly would prefer to ignore international political movements. As a stated goal, this policy is admirable. Unfortunately, avoiding the po-litical turmoil that besets the world is impossible. The clearest example of this is, of course, the Munich, Germany, raid on the 1972 Olympics by Arab terrorists of the Black September movement.

Even before 1972 the Olympics had been forced to deal with political situations. In 1936, Hitler had hoped the Berlin Olympics would demonstrate the superiority of his "master" race. The boy-cott against South African apartheid was reluctantly joined by the Olympics in 1968. In 1972, the Munich, West Germany Sum-mer Olympic Games were brought to the forefront of the inter-national political arena when they were disrupted by the invasion of the Israeli housing area by Arab terrorists who killed two ath-letes. The next day, the terrorists battled with the police and nine other Israeli athletes were slain

Although it is impossible to comprehend how the terrorists thought that there was a propaganda victory to be won, the Olympics had become an important arena for political statement. The 1976 Olympics were characterized by the absence of several countries that were boycotting South Africa's inclusion in the Games. The United States, which provides one of the largest con-tingents to the Olympics, boycotted the 1980 Moscow Games in protest over the Soviet invasion of Afghanistan. More recently, the 1994 Olympics in Norway were haunted by the recognition that the teams from Bosnia and Herzegovenia, places that were embroiled in an incredibly bloody civil war, would return not to their nations as heroes, but to refugee camps; their homes had long since been destroyed. The high spirits of the Olympics of 1984 in Sarajevo have also been dealt a death-blow, as ten years after the event television and newspapers recorded the kill-ing, brutality, and destruction at the site where the games were held.

Additionally, the IOC, and the national Olympic governing boards (NGBs), also have to deal with the way social movements impinge upon the Olympics. The 1996 Olympics, scheduled for Atlanta, Georgia, is, as of 1994, the site of unrest over the treat-ment of homosexuals. County commissioners in the site chosen for the volleyball championships, Cobb County, passed a resolu-tion declaring that the "life style advocated by the gay community

. . . [is] incompatible with the standards to which this community subscribes." Although the resolution does not ban homosexuals from the county, there is a strong effort from the American gay and lesbian community to insist that this particular venue be moved. In an effort to keep the site of the volleyball competition in the county, officials of Cobb County have "pledged to welcome everyone, including gays. . . ." The IOC has maintained that it has no responsibility to the political agendas of the localities in which it holds its contests. On the other hand, the homosexual community clearly believes that to hold its contests in such a place is an insult to gay and lesbian athletes.

Still another issue arising from the Atlanta site of the Games will be the matter of the Georgia state flag, which bears the confederate symbol. Earlier moves in the statehouse to change the design of the flag because it is offensive to blacks have been rebuffed. With the attention of the world focused on Georgia, the IOC and the USOC might have to deal with this issue.

A more general issue is facing the USOC, brought to light by the attack on figure skater Nancy Kerrigan before the 1994 Olympics— to what extent can and should a sports association (of which the USOC has more than 25 as members) enforce a code of ethics that may be at odds with American law and/or the United States Constitution?

After Nancy Kerrigan was attacked, but before the 1994 Olympics began, Tonya Harding let it be known that she had been aware of, but not reported, the involvement of her former husband in the attack on Kerrigan. Although her failure to report her former husband was likely a violation of criminal law, no guilt had been established in a court of law. When the Figure Skating Association (FSA) scheduled hearings on Harding's involvement, Harding went to court to prevent the FSA from holding a disciplinary hearing. Following the Olympics, a similar situation developed when the FSA action jeopardized Harding's possible place in the World Championship competition in April 1994.

The issue of the FSA's authority was rendered moot, at least for the time being, by Harding's eventual plea agreement to impeding justice; part of her penalty was to resign from the FSA, and thus not participate in further FSA-sanctioned events. The issue remains unresolved, though it is almost certain to come up again in the future, either within the FSA or within some other national sports association.

Should Harding have been suspended for unethical behavior when she had not been convicted (and in fact had not even been indicted) but had possibly violated her sport's code of ethics? For that matter, should a sports administration (either an association or, in the case of professional athletes, a team owner or league) have ethics and conduct rules different from, and usually stricter than, those rules that we have chosen to legislate into law?

Professional Sports

Professional sports are the most visible athletic contests in the United States. Despite the enormous growth of college "money sports" (usually basketball and football), the professional categories most contribute to how we define sports.

Our expectations of professional sports are outgrowths of what we see as the "rights of fans." We have been taught by the professional sports owners that sports exist to please us. We are encouraged to root for our "home team;" a team and its players are presented to us as heroes available for our worship. In 1993, two San Diego Padres fans sued the baseball club following the trades of two important players whom the team had promised to keep in a letter to season ticket holders. The suing fans also cited the team's media guide, which stated that the team "is committed to building a strong and cohesive team, a team consisting of strong management and talented players with the desire to win."[22]

When professional sports organizations behave in ways that strike us as inappropriate, our reaction is to believe that their particular behavior is aberrant, and that we have been individually and collectively betrayed. Those making the decisions undoubtedly have different things on their minds than only our interests. They're concerned with profitability—not an inherently bad concern for *business organizations*.

The oldest sport still played professionally in the United States is baseball. The modern league organization came into being in the 1870s, but it wasn't until 1903, when the first World Series was held involving the American and National Leagues, that these came to be recognized by both the players and the fans as the authoritative baseball structure.

In 1915, an agreement between the American and National Leagues and seven out of eight teams from a rival, upstart group, the Federal League, established the pattern of affiliated minor-league clubs. (The Federal Base Ball Club of Baltimore was the only team that had not joined the agreement.) At the same time, the Reserve Clause came into being as part of the agreement, mandating that players "belonged" to a particular team; players were automatically renewed each year, with or without salary negotiations, into the team they had played for the year before. This clause, which was to sustain the way the owners ruled baseball for more than 50 years, tied a player to a team, unless he was traded, for the length of his major-league lifetime.

In 1922, as a result of Baltimore's complaint that the new Reserve Clause was destroying its team, the Supreme Court ruled on baseball's relationship to the laws on interstate commerce (*Federal Baseball Club of Baltimore, Inc. v. National League of Professional Base Ball Clubs et al.*, argued 19 April 1922, decided 29 May 1922). By deciding that baseball was only tangentially involved in interstate commerce, baseball was effectively granted an antitrust exemption. Regardless of where games were played, the Supreme Court said, baseball was a local game and not subject to anti-monopoly laws and regulations. Warren Friedman notes that, "of all the professional sports rampant on the American scene today, only the professional sport of baseball is the proud owner of an exemption from the antitrust laws."[23]

Marvin Miller, a executive from the steel industry union, was recruited by the baseball players to head their nascent union in 1966. The relationship between players and the owners was, by trade union standards, incredibly primitive. What passed for a union at that time was an organization completely paid for and run by the owners. Salary negotiations and collective bargaining were practically nonexistent; players had little option except to sign whatever contract was tendered to them.

Miller immediately began to organize the major league players into an organization that more closely resembled a modern union. His changes, hardly revolutionary by the standards of any other union, included having players support their union through payment of union dues, holding regular meetings with the players, and demanding that the owners negotiate individual contracts with players while observing a collective bargaining agreement with the union.

The Reserve Clause, which Miller could not negotiate out of the contracts, remained as the major hold of the teams upon the players. Because of the Reserve Clause, if a player did not sign a contract offered to him, he could not play anywhere. In 1970, after being traded without consultation, Curt Flood sued organized baseball, charging that the Reserve Clause violated Federal "antitrust laws and civil rights laws, as well as the imposition of peonage and involuntary servitude, violative of the Thirteenth Amendment of the Constitution."[24] Though the Supreme Court found against Flood, the case had opened the way for reexamination of baseball's antitrust status and the Reserve Clause.

In 1975, when Andy Messersmith and Dave McNally could not reach agreement with their clubs over contracts, there was another lawsuit. Seemingly unnoticed for 50 years was the fact that the Reserve Clause only restricted a player for one year after he failed to renew a contract; following that period, there was no reason whatsoever why a player could not be thought of as a free agent. The acknowledgment of that fact by an arbitrator, Dave Seitz, was eventually upheld by the courts, though the antitrust exemption remained.

As a direct result of the Flood and Messersmith-McNally cases, coupled with the coming of an effective players' union, modern baseball was propelled into the present situation in which players are now paid salaries that some consider astronomical, others consider the salaries merely inflated, and still others believe they are realistic and equitable.

The clubs do make money for their owners, although the past two years have been difficult for them. According to a report issued at the end of 1992, industry-wide profits have fallen 31 percent from $142,867,000 to $98,953,000. 1989 was a year of record profits; figures have fallen off since then. Losses were expected in 1993 and 1994.[25]

Miller, in his autobiography, makes the point that the players are the very best in their fields. Top executives, earning millions of dollars for their companies, are compensated as well as the players are.

The owners insisted, at the start of the new era, that the new system of free agency would wreck the game. Miller and the union insisted, just as vocally, that the players would be finally receiving their fair share of the enormous profit that baseball makes.

The coming of the unionized age to baseball has spawned several labor strikes and an owners' lockout of players. (Late in the 1994 season, players went on strike through the end of the season.) On Miller's retirement, he was replaced by his assistant and chief counsel, Donald Fehr. Though Fehr is much more willing than

Miller was to be in the public eye, he has the same commitment to his charges that his predecessor had.

In other sports, the example of the baseball players inevitably caused comparisons and the formation of union-like players' associations. Football and basketball also are now in a situation where players generally have free agency and individual negotiating rights (with various restrictions negotiated into the uniform bargaining agreement between management and the union).

The business dealings between professional team owners and the athletes who play for them frequently have an other-worldly quality about them. The annual demands of the players, the complaints from the owners that the players are out to bankrupt them, and the eventual financial success of both sides are more than a little reminiscent of nineteenth-century labor relations. Professional basketball, though as much a business as any other professional sport, seems to develop less vituperation at contract time than other sports, perhaps because there is no long history of owner paternalism cum abuse—both sides seem to recognize that a mutually satisfactory negotiation is essential to getting on with business.

In baseball's response to free agency, owners began to share among themselves, in 1985, a database of league salaries; the discovery of this database led to charges of collusion from the union. In 1990, after arbitrators had ruled on three cases, the owners agreed to settlements totaling over $280 million.

From the beginnings of professional baseball and other sports, there has always been an effort by the owners to increase their profits, sometimes by changing the playing rules to increase the excitement. Most organized sports have done the same thing, even if they have publicly claimed to be changing the rules to make the game more of a challenge. The three-point goal in basketball, for example, is only a few years old. Football has fiddled with its rules constantly, and will be instituting a two-point-conversion rule in the 1994–1995 season.

Although the players' unions garnered a rapid increase in players' salaries in professional sports, there is some evidence that the owners are beginning to learn how to work with the system of free agency, and within the law, in order to control costs. In early 1994, a *Wall Street Journal* article reported that, although certain star players are receiving extremely large salaries, there are a number of major league players of moderate ability who are being offered contracts at significantly lower amounts than they enjoyed several years earlier. For example, Harold Reynolds, who received a salary of $2 million in 1990, is now playing with a contract that nets him about $200,000 (the negotiated minimum major league salary is over $100,000). Of the 49 players who had million-dollar salaries or more in 1993 and who then became free agents, only 16 achieved higher contracts in 1994, and 26 took pay cuts.[26]

Baseball and other professional sports have made business mistakes before. Sports history is filled with examples of business decisions gone bad, the most famous being the trade of Babe Ruth by the Boston Red Sox, in 1928, to the New York Yankees. The Red Sox haven't won a pennant since then, supposedly because of the "Babe's curse."

Because we are accustomed to thinking of sports almost as a public service, the businesslike actions of the owners (and of the players) sometimes strike us as inappropriate. It is likely that if we realize that professional sports is a business designed to make money for the participants (not necessarily a bad thing), we will be able to accept certain ways of doing things that we now see as inimical to "the sporting spirit." We have learned to accept, for example, that advertising on outfield walls is just another part of the game.

In 1994 seven American League baseball clubs decided to allow the use of advertising behind home plate (the National League still has a rule against it); when games are televised, the advertising will almost have to be shown, unless television stations change their methods of shooting the games. American League teams are concerned that there may be a conflict if two teams sponsored by the same type of product (such as beer) play, but only one type of beer is advertised. While many of us may believe that "a beer is just a beer," this is a matter of high seriousness to the clubs, their advertising departments, and their public relations staffs.[27] If a sports organization is a public service, advertising is flatly wrong. If the organization is a business just like any other, the owners are entitled to earn their money almost any way they wish.

As fans, we have generally been convinced that professional sports are operated purely for our benefit; that sports are a public service to the community; and that professional sports deserve the very same support, both psychological and financial, that communities devote to schools, hospitals, and police and fire departments. These assumptions are what made the 1989 movie *Major League* such a hit. A team owner, a strident businesswoman with no interest in her community, tries to make her team do so poorly that a move to Florida is within the limits of her commitment to the league. The players, inspired by the heresy, turn themselves into champions in order to show the owner that they want and deserve to stay where they are.

While on-field or on-rink advertising is not new for many sports, especially ice hockey and basketball, it is a bit of a shock for the baseball fan, who tends to believe that he has a right to watch a game on television without the intrusion of advertising. However, watching a game on television means accepting the broadcast service of a business that has paid the home team or the league for the right to broadcast, and which has accepted money from advertisers who wish to run their commercials during the game. People attending a game *might* have a better claim to a desire for a commercial-free atmosphere; theoretically, their admission fees cover the cost of providing the stadium and the seats, as well as a profit for the teams. Except in baseball and a few other sports, however, advertising in the stadium has long been an accepted way of doing business, and will probably be universal in the near future.

Still another example of the businesslike management of professional teams is their movement from one location to the other. Although, as Joan Chandler has pointed out, television is usually considered the culprit for encouraging teams that have been loved and cherished by various localities to move to different locations, teams move for several reasons, not the least of which is that the modern age, with its high-speed transportation, makes such movement possible.[28] Despite the 1992 threatened move of the Los Angeles Giants, few teams have relocated in recent years. It is here, if anywhere, that one finds some indication that professional teams do allow themselves an unbusinesslike, sentimental aspect.

Specific Controversies

Role Models

Should athletes, or any other public figures, be role models? It seems to be a natural tendency for the public audience to make role models of the famous and successful. Every politician worth his vote, for example, knows that having a well-known entertainer or film star's endorsement is going to pay off at election time. It is not surprising, then, that our society quickly slots well-known athletes into role-model status.

If the athlete truly is an exemplary figure, both in his or her athletics and his or her way of life, there may be some benefit to both children and adults in seeing the athlete as an example of responsible behavior. Indeed, some athletes seem willing and pleased to accept the assignment. The late Roberto Clemente, for instance, is frequently cited as an example of a man who lived an exemplary life by using his position as a baseball hero to assist people in need. Clemente died on New Year's Eve in a bad-weather air accident in 1972 while delivering relief goods to Nicaraguan hurricane victims. Before then, he had been active in youth outreach programs, especially in his native Puerto Rico. Twenty-five years later, his son, Roberto Clemente Jr., continues his father's efforts on behalf of poor children. The Roberto Clemente Foundation, run by his son and widow, is extremely active in charitable affairs, and the positive effect of his efforts and intentions has become an enduring legacy.

Dave Winfield, a highly regarded baseball star, has said, "Athletes are a key role model for many people, and they can and should be. . . ." Winfield, however, continues to say that "in an ideal situation they should not be the primary [role models]. The parent should be first, the teacher should be second, and then maybe the athletes or other non-family members. You can fit a lot of people in that last category. Unfortunately, in this day and age, it doesn't necessarily work like that. So athletes do impact and influence a lot of people, whether the athlete wants to or not."[29] Winfield recognizes that parents, not athletes, entertainers, or politicians, should be the role models for children. He also recognizes the difference between the ideal and the actual—how athletes deport themselves, on the field and off, does have an effect on youngsters (and adults) and that athletes need to recognize and deal with that fact.

Some role models, on the other hand, cannot live up to the standards set for them. How useful is it for a youngster to have to ask, as in the classic story about the "Black Sox" scandal, "Say it ain't so, Joe?" It is not only the youngster who learns, for better or worse, from the role model: An admirable or despicable act or gesture can affect adults as well.

In some instances, the role model is not what he seems to be. Babe Ruth, for example, was indeed a magnificent ballplayer;

many rightly aspire to equal or surpass his athletic achievements—that's part of the healthy spirit of sports competition. Off the field, however, Ruth was not always the type of person we would want to be like. Frequently a hard-drinking, womanizing, rude, and compulsive personality, he was also a charming, chivalrous, and generous person. Ruth's justly acclaimed achievements on the field were sometime offset by behavior that would offend most of us if practiced by the man down the street.

Ruth, of course, was not the only sports figure to engage in less than high moral practices. What should we think of an athlete like Pete Rose, who spent time in jail for income tax evasion? Or of the legendary Vince Lombardi, who is known for saying (though he may not have really said it) that "winning isn't everything—it's the *only* thing." Or of the baseball players who thought it was a fun idea to throw a large firecracker into the crowd after a game?

Robert Lipsyte is one of many sportswriters who ask if the actions of those who are considered role models and heroes are what is really desired by the fans. He includes in his list of dubious inspirations:

> The Boston Bruins, the Cincinnati Bengals, and the New York Mets, some of whose members have recently been accused of sexual crimes?
> The Mississippi State football coach who allowed a bull to be castrated in front of his team to pump up their pre-game testosterone?
> The Cal basketball coach who was fired for abusive behavior toward his players?
> High school coaches who leave a tampon in the locker of a player they want to motivate to get tough?
> All those peewee league football coaches who teach kids to block and tackle with their heads?[30]

Still another writer, Ira Berkow, has provided his own list of problems that have shocked and appalled the public:

> Pete Rose was banned from baseball for betting on games; Magic Johnson, who says he had sex with thousands of women, contracted the virus that causes AIDS; boxer Mike Tyson was convicted of rape, and Steve Howe was banned from baseball after six previous suspensions and after pleading guilty to a cocaine change. Now comes the Bengals case. [The Bengals case involved accusations by a "Victoria C." who charged that she had been gang-raped by "approximately 15

football players who are or were members of the Cincinnati Bengals
football team on or about October 4, 1990. . . . "][31]

Even on the field, professional athletes do not seem to be
doing well at setting a good example of professional behavior. The
image of the baseball player arguing with an umpire is, sadly,
almost part of American folklore. Practically no professional ice-
hockey game is complete without at least one, and usually more,
fistfights on the ice involving, if not most of the players on both
teams, at least the one player on each team unofficially designated
as an "enforcer" because of his ability to fight as well as his hockey
ability. In recent years, bench-clearing brawls have occurred with
increasing regularity in both baseball and basketball. In May 1994,
organized baseball found on-field violence enough of a problem to
form a study committee involving both the owners and the Players' Association. While the idea of rejecting authority is part of
American myth, this image teaches that authority can and should
be made light of, rejected, and intimidated. The alternative, especially in a sport situation which depends upon at least the sem-
blance of objective decisions about achievement, is anarchy.

It may be that merely enforcing the rules, or instituting new
rules, will not change this behavior much. If balls thrown at a
batter's head, illegal tackling or checking, and disrespect for refer-
ees and umpires are considered part of the game, then there is no
way that the game is going to change. It is curious that we so often
seem to tolerate on-field violent behavior while seeking role-
model quality behavior off the field. We seem, regrettably, quite
willing to accept behavior on the field that, anywhere else, would
be considered antisocial if not criminal. At the same time that we
want our athletes to be ideal members of society, we almost expect
them to defy authority in the same way that teenagers are expected to be somewhat rebellious.

Perhaps being a role model is inescapable for a professional
sports star, and a conscious awareness of one's responsibility to
the fans is an integral part of this job. Donald Fehr, head of the
Professional Baseball Players' Association, has observed that "anybody who is in the public eye is foolish if he doesn't recognize that
he or she is paid attention to by other people and by kids if you're
in sports or entertainment."[32]

Major League Baseball (MLB; the business organization
comprising the National and the American Leagues) can supply

questioners with a fairly complete list of off-field benevolent activities of professional baseball players. Another list provides the organized activities of the clubs. Though some of the items on the lists may be mere fluff, there are genuinely good works listed—in this sport, at least, it seems clear that some if not all of the athletes are willing to assume a social responsibility. Athletes in other sports besides baseball have also been recognized for their off-field deeds.

Off-field behavior is indeed important to those involved in sports administration. Every organized sport has its own statement of ethics, and violations can result in punishment ranging from a minor fine to a lifetime suspension from the sport. Most professional sports players, for example, even have an "ethics clause" in their contracts, legally binding them to behavior that the owners have determined is appropriate. Organized sports is, at least some of the time, understandably concerned about what its players do off the field. The National Football League, for example, puts forth an impressive effort to reach out to players to convince them that their behavior, both on- and off-field, is important. NFL Commissioner Paul Tagliabue has noted that:

> We hope to make clear to the players that there are a set of standards that are expected of them in regard to personal conduct on and off the field. . . . We hope to make it clear that they have a responsibility to the league, to the clubs, to their families, and to themselves. It's a matter of education, or of communication. It starts with the clubs, and particularly the coaches and assistants, the people with the closest contact with the players . . . You have to be careful. There's only so much a league or club can do. You must be careful about compromising a player's privacy.[33]

There are athletes like basketball's Charles Barkley, who has twisted himself into an ethical möbius strip, playing both sides of the role-model issue. Barkley told an interviewer in 1992 that "I'm not a role model." Another, contradictory platform for this statement was a 1993 television advertisement for sneakers, for which he received several hundred thousand dollars. The purpose of the ad, of course, was to sell sneakers to those who see Barkley as a role model. There's nothing wrong with selling shoes; perhaps Barkley has every right to take a large sum of money from the manufacturer if it is offered.

In the same interview, Barkley asserted that the role-model assignment is given by the media, which:

holds athletes to higher standards than anybody. There are two reasons why I don't think athletes should be role models: Number one, the ability to run and dunk a basketball should not make you God Almighty. There are a million guys in jail who can play ball. Should they be role models? Of course not. Two, they got people modeling themselves after something they can never be. Kids can't become Michael Jordan. Parents and teachers should be role models.[34]

Certainly, Barkley and other athletes have the right to eschew the active role-model assignment. But, in the instance of Barkley, is the denial of responsibility sufficient notice to the world that he considers his endorsements meaningless? If one doesn't want to be a role model, is it sufficient to say so, or should one also avoid all situations where one's words are taken with more weight than the words of others? As Robert Lipsyte of the *New York Times* has asked: "If you aren't a role model, why are you trying to tell us what shoes to wear?"[35]

In writing about the *Sports Illustrated* 1987 Sportsman of the Year Awards, Frank Deford noted that

many athletes are uncomfortable with this reality and try to evade what it means. It's their contention that as long as they go out and play ball, noting else is required of them. This is fallacious on a number of counts. First, star athletes are part of a business that is in the public eye. Scrutiny goes with the whole luxurious territory. Second, athletes are rewarded commensurate with their fame, not their intrinsic talent, and they should be obliged to pay back in that same popular currency. And finally, as glib as this may sound nowadays, it still obtains: To whom much is given, much is expected.[36]

Perhaps the ethical standards of athletes would not be such an issue if other, nonathletes involved in sport were held to the same ethical issues. George Steinbrenner, for example, the principle owner of the Yankees, was involved in an arrangement with a known gambler in an effort to collect negative information about Dave Winfield. He was, supposedly, banished from baseball. Yet, in 1993, he resumed his role as the lead administrator of the team—his "banishment" was lifted by the other owners.

A player with connections to known gamblers would usually be in hot water, as was the case with Pete Rose, but Steinbrenner and other owners, in baseball and in other sports, who have been unethical seem to have gotten away with the proverbial slap on the wrist. While professional ballplayers sign a contract with an "ethics clause" in which they pledge to "conform to high standards of personal conduct," owners seem to be removed from such a commitment. (See chapter 4, page 123, for a standard ethics clause.)

Do we want or need to require standards of conduct of our athletes that we do not require of our neighbors or ourselves? There can be unfortunate results from blindly making heroes out of public figures, and making gods out of sports heroes. Is it enough that an athlete can run, throw, jump, catch, or lift better than 99.9 percent of the population? Or does the competitive display of these skills also require an exemplary level of behavior not found in our everyday lives?

Racism in Sports

Although many of the more obvious forms of racism, such as Jim Crow laws, are gone from American society, there is still a quiet, more subtle racism at work, both in society at large and in sports.

Tommie Smith and John Carlos were two black track athletes who celebrated black achievement and protested racism in society by raising their gloved fists at the 1968 Olympic awards ceremony for their achievements in track. The public response was severe. Looking backwards after more than 25 years, the response would seem comical were it not that the careers of these two fine athletes were disrupted.

At best, Smith and Carlos, under the influence of the Olympic Committee for Human Rights (which had originally called for a boycott of the Olympic Games), had found a highly visible means of protesting rampant racism in amateur sports. At worst, the two athletes were guilty of an act of a highly visible protest, with which the public did not agree—hardly justifying the heavy-handed reaction. Much as patriotic fans like to itemize overall medal counts, and believe that the Olympic Games exist to showcase a country's best face, most athletes, patriotic though they may be, compete in the Olympics and in other events for their own benefit and glory. This is not a bad thing, as Dr. Robert Voy, former Olympic physician, has pointed out, the "gold-medal mentality" makes heroes out of sports figures who are doing what they like to do and what they do well. Alan Guttman's analysis of the Smith and Carlos demonstration (and its consequences) is that the furor over the demonstration missed the important point:

The critiques and the protests were less radical than they seemed. Whether their revolt took verbal or behavioral forms, activists ... acted in conformity with the inner logic of modern sports. Common to nearly all of the American protest was the axiomatic assumption that equality of opportunity to participate in sports is a fundamental human right. Excluded groups demanded inclusion. Blacks and women wanted their "piece of the pie." Few critics asked, "What kind of pie?" Hardly anyone this side of the Atlantic wondered, "Is this pie really good for you?"[37]

Regardless of the appropriateness of their protest, Smith and Carlos did have something about which to protest. Though there has been some change, there are still serious indicators that a good portion of American sports is racist in nature.

One clear measure of discrimination is the number of blacks and Hispanics employed in management and off-field jobs in professional sports. Compared to the rate of white employment, the numbers are appalling.

A recent "report card" issued by the Northeastern University Center for the Study of Sport in Society (CSSS), for example, provides an analysis of minority hiring of administrators (coaches and higher) in the three major professional sports areas—baseball, football, and basketball. In the NBA, opportunities have been brightest, but even here the number of blacks in management is nowhere near reflective of the number of blacks playing the game, or the number of blacks in the population at large. In 1991, the CSSS found black general managers in five teams, and several black coaches in six teams. At the same time, 72 percent of the NBA's players are black. The CSSS found similar conditions, though not quite as good, in both baseball and football.[38]

Baseball, more than the other sports, might be expected to do better. As the *New York Times* writer Claire Smith points out, "No other sport dares call itself the national pastime, or reminds constantly that it is the sport of Jackie Robinson and that it integrated before the country itself, therefore becoming an industry leader in this area."[39]

Sports hero Henry "Hank" Aaron has made no secret of the racial abuse he took as he approached baseball's record for the greatest number of hits. Aaron, now a vice-president with the Turner Cable Network, feels that racism in hiring practices has held his career back, and that racism is still a reality for many minorities:

> But it's basically right to hire blacks and Hispanics. Henry Aaron, Jackie Robinson, and Willie Mays made their marks on the field. That alone should give us a chance in the front office. We deserve a chance just as much as Stan Musial and Ted Williams. Baseball gave Williams a managerial job even though he couldn't fill out a lineup card. When Stan Musial got out of baseball, the St. Louis Cardinals gave him a general manager's position."[40]

Other instances of racism are apparent in the sports universe. "Stacking," for example—the practice of assigning certain racial minorities to some positions and not to others—is a relatively common phenomenon, though less so than it was several years ago. On football teams, one can usually expect to find that the quarterback is white, while defensive linemen are usually black.

Even without comparison to management ranks, another side of racism is shown by the huge number of blacks playing in various sports. According to Richard Lapchick of the CSSS, NCAA Division I schools field basketball teams

> that are 56 percent black, in comparison to a student population that is 7 percent black (and a faculty that is 1.56 percent black). White athletes are twice as likely to graduate as black athletes. The dropout rate after 4 years of school is 28.5 percent for blacks compared to 10 percent for whites. Arthur Ashe, the former black tennis star who died recently, considered figures such as this evidence of "blatant hypocrisy."[41]

Figures in professional sports, especially basketball, would probably show similar skewing from the general American population. There are a number of possible reasons for the black predominance among sports players, none of which reflect very well on colleges and professional management. Is it possible that sport organizers believe in the expression that became a hit movie title, "white men can't jump?" If blacks are considered most fit for sports stardom, does that mean that other racial groups are fit for other pursuits, such as management? Have poor black youths bought into the myth that sports is a way out of poverty—perhaps the only way? Lapchick has asserted that "there remains this prevailing belief in black communities that you can make it to the pros when, in fact, the odds of that happening, depending upon what sport you're talking about, are about 1 in 10,000."[42]

Another aspect of racism in sports is the national willingness to allow youngsters to believe that sports are a way out of poverty.

The number of successful professional athletes who have left the ghetto by virtue of their talent in sports is minimal. In *SportsWorld*, Lipsyte addresses the question in relation to black youth, but his observations are true for all minorities:

> This is one of the crueler hoaxes. . . . Sports success probably has been detrimental to black progress. By publicizing the material success of a few hundred athletes, thousands, perhaps millions, of bright young blacks have been swept toward sports when they should have been guided toward careers in medicine or engineering or business. For every black star celebrated in *SportsWorld*, a thousand of his little brothers were neutralized, kept busy shooting baskets until it was too late for them to qualify beyond marginal work.[43]

Although it is possible to imagine that racism is on the decline, there have been too many instances in recent years of both statements and actions indicating that racism is still alive. Radio commentator Jimmy "The Greek" (a gambler hired to report on sports) managed to ruin his new career when he told his audience that blacks are more athletic than whites because blacks were bred to be strong by their owners before the Civil War. Al Campanis, a vice-president for player personnel of the Los Angeles Dodgers contended on national television in 1987 that blacks "may not have some of the necessities" to handle management assignments.

In 1990, the Professional Golfers Association (PGA) announced that it would not hold tournaments at clubs with anti-black policies. One year after, William A. Henry III investigated the status of discrimination in the golf world. Despite the PGA position, discrimination is far from eliminated in the golf world. Henry cites industry experts who estimate that there are 5,232 private golf and country clubs in the United States that have no black members. Among the specific examples that he cites, there are 74 clubs in the Chicago area, of which only 10 have black members and only 26 enroll women. In Westchester County, New York, there are black members at only 11 of 39 clubs. In metropolitan Detroit, only 11 of 38 clubs have black members. [44]

Women are denied membership as well as blacks and Hispanics. Henry also cites the case of Marcia Welch who had been a member of Pittsburgh's Wildwood Country Club. After she was divorced, the club told her to reapply and pay a new membership fee. The Lady's PGA tourney in 1991 was held at Highland

Meadows, Sylvania, Ohio, where women are not allowed to be voting members.[45]

More recently, in 1992, Marge Schott, owner of the Cincinnati Reds baseball team, made some very public, very obnoxious antiblack and antisemitic statements. After a year's suspension from baseball, Schott is now back with her team. Ironically, Schott's organization may be more racially aware than the other teams in baseball. According to the Reverend Jesse Jackson, who had recently formed the Rainbow Committee for Fairness in Athletics, Schott had established an affirmative-action plan for her team, hired one of two Hispanic managers in the majors, and employed minorities in the front office and in the Reds' minor league teams. "In a kind of irony," Jackson said, "she may . . . actually have a better racial record than most of the other 27 major league teams. . . ."[46]

There is little evidence that very much has changed in the rest of baseball in the wake of the Schott suspension, or that other baseball owners see her as anything more than a potential public relations embarrassment, rather than as one sign out of many that professional sports may need to reevaluate its attitudes and practices.

More recently, there has been some serious attention paid to complaints by American Indians that the team names and mascots of baseball's Braves and Indians were insulting to them. Arguing that the names and the fans' "tomahawk chops" perpetuated a negative stereotype, there have been written and televised discussions. There are five teams in professional sports with Indian names: the Atlanta Braves and the Cleveland Indians in baseball, the Kansas City Chiefs and Washington Redskins in football, and the Chicago Blackhawks in hockey.

Indian spokesmen believe that the portrayal of one-dimensional comic-book Indians is highly derogatory. They object to phony Indian dress, fan chants, foam-rubber tomahawks, and outmoded stereotypes. As one activist pointed out to an interviewer, "It's analogous to somebody dressing up as the pope, going out on the field, waving a cross, and performing a mock communion." Although the team organizations have insisted that they mean no harm and have no plan to change the team names, there have been several changes which show a certain amount of sensibility to the issue. The Redskins marching band no longer uses tom-toms, and the Chiefs no longer have an Indian-costumed mascot on horseback.[47]

Women in Sports

Discrimination against women has long been an aspect of American sports, and it took the weight of national law to *begin* to set the situation straight. Although there have always been superb women athletes, women who competed were viewed, for many years, as being, at the very least, socially inept or incompetent, if not guilty of a variety of moral turpitudes.

World War II began to change women's role in sports, much as it changed everything else. Our society began to accept a woman's right to go to work and earn a living, and it also gave us a view of women as entitled and welcomed to participate in sports both for pleasure and for competition. Though women athletes are very obvious in today's society, women are still discriminated against.

One clear example of current attitudes toward women is the annual "Swimsuit Issue" of *Sports Illustrated*, the most widely sold issue of the most popular sports magazine. The pictures themselves aren't particularly risqué—by 1990s (or even earlier) standards, the photographs are downright conservative. What's more important, however, is that the swimsuit issue represents some of the few times in the past year that a woman has made the cover of *Sports Illustrated*. Out of 52 issues, 1993 saw only six women on the cover.[48]

If you attend a Little League game, you are likely to see some excellent young girl players. And, in most cases, no one playing or watching the game thinks anything of it. Girls are, at least today, as entitled to play as boys are. It wasn't always so, however. As recently as 1972, girls were prohibited from playing in Little League (and in other sports as well). It took a spate of lawsuits to get girls admitted. When the national organization finally decided that girls would be allowed, hundreds of all-male teams in New Jersey, where the issue first went critical, actually threatened to not play. It is hard to believe that the following was the attitude of only little more than 20 years ago:

> Our younger male population has not become so decadent that boys will experience a thrill in defeating girls in running contests. . . . It could well be that many boys would feel compelled to forgo entering track events if they were required to compete with girls. . . . With boys vying with girls . . . the challenge to win and the glory of achievement, at least for many boys, would lose incentive and become

nullified. Athletic competition builds character in our boys. We do not need that kind of character in our girls.[49]

In 1972, Title IX of the amendments to the Education Act mandated that colleges and universities give women equal access to sports funding. It wasn't until 1979, however, that the Department of Health, Education, and Welfare finally promulgated rules by which equal opportunity would be judged.

The 1979 federal rules required that women be given equal opportunity in such matters as coaching, facilities, equipment and housing. If a men's basketball team receives funding for a locker room with modern facilities, for example, the women's team (in either basketball or in another sport, if the women do not want to play basketball) should have the same type of modern facilities. Although some people predicted that such equal treatment of women would be the end of society, what has actually happened is that college women receive, in many if not most cases, equal access to coaching, facilities, and the opportunity to play. There are indications, however, that Title IX is not working the way it was intended to work, and that women are still being shortchanged.

Women are perhaps still resented in some places because the allocation of resources to women means that the money-making men's sports are often receiving less financial attention than they did before Title IX. While there *may* be a difference in the amount of dollars that men's teams can bring to a college because of Title IX, the issue of returned dollars really begs the question: What is the purpose of college athletics?

If there ever was a defining moment in dealing with discrimination against women in sports, it was the Billie Jean King-Bobby Riggs tennis match of 20 September 1973. Loudly proclaiming that men were superior to women, Riggs challenged any woman tennis player to try to disprove him. King did, of course, through a combination of youth and ability. Though the match was almost undoubtedly a publicity event for Riggs, and though King may have laughed secretly at the noise and fuss over the match, there was never any sign that Riggs really thought that he would lose. King trained properly for the match, and her playing was exemplary.

After losing the match, Riggs was gracious: "She was too good. . . . She played too well." King felt that the match would serve to alert people that women could and would do well in sports. Several days before the match, King had noted that "women can be great athletes. And I think you'll find in the next decade that women athletes will finally get the attention they've deserved through the years, that people will treat us as athletes . . . [I]n particular, businessmen are realizing that we're marketable."[50] King was right. The match did establish that women have a right to be considered serious professional contenders in sports, and that they can attract enough public interest to earn significant money from their professionalism.

Financially, the fortunes of women tennis professionals increased greatly following the Riggs-King match, as King predicted. Where previously they had competed for prizes roughly one-tenth the size of the men's awards, women's prizes today, though still not completely comparable, are much closer. Additionally, King's example inspired major funding for women's tennis tournaments, including the now-recognized and important Virginia Slims Tournament, held annually for a first-place purse that, in 1993, reached $3.5 million.

Women had been competing in athletics, seriously and well, long before the King-Riggs match. Historically, however, American society has usually found it convenient to impugn the femininity of those women who do well in sports.

Mildred "Babe" Zaharias, for example, was the preeminent woman athlete of the first half of the twentieth century. Despite her awesome string of achievements in track and field and other sports, and, ultimately, in golf, stories and articles about her usually noted her appearance and subtly hinted at her being less than a typical woman.

Sexuality continues to be an issue in sports; the suggestion that a female coach or manager might be a homosexual is suffficient to influence some women athletes to avoid a particular college or university; there has been at least one court case in which a woman coach successfully sued her college because an administrator, in an effort to sabotage the coach, had spread rumors that she was a lesbian. Pat Griffin, a former swimming coach and now an associate professor of social-justice education, agrees: "The stereotype is used anywhere to keep women out. . . . Because of the homophobia, the bigotry, the incredible stigma, it is an effective tool, particularly in athletics, where the label sticks so easily."[51]

In 1992, the hit movie A League of Their Own reacquainted Americans with the history of The All-American Girls Professional Baseball League. Begun during World War II, women's baseball actually flourished until 1950. But in the same way that Rosie the Riveter was told to go home and put on her apron again after the war, women professional baseball players found that few fans were interested in seeing them play ball. (There were other reasons, too, for the failure of the league, including a decline in interest in all spectator sports after the war. The postwar economic boom gave many people enough money to lead more active lives away from the ballpark, radio, and television.)

Several books about the women's professional league appeared at about the same time as the movie. That their playing was exceptional and that the leagues should be remembered as an important part of sports history, are not surprising revelations in the mid-1990s. What is surprising is that the movie and the books were able to ambush such a large number of viewers and readers into finding out about a "lost" segment of American sports history. The topic should not have been obscure; the women who played were not a small number of women in a small town in a small midwestern state. Nevertheless, the story of the women's leagues had vanished as surely as the town of Brigadoon.

In 1994, a professional minor-league team of women players began to compete, coached by former major-league star Phil Niekro. Whether the women achieve the success they seek, or are forced to disband because of lack of interest, it is certain that women will indeed have a role in professional baseball someday.

In other previously all-male sports, a few women are competing, and competing well. There have been at least three women who were at least suggested for professional contracts in basketball in the past 15 years. Additionally, there is one woman, Lynette Woodward, now playing for the Harlem Globetrotters basketball team. Serious women's amateur boxing is developing rapidly. While it may be interesting and notable that there are some women able to compete with some men, what is really important is that women are gaining access and the right to participate in sports from which they had previously been shut out automatically.

Drug Abuse

Under what conditions, if any, should the use of performance-enhancing drugs be permitted in either professional or amateur sports?

The 1980s saw a tremendous increase in the use of drugs by athletes. Anabolic steroids, especially, became increasingly popular among a large number of athletes; one estimate of drug use in the 1988 Olympics, for example, suggested that 50 percent of the competitors were using some type of drug. Though this percentage is probably higher than the true figure, there is no doubt that drugs were not uncommon. The disclosure that Ben Johnson had tested positive for steroids following enormously successful Olympic track competitions in 1988 sparked the movement to test for and prevent the use of drugs.

The Olympics, as do almost all organized sports, now forbid the use of these and other drugs. Drug testing, however, is frequently controlled by national Olympic committees, and in many cases, including that of the United States Olympic Committee (USOC), the ability to test carefully and fairly for drugs has frequently been questionable.

Olympic testing, both at the national and international level, came after 1988, and the debate over testing led at one point to the resignation of Dr. Robert Voy, a vigorous proponent of testing. Dr. Voy is highly respected today as a leading figure in the movement for fair and effective testing, but he has expressed the thought that perhaps he could have done more had he stayed with the Olympic movement: "My one regret is that I didn't tough it out," he noted recently.[52]

In 1993, the USOC voted for a stricter drug policy that allows any Olympic athlete to be tested for steroids, beta blockers, and masking agents up to four times a year on a random basis; additional testing required by individual sports federations would still be allowed.[53]

Steroids and other performance-enhancing drugs are banned for several reasons. If they are effective, they provide an artificial enhancement to an athlete's abilities, and prevent the competition from testing what an athlete can really do. Just as importantly, there is a rapidly accumulating body of evidence that steroid use leads to a variety of serious medical problems.

According to the American Medical Association (AMA), steroid abuse can lead to such medical problems as impaired liver function, cholestatic hepatitis with jaundice, blood-filled hepatic cysts, benign hepatomas, potentially malignant hepatic tumors, testicular atrophy, changes in prostate and/or seminal vesicles resulting in urinary obstruction, and, when taken before puberty, growth problems such as permanent short stature.

The AMA also lists several possible side-effects, many of which less-cautious but otherwise conservative physicians might consider more likely to occur than not. Among the symptoms considered likely are fluid retention, hypertension, thickened skin, elevated circulating concentrations of low-density lipoprotein and reductions in high-density lipoproteins, cardiovascular difficulties (including a link to myocardial infarctions), colonic cancer, marked affective and/or psychotic syndrome, and severe acne. In women specifically, potential difficulties include menstrual irregularities, permanent hypertrophy of the clitoris, lowered voice pitch, and changes in hair growth patterns.[54]

Several authors have suggested that, since competitors are not required to take drugs, there is no reason why an athlete who wants to take steroids should be prohibited from doing so. In this view, drug use is merely one more way to improve performance, much the same as working out, weight training, and practice. Still another possibility, though one that seems least likely to happen, is to allow athletes to compete in two groups—one group for those who use steroids, another group for those who do not.[55]

More recently, the evidence that steroids are out-and-out harmful has grown to be almost unavoidable. Is this sufficient reason to ban them from competition? Should athletes have the right to do harm to themselves in the pursuit of excellence in sport? Or, should the organizers and owners of sports take a firm stand against drugs that parallels the stand our society at large has taken against such drugs as cocaine and marijuana?

Most athletic codes contain prohibitions against drug use, and in response to various scandals or whispers of scandals, even professional athletics have clearly prohibited drugs. Major League Baseball and the National Football League, for example, have antidrug conditions written into their collective-bargaining agreements. In addition, there are extensive testing and rehabilitation provisions in the agreements. In addition to steroids, there are prohibitions against and testing for illegal street drugs such as cocaine and marijuana. Some amateur sports organizations, such as the National Junior College Athletic Association, also ban smoking at athletic events.

Media Relations

Sports have traditionally had an unusual relationship with the media. For many years, sports writers were expected by readers and athletes alike to be no more and no less than partisans of the teams and sports they covered.

Many professional journalists, on the other hand, rarely saw sportswriters as fellow news-people; sportswriters were seen as people who had fallen into journalism as a way of continuing their lifelong pursuit of being professional fans, people who had no real sense of news. As one editor said in a private conversation, "An editor's worst dream is having only sportswriters around to cover a news event that occurs during a game. The story would undoubtedly look something like 'Play in today's very critical game had to be suspended for two-and-a-half hours while the bodies of the victims of the air crash were removed from near the line of scrimmage. Commenting on the delay, Coach Jones protested that his players had lost the edge with which they began the game and. . . . ' "

Today's sportswriters, however, are serious journalists, and there is no doubt that many sportswriters produce excellent reporting and analysis. The writings of such sports journalists as Robert Lipsyte, Frederick Klein, and many others are excellent examples of reporting and analysis that stand up to comparison with any other field of journalism. And, despite the traditional attitude, there is a large body of fine writing, going back to Damon Runyon, moving through Red Smith, and coming up to the present.

While sports journalists may have become capable professionals, it is difficult for the athletes themselves, if not the fans, to accept sports journalists as serious writers. Journalists are often expected by athletes and fans to be cheerleaders for the teams and sports they cover, and establishing one's independence is a difficulty any sportswriter must face.

Many television sports broadcasters are either paid by or approved by the teams on which they report. Even an ethical, well-intentioned broadcaster is likely to be chosen for his or her technical knowledge, audience appeal, dedication to the home team, or lack of serious concern for disruptive issues that may arise during the broadcast season. For the average fan, as for the player, it is difficult to distinguish the "selected" media who are congenitally favorable from the rest of the media who are trying to fulfill their obligations to get a story, regardless of the light in which the story puts the players and their teams.

Even a sports journalist's own colleagues often fail to see the challenge of good sports journalism. In a review of television sports, the *New York Times* writer Richard Sandomir had this to say about a televised game: "NBC generated a 9.3 overnight Nielsen rating for Saturday's Notre Dame-Boston College game. The work of the director, Joe Aceti, and the producer, Tommy Roy, sparkled on all levels, making the game move like a filmed story. . . ."[56] Though Sandomir, an experienced professional journalist, was complimenting the broadcast, his remark shows how easy it is, even for a journalist, to fall into the trap of expecting only entertainment from television journalism. When television journalists do produce serious news stories about sports, it may be difficult to realize that they have been acting as journalists should act, and not as producers of a fictional account.

Instances of players and coaches barring journalists from locker rooms or refusing to permit journalists to cover their beats occur with a weary repetition each year. Cases of players threatening or actually doing bodily harm to journalists are almost as frequent. In 1993, for example, one baseball player threw bleach at a reporter, supposedly as a way of expressing his distaste for the reporter's work.

When the journalist is a woman covering male athletes, there is frequently the added element of sexism thrown into the pot. In 1992, for example, Lisa Olson, a writer for the *Boston Herald,* was harassed by several football players on the New England Patriots football team while she was trying to do a postgame story. Olson's later complaints about her treatment became a major focus of interest, mostly because she had received little or no support when she first announced that she had been harassed. Team owner Victor Kiam, for example, found nothing surprising or disturbing in Olson's treatment. His response was to make light about the matter with an off-color joke. (In fairness, the team and the players were fined by the NFL, and Kiam apologized publicly for his attitude).

It is hardly surprising that athletes frequently see newspeople as, at best, nuisances to be dealt with. In the case of television sports, where a professional athlete's salary is largely the direct result of large contracts provided by the networks to the league or team, it is understandable that an athlete would expect a journalist's opinions and presentations to be shaded in a positive manner. Print journalists, who make no obvious contribution to an athlete's salary, likely are seen as nuisances and troublemakers.

Sometimes, however, the sportswriters are even hired by the same people who own the team, as is the case with baseball's

Chicago Cubs, owned by the Tribune Company. Some players might feel confused or double-crossed to discover that reporters are not merely colleagues who happen to be wearing ties and toting pens and pencils. The problem is not with the reporters, but with athletes who can not or will not understand the job of a journalist. (There is, of course, an ethical question about whether a large news organization should count a baseball team among its holdings. More than likely, these reporters conduct their operations under an explicit, strict, "management hands off" policy, but that may or may not be a sufficient solution. The ethics of the news business, however, are outside of the scope of this book.)

Additionally, problematic interactions between athletes and the media often seem to occur when the athlete is not guarded by press relations people from his team and league. To avoid such embarrassing situations, players, coaches, and managers are prevented from getting an accurate picture of the role of the press. Murray Sperber has noted, with only a little overexaggeration, that "if a football coach spits into the wind, a sports information person is there to gauge the velocity, wipe off the coach's face if necessary, and interpret the move for the media, as well as provide 8-by-10 glossies of the event and samples of the spit."[57]

Understandably, management makes every effort to see that players and their sports are seen in the best light possible. The NFL, for example, has given instructions to its players on how to deal with the press in an attractive eight-page brochure called "Media Relations Playbook." The pamphlet explains in detail why the NFL finds good media relations important, and even includes two lists of ten items: "interview 'do's' " (be prepared, be positive, praise your teammates, talk in sound-bites, etc.) and "interview 'don'ts' " (don't say "No comment," don't talk about money, don't be negative, don't hide, don't lose your cool, etc.). The standard NFL contract includes a requirement that players make themselves available for interviews and discussions.

The media themselves have contributed to the problem. In television, the number of former athletes who are hired as commentators is gigantic. And though the perceptive fan might be aware that one commentator or another is there to "do color," most people, athletes included, cannot distinguish between the real journalist and the person hired to tell stories out of school. When the athlete on the field knows that the television sportscaster is either being paid by the home team, or that the team has "permitted" a commentator's assignment, the athlete will likely have pleasant expectations of his treatment by sportscasters.

Print journalists have by and large allowed themselves to become part of the game they cover. Baseball Hall of Fame elections, for example, are determined by the votes of sportswriters. Football "dream teams" are based on the votes of writers. In college basketball, the Associated Press poll of sportswriters yields a weekly listing of team placements that has become of great importance to the college sports establishment. To their credit, some sportswriters have protested that they should not be the ones deciding who enters the Hall of Fame; some newspapers, such as the *New York Times*, have policies prohibiting their sportswriters from participation in such votes.

Professional Sports and Antitrust

The question is open as to whether professional sports benefit by antitrust exemptions; baseball has one, and basketball and football operate as if they did. There are periodic attempts by Congress to examine and reverse the monopoly status of baseball, the most recent being a set of hearings held in March 1994 by Senator Howard Metzenbaum of Ohio. The more that organized baseball reveals itself to be acting like any other business, and not an operation run for the benefit of the fans, the more likely it is that its monopoly status will be lifted.

In 1992, when the Senate Antitrust Subcommittee held hearings on baseball, one of the major issues was the way organized baseball had mismanaged the potential franchise relocation of the San Francisco Giants. The Giants had announced that they wanted to leave California and were seeking bids from other localities. After seeming to accept a $115-million bid from the Tampa–St. Petersburg, Florida, area, the Giants changed their minds, accepted a $100-million package from San Francisco, and decided to stay put. Californians, especially Angeleños, were left with the impression that they had been conned by a phony threat into putting up more money. People in Florida felt that they had been pawns in the con game, and that organized baseball had never intended to locate a team there.

Among other issues about which the subcommittee was concerned were:

- An increased number of games being shown on pay television and a decreased number of games on nonpay television.

- Restrictions on pay-television showings of some games.
- Baseball's hiring policies vis-à-vis minorities.
- The effectiveness of baseball's antidrug policies, especially after pitcher Steve Howe's reinstatement following seven disciplinary actions dating back to 1979.
- Continuing demands from teams for financial concessions from their localities at a time when local budgets were generally overextended. Senate Subcommittee Chairman Howard Metzenbaum said that "if decisions about the direction and future of Major League Baseball are going to be dictated by the financial interests of team owners, then maybe baseball should be required to operate under the same business rules as any other sport."[58]

In September 1994, upset by a baseball strike that seemed to have no end in sight, the Senate Antitrust Subcommittee considered limiting the antitrust exemption if the owners tried to unilaterally impose a salary cap on their players. Because the strike was continuing, the proposal was tabled, and will again be reviewed by the subcommittee in early 1995.

Removing the monopoly rights of baseball will not, of course, lead hundreds of entrepreneurs to form their own leagues and force increased competition for players, coaches, and managers. What it will do, however, is give players the same rights as other employees in corporations across the country, and force league ownership to deal with the players and the fans (i.e., the consumers) in a way that parallels the way any American corporation is expected to treat its employees and customers. And, perhaps more importantly, it will force fans and spectators to realize that what they see when they go to a game or watch a game on television is an economic enterprise—the object of which is to make money for the business owners, and not solely to satisfy the interests of the fans.

Notes

1. Thomas H. Kean, foreword to *Sports Ethics in America: A Bibliography, 1970–1990* (New York: Greenwood Press, 1992).

2. Harvey Araton, "Jordan's Situation Good One, Says Stern," *New York Times*, 1 November 1993, C:4.

3. Debra Blum, "Defending College Sports," *Chronicle of Higher Education* 40, no. 25 (23 February 1994).

4. Don Atyeo, *Violence in Sports* (New York: Van Nostrand Reinhold Company, 1981).

5. Felicity Huntingford and Angela Turner, "Aggression: A Biological Imperative?" *New Scientist* (4 August 1988): 44–47.

6. David Gough, "Ethics Transcend Mere Rule-Following," *The NCAA News* (3 March 1993).

7. Robert Lipsyte, "Where, Oh Where, Is Roar of the Athletes?" *New York Times*, 7 February 1993, VIII:8.

8. Sally Jenkins,"Persona Non Grata," *Sports Illustrated* (23 August 1993), 32.

9. Lyle J. Micheli, M.D., with Mark D. Jenkins, *Sportswise: An Essential Guide for Young Athletes, Parents, and Coaches* (Boston: Houghton Mifflin, 1990), 187–188.

10. Curt Brown, "Playing Hurt: Injuries in Youth Sports," *Minneapolis Star Tribune*, 1 November 1992, 1S+.

11. Rick Wolff, *Good Sports: A Concerned Parent's Guide to Little League and Other Competitive Youth Sports* (New York: Dell, 1993), xii.

12. Gary Alan Fine, *With the Boys: Little League Baseball and Preadolescent Culture* (Chicago: The University of Chicago Press, 1987).

13. Kostya Kennedy, "Moving On: Dream Dies for a Young Basketball Coach," *New York Times*, 20 March 1994, VIII:9.

14. Murray Sperber, *College Sports Inc.: The Athletic Department vs. The University* (New York: Henry Holt and Company, 1990).

15. Arthur A. Fleisher, Brian L. Goff, and Robert D. Tollison, The National Collegiate Athletic Association: A Study in Cartel Behavior (Chicago and London: The University of Chicago Press, 1992).

16. Sperber, 18–29.

17. Bill Brubaker, "The Sneaker Phenomenon: In Shoe Companies' Competition, The Coaches Are the Key Players," *Washington Post*, 11 March 1991, A1+.

18. Brubaker.

19. John Weistart, "The 90's University: Reading, Writing, and Shoe Contracts," *New York Times*, 28 November 1993, VIII:9.

20. E. Gordon Gee, *New York Times*, 1 January 1990, 25.

21. David Salter, "Playing Ball with Colleges," *USA Weekend* (21–23 January 1994): 8.

22. Murray Chass, "Without a Commissioner, Padres Unload Their Stars," *New York Times*, 27 June 1993, VIII:6.

23. Walter Friedman, *Professional Sports and Antitrust* (New York: Quorum Books, 1987), 31.

24. *The Guide to American Law: Everyone's Legal Encyclopedia*, vol. 2 (St. Paul, MN: West Publishing Co., 1983), 49.

25. Murray Chass, "Thud! Economic Report Lands on Baseball's Desk," *New York Times*, 7 December 1992, C:2.

26. John Helyar, "Squeeze Play: Baseball's Journeymen Face a New Challenge: The Low-Ball Salary," *Wall Street Journal,* 4 April 1994, A:1.

27. Richard Sandomir, "Sports Business: To Every Advertisement, Turn, Turn, Turn," *New York Times,* 7 January 1994, B:13.

28. Joan Chandler, Television and National Sport: The United States and Britain (Urbana and Chicago: University of Illinois Press, 1988).

29. Claire Smith, "The Debate: Athletes as Role Models," *New York Times,* 23 July 1993, I:9.

30. Robert Lipsyte, "Must Boys Always Be Boys?," *New York Times,* 12 March 1993, B:7.

31. Ira Berkow, "Troubled Times beyond the Lines," *New York Times,* 20 July 1992, C:1.

32. Smith, I:9.

33. Berkow, C:1.

34. Larry Platt, "Charles Barkley" (interview), *Sport* (February 1992), 31–32+.

35. Robert Lipsyte, "Council Needs Action More Than a Hero," *New York Times,* 25 June 1993, B:12.

36. Frank Deford, "A Little Lower Than the Angels," *Sports Illustrated* 67, no. 27 (21 December 1987): 12–15.

37. Allen Guttman, *A Whole New Ball Game: An Interpretation of American Sports* (Chapel Hill: University of North Carolina Press, 1988), 182.

38. Associated Press Newsfeatures, "Pro Basketball Ranked Best in Minority Study," *Sun-Sentinel* (Ft. Lauderdale), 23 July 1991, 1C+.

39. Claire Smith, "Hold the Game to a Special Moral Standard," *New York Times,* 3 June 1992, B:11.

40. William Ladson, "Hank Aaron" (interview), *Sport* (February 1993): 71–75.

41. Robert Lipsyte, "Blacks on the Court; Why Not On Campus?" *New York Times,* 27 March 1992, B:9.

42. Andy Rierden, "Boy's Dream Becomes Man's Pain," *New York Times,* 15 March 1992, Connecticut Section, XII:1.

43. Robert Lipsyte, *SportsWorld: An American Dreamland* (New York: Quadrangle/ The New York Times Book Company, 1975), xi.

44. William A. Henry III, "The Last Bastions of Bigotry," *Time* (22 July 1991): 66–67.

45. Henry, 66–67.

46. Claire Smith, "Owners' Ruling on Schott Is Assailed and Lauded," *New York Times,* 4 February 1993, B:11.

47. Richard L. Worsnop, "Native Americans," *CQ Researcher* (8 May 1992): 387–403.

48. Lynda Truman Ryan, "Swimsuit Models or Victim Stories, Who Will Cover for Me," *New York Times,* 20 February 1994, VIII:11.

49. Judge John Clark Fitzgerald, New Haven Superior Court. Quoted by Allen Guttman in *A Whole New Ball Game*, 154–155. Originally cited by Bil Gilbert and Nancy Williamson, "Sport Is Unfair to Women," *Sports Illustrated* 38 (28 May 1973): 95.

50. Neil Amdur, "She Played Too Well, Says Riggs of Mrs. King," *New York Times*, 22 September 1973.

51. Debra Blum, "College Sports' L-Word," *Chronicle of Higher Education* 40, no. 27 (9 March 1994): A35.

52. Robert Lipsyte, "Rx for Olympic Athlete: Heal Thyself," *New York Times*, 26 June 1992, B:12.

53. Filip Bondy, "Not So Fast on Competition Changes," *New York Times*, 14 February 1993, VIII:7.

54. Council on Scientific Affairs of the American Medical Association, *Journal of the American Medical Association* 264, no. 22 (12 December 1990): 2923–2927.

55. Drew A. Hyland, *Philosophy of Sport* (New York: Paragon House, 1990): 47–67.

56. Richard Sandomir, "TV Sports: 'No Pain, No Gain' Not a Network Motto," *New York Times*, 23 November 1993, B:17.

57. Sperber, 72.

58. Claire Smith, "At Capitol Hill, It's Batters Up," *New York Times*, 10 December 1992, B:19.

2

Chronology

1869   The first professional baseball team, the Cincinnati Red Stockings, wins 91 out of 92 games in their first season.

1871–   A loose league of baseball teams flourishes. Along with estab-
1875   lishing the idea that baseball teams could have professional standards of play, professionalism means the beginning of owner–player labor disagreements.

1876   Baseball becomes a business as team owners form the National League of Professional Base Ball Clubs.

1879   Owners of the National Baseball League create the Reserve Clause as a standard part of the usual baseball contract. The clause ties players to a particular team and renews contracts automatically whether or not a player actually signs a contract. The Reserve Clause is not challenged for nearly 100 years.

1885   Baseball players form the National Brotherhood of Professional Ball Players to combat the owners' control of salaries caused by the Reserve Clause. Although it is the first organization designed to further the interests of the athletes, its strength, like that of most labor organizations of the period, is dwarfed by the strength of the owners.

1889   Rutgers and Princeton play the first intercollegiate football game in the United States on 6 November. Each side uses 25 players, and only goals (rather than touchdowns or other present-day ways of scoring) count toward the final score.

1889
(cont.)   Other colleges and universities soon begin to field football teams. By 1889, under the guidance of Walter Camp there are several innovations which bring the game closer to the way it is played today, including decreasing the size of the team on the field to 11 players and having the quarterback receive the ball from the center on the line of scrimmage. The first All-America football team is selected, furthering the marking of individual players as sports heroes.

1890–1892   The National Brotherhood of Professional Ball Players operates the Players League. The increased competition that the new league offers the owners of National League teams leads to an increase in salaries, but the Players League is too weak financially to continue to operate.

1894   The Western Association, a minor league, is reorganized under the control of Ban Johnson and Charles Comiskey.

1900   The Western League changes its name to the American League and moves a number of franchises east to compete financially with National League teams.

1903   The National League and the newer American League agree to hold a postseason tournament (the first World Series) and cooperate in advancing the cause of professional baseball.

1904   Because of animosity toward the American League, New York Giants owner John T. Brush refuses to allow his National League team to engage the American League's Boston Pilgrims in a postseason tournament. The public outcry over the decision leads Brush to propose, for future seasons, a best-of-seven-games competition.

1905   Amateur football is recognized as extremely dangerous (there were 18 deaths and 159 serious injuries in 1905), and several states consider banning football. In response, President Theodore Roosevelt, an avid football fan, invites the college presidents of Harvard, Princeton, and Yale to the White House to discuss safety issues in college football. Roosevelt meets twice with college representatives, gaining promises of rule changes.

On 28 December, 62 colleges meet to form the Intercollegiate Athletic Association of the United States (IAAUS).

1906   The newly formed IAAUS meets with the Intercollegiate Football Rules Committee (this committee will soon join the NCAA) on 12 January, and reforms several aspects of football for the upcoming season. The new rules recognize the forward pass, require that 6 of 11 players be at the line of scrimmage before a play, and extend the first-down requirement from 5 yards to 10 yards.

1910   The IAAUS changes its name to the National Collegiate Athletic Association (NCAA).

1919   The trial of eight members of the Chicago White Sox on charges of conspiracy to throw the 1919 World Series leads to the appointment of Judge Kenesaw Mountain Landis as baseball's first commissioner. Landis, granted extensive powers by the owners, desperate to save professional baseball's reputation, suspends the eight players permanently and enforces strict rules of deportment with other suspensions and fines.

The first professional football league is formed following a conference in Canton, Ohio. The first league president is Jim Thorpe, the American Indian star. Football did not achieve its current popularity until the 1950s, following the growth of television and the expanded use of the passing game.

1935   The first professional night baseball game is played on 24 May at Crosley Field between the Cincinnati Reds and the Philadelphia Phillies. President Franklin D. Roosevelt turned the lights on by pressing a button in the White House that was connected to the field in Cincinatti. The night game is introduced to allow more fans to attend games and thus allow a greater gate for the owners.

Testosterone, the male sex hormone and the first anabolic steroid, is synthesized. Some medical authorities suggest that the substance might be used to improve physical performance.

1939   The first Little League game is played on 6 June in Williamsport, Pennsylvania. Organized by Carl Stotz, the modest effort began with Stotz asking some local boys if they wanted to play baseball "on a regular team with uniforms, a new ball for every game, and bats you can really swing," and will grow to international proportions to become the largest youth sports organization in the world.

1947   Jackie Robinson becomes the first black player to join the major leagues on 15 April, making his debut with the Brooklyn Dodgers at Ebbets Field. Although some owners are in agreement with team owner Branch Rickey that Robinson's playing is a matter of ethics, the move is motivated both by ethics and the desire to include black fans in professional baseball's audience.

1948   The NCAA convention adopts the Sanity Code, prohibiting scholarships based only on athletic ability. A Constitutional Compliance Committee is formed to enforce the rule, but the only available punishment is expulsion from the NCAA.

1950   Professional baseball signs its first major television contract, receiving $6 million for the World Series. Baseball, and other sports afterwards, develop a relationship with the television media that has since been both praised, for making professional sport a financially viable business, and criticized for making sport too dependent on money provided by television (franchise movements, for example, are frequently motivated by a team's desire to move to a bigger and/or better-paying television market).

1951   A variety of charges of college basketball point-shaving scandals appear throughout the year, most investigated by New York City District Attorney Frank Hogan. Ultimately, Hogan's probe reveals that 32 players from seven schools fixed 86 games in 23 cities between 1947 and 1950. The seven schools were Kentucky, City College of New York, Long Island University, New York University, Manhattan, Bradley, and Toledo.

The NCAA's Constitutional Compliance Committee reports that the Sanity Code does not work because members refuse to expel other members. The rule is repealed. Walter Byers is hired as the new executive director. Enforcement becomes a priority under Byers, and criticism of the NCAA's investigative powers begins to grow from the time of his appointment (and is still an issue in the mid-1990s). Byers serves until 1987, building the NCAA into a major force in college athletics.

1954   The *Brown v. Board of Education* decision is handed down by the Supreme Court on 17 May. The historic decision provides tremendous impetus to desegregating college athletics by effectively forcing colleges to review enrollment and scholarship practices and to enroll minorities. With racially mingled

1954
(cont.) student populations, improper treatment of minorities becomes much more difficult to ignore or remediate than previously. Although not solving the racial problems of either the schools or the nation, the decision provides significant access to blacks, in sports and elsewhere, for the first time in the United States.

1966 Marvin Miller, a former economist for the steel workers union, is hired as the director of the Baseball Players' Association. Miller brings baseball labor relations into the twentieth century and inspires labor movements in other professional sports.

1970–
1972 Curt Flood files an antitrust suit against Major League Baseball on 17 January, asking that the Reserve Clause be invalidated, along with his October 1969 trade from the St. Louis Cardinals to the Philadelphia Phillies. The case reaches the Supreme Court in 1972, where baseball's antitrust status is upheld. Flood's suit, however, forces reexamination of the Reserve Clause and the "discovery" that the Reserve Clause could not be in force for more than one year after a player refuses to sign a contract, opening the door to free agency.

1972 On 1 April, under the direction of labor leader Marvin Miller, the first strike in modern baseball history takes place. Eighty-six games at the beginning of the season are lost before a back-to-work agreement is reached. There will be several labor actions in the coming years, the most serious culminating in the end of the 1994 baseball season at midnight, 11 August.

President Richard M. Nixon signs the Higher Education Act of 1972 on 23 June. Title IX of the act forces colleges to spend increased money on women's sports. The Association for Intercollegiate Athletics for Women (AIAW), which is the most-significant organization for women's collegiate sports, suddenly becomes more powerful because of the larger amounts of money involved. Over the next several years, Walter Byers will try to integrate the AIAW into the NCAA, eventually rejecting a proposed arrangement giving two votes in the NCAA to each member college, one for men's sports and one for women's sports. Title IX will go into effect on 21 July 1975.

On 4–5 September, eight Arab terrorists invade the living quarters of Israeli athletes at the Munich, West Germany, Olympic Games, killing two athletes and taking nine hostage

1972
(*cont.*)
(4 September). The following day, in a shootout with police, nine Israeli athletes, five terrorists, and a West German policeman are killed. It is decided to continue the Olympic Games rather than capitulate to terrorism.

1973
In February, baseball players are locked out of spring training by the owners after a failure to resolve a dispute with the Players' Association about the reserve system. The eventual agreement creates a salary arbitration system in which, if a player and his team do not agree on a salary, an arbitrator is required to choose one of the two proposed salaries.

On 20 September, Billie Jean King captures a winner-take-all purse of $100,000 for beating Bobby Riggs in the "tennis match of the century" at the Houston Astrodome. Despite the hoopla surrounding the event, it establishes once and for all in the minds of the American public that women are capable athletic competitors.

1974–
1975
In October, Little League announces that the Little League World Series, which had been won by Taiwanese teams over the past four years, would be limited to teams from the continental United States. The decision is not popular and is reversed in December 1975. The rescinding of the rule brings about a regulation limiting Little League teams from drawing players from areas greater than 15,000 people, among other changes.

1975
Professional baseball's Reserve Clause is challenged once again, and arbitrator Peter Seitz rules on 23 December that Andy Messersmith and Dave McNally are free agents, having gone a year without signing a new contract.

1980
Major League Baseball is hit with an eight-day strike during spring training, resulting in increased salaries and the first serious constraints in modern times on owner treatment of players. While actions that look like run-of-the-mill union activity dim baseball's romantic image, the labor agitation brings owner-player relations into line with the reality of the late twentieth century.

1981
The Baseball Players' Association strikes for the second time.

1981–
1982
The NCAA schedules women's championships at the same time as AIAW tournaments and offers to pay expenses for schools competing in NCAA women's events. The AIAW cannot hold its membership against this offer, but files an antitrust suit against the NCAA.

1982
On 21 September, in mid-season, NFL players go on strike for the first time; it lasts for 57 days and is the longest strike in the history of professional sports. The Players' Association does not achieve very much financially, but manages to demonstrate to the players that there is a place in professional football for professional labor negotiations. The strike discomfits many fans for the same reasons that baseball's strikes do—the strikes show fans that the players are not playing only for the pleasure of the game, but are professionals who want to be paid as professionals. When an agreement is reached on 16 November, the nation's view of the reasons professionals play football is changed dramatically.

1984
On 28 February, the scope of Title IX is limited by a Supreme Court decision, *Grove City College v. Bell.* The Court rules that Title IX only applies to programs that receive federal aid directly.

The AIWA folds, but its antitrust suit against the NCAA continues until 19 May, when a federal appeals court refuses to reverse an earlier, lower-court decision favoring the NCAA. The voluntary nature of NCAA membership, according to the decision, means that the NCAA is not a trust.

1985
The Baseball Players' Association strikes for the third time.

1987
Walter Byers leaves the NCAA in June, having built the enforcement division to its modern proportions and overseen a tremendous growth in cash flow to the national organization as well as its member colleges. The new executive director, Dick Schultz, is a former athletic director and far more outgoing than the reclusive Byers. Colleges look to the popular Schultz to resolve their problems with the NCAA organization and its enforcement division. Schultz agrees that there are many difficulties to deal with, typical of any large bureaucracy, but says he sees no difficulty in the enforcement division.

1988   On 22 March, Congress overrides a veto by President Reagan to pass the Civil Rights Restoration Act. The law nullifies the Grove City College decision and prohibits sex discrimination in any educational institution that receives federal funding.

Ben Johnson, a star Olympic runner, loses his gold medal on 27 September (from the 100-meter race on 24 September) after postrace testing discloses that he had used stanozolol, an anabolic steroid. Though certainly not the first athlete to engage in substance abuse, Johnson's rapid loss of his star status triggers careful examination of steroid abuse throughout the athletic world. It is now clear even to the most optimistic sports administrators that drug abuse is a serious problem that cannot be wished away. Carl Lewis, Johnson's main competitor who finished second in the race, hinted at an earlier race that Johnson might have been using drugs.

1989   On 25 August, Baseball star Pete Rose agrees to a lifetime banishment from baseball as the result of an investigation which concludes that he is guilty of tax evasion. The commissioner, Bart Giamatti, asserts at a press conference that he is certain Rose had made bets with professional gamblers on baseball games.

1990   On 23 February, Louis W. Sullivan, Secretary of Health and Human Services, calls for an end to cigarette manufacturers sponsoring sports events such as the Virginia Slims tennis tournament.

In an extremely strong statement, Sullivan asserts, "An athlete or sports figure should not allow his or her good name, hard-earned image or integrity to be exploited by the tobacco industry to push a product that when used as intended causes death. This blood money should not be used to foster a misleading impression that smoking is compatible with good health."

The Virginia Slims tournament had been forced off campus from its earlier location at George Washington University in Washington, D.C. by an administration that had held similar views to Sullivan's. In 1990, the tournament was again to be held at the university, which stood to gain scholarship money for women medical students and free tickets for some young people in the area. A statement issued by the university's athletic director said, "We seriously considered the pros and cons before making the decision to house the tournament . . . and

1990
(cont.) concluded that we would do more good for the community by having it here than not."[1]

A preemptive lockout of players by the owners in Major League Baseball (MLB) heats up the union-owner controversy.

In June, discrimination in professional golf erupts as a major issue when the founder of the Shoals Creek Country Club, Alabama, scheduled to host the Professional Golfers' Association championship in August, says in an interview that blacks are not members of his country club because their membership would be unacceptable in Alabama. He states, "The country club is our home and we pick and choose who we want . . . that's just not done in Birmingham."[2]

After falling under the influence of noted boxing trainer Cus D'Amato, Mike Tyson becomes one of the most impressive boxers in history, winning the heavyweight title at the unprecedented young age of 20 on 1 August.

1992 On 26 March, Mike Tyson, former World Heavyweight Boxing Champion, convicted in February of one count of rape and two counts of criminally deviant conduct, is sentenced to ten years in prison, with the final four years suspended. With time off for good behavior, Tyson will spend between three and six years behind bars.

Tyson has a history of minor crimes as a child, and was involved in, but never convicted of, several incidents involving the mistreatment of women, including his former wife. There is some controversy about the fairness of the trial before an all-white jury; there is also evidence that a substantial portion of black males believe he is unfairly convicted.

The "Dream Team," made up of professional basketball players, competes for the United States in the Olympics, demonstrating the commitment of the Olympic Games to allowing the best players in each country to compete, regardless of their amateur or professional status.

Darryl Strawberry of the Dodgers puts his byline on a biographical book manuscript that he acknowledges he did not read before publication.

1993 Dick Schultz announces on 11 May that he will resign as executive director of the NCAA in the wake of an investigation

1993   against the University of Virginia, where he had been athletic
(*cont.*)   director. Regardless of their truth, suggestions that Schultz
might have known about, but not reported, improper loans to
athletes would seriously undercut NCAA enforcement efforts. Schultz is replaced by NCAA secretary-treasurer Cedric
Dempsey (appointed January 1994). Earlier in his career,
Dempsey served as athletic director at the University of Arizona, where he gained a reputation as a strict and careful
observer of NCAA regulations.

1994   Unable to reach an agreement on a new contract, the Major
League Baseball Players' Association calls a strike at midnight,
11 August, against Major League Baseball. Slightly more than
one month later, Acting Baseball Commissioner Bud Selig
declares an official end to the season. Publicly reported negotiations are few, and the major sticking point seems to be the
owners' demands for a salary cap.

One gesture by the owners in the first month of the strike
is notable: Matt Turner, a player suffering from Hodgkins
disease, is released by his team, the Cleveland Indians. By
releasing Turner, which requires paying him the balance of his
1994 contract salary, the team guarantees that Turner will not
lose any money in 1994 as a result of the strike.

In September 1994, upset by a baseball strike that seemed to
have no end in sight, the Senate Antitrust Subcommittee considers limiting the antitrust exemption if the owners try to
unilaterally impose a salary cap on their players. Because the
strike is continuing, the proposal is tabled and will again be
reviewed by the subcommittee in early 1995.

Notes

1. *New York Times*, 24 February 1990, 12.

2. Ira Berkow, "Sports of the Times; an Upright Man Named Watson," *New York Times*, 1 December 1990, 45.

3

Biographical Sketches

Arthur Ashe (1943–1993)

If recent sport history has ever provided us with a black cultural hero, it has to be Arthur Ashe. Competing in a sport that was traditionally a bastion of whiteness, Ashe's calm skill and determination overcame his opponents and he became the first black man to win the U.S. Amateur Singles in 1968. Ashe went on to an enviable career in professional tennis, winning the Australian Open in 1970, and at Wimbledon in 1975. He played until 1979 when he developed a heart condition and had to retire from the game.

Though his outstanding tennis career made him a prime target of racist abuse from those who could not abide the idea of a black sports champion, Ashe was convinced that the best way to combat racism was to demonstrate his ability at sport; Ashe was occasionally criticized during his career for not being more aggressively militant against racism.

Following his heart attack, Ashe did concentrate on civil rights issues in sport, though again, not as militantly as some wanted. His history of blacks in athletics, *Hard Road to Glory* (1988), is a well-researched work that makes the black experience in sports a reality for any reader who's not aware of what African-Americans have had to deal with in American sports.

When Ashe announced in April 1992 that he had contracted Acquired Immune Deficiency Syndrome (AIDS) from an earlier heart bypass operation, the story had already surfaced in the press, and Ashe's announcement was intended to set aside speculation about his personal life. He probably would have preferred to have had no public mention made of his illness, and just disappeared from the public spotlight.

Above all, he was a quiet, gentlemanly person who, because of his status in sport, was never able to achieve the privacy that many successful people in other fields can attain. Ashe died in early 1993, idolized and mourned by many; in his death he was able to finally go beyond the undoubted racism that he and so many others had experienced.

Walter Camp (1859–1925)

As an undergraduate and graduate medical student at Yale University, Walter Camp had played halfback on the Yale football team and had also been his team's captain, an assignment comparable to head coach.

Beginning in 1880, Camp made several suggestions to improve the game (and also to help develop it as more than an offshoot of football's immediate ancestor, rugby). Camp's innovations contributed many of the characteristics of the modern football game, including 11-man teams, a required number of plays in which to advance the ball, and different points for different achievements on the field (such as touchdowns or safety plays).

In his later career, Camp published the first lists of "All-America Teams," although he credited his colleague, Caspar Whitney, with doing the choosing in the early years. The tradition of naming All-America teams continued after Camp's death.

Roberto Clemente (1934–1972)

Although Clemente was a sensational baseball player with a string of impressive playing records, he is remembered best as the modern ballplayer with a fully developed sense of his responsibilities to society.

Playing for the Pittsburgh Pirates for 18 years, beginning in 1954, Clemente accumulated more than 3,000 hits in his career (a feat equaled by only 4 other players), was the National League batting champion 4 times, and received the Golden Glove award for fielding prowess 11 times. He was the Most Valuable Player in the league in 1966, and in the World Series in 1971.

Clemente never forgot his roots in Puerto Rico, and was well known there as Puerto Rico's most important citizen. Additionally, he participated in numerous charitable activities in the United States. On New Year's Eve, 1971, he died in a plane crash while attempting to take supplies to survivors of an earthquake in Nicaragua.

Clemente has not been forgotten by the people of Puerto Rico or by other people who know about or witnessed his efforts on behalf of those in need. His wife and his oldest son, Roberto Clemente, Jr., operate the Roberto Clemente Foundation, committed to helping others and serving society in the same fashion that Roberto Clemente would have desired.

Baron Pierre de Coubertin (1863–1937)

Founder of the Olympic Movement, Coubertin was an educator who toured both the United States and Greece; in Greece he observed excavations of the ancient Olympic Games sites. In 1892, at a conference of the French Athletic Sports Union, he proposed the idea of reviving the Olympic Games.

With his assistance and encouragement, the first modern Olympic Games were held in Athens in 1896. There has been speculation that Coubertin suggested the Olympic Games as a way of encouraging French youth to be fit in order to meet the challenge of the next war against France's traditional rival, Germany. Though this may well have been so, Coubertin sincerely believed that the idea of the Olympic Games would help reduce world tension.

Cedric Dempsey (b. 1932)

Appointed the third executive director of the NCAA in November 1993, Dempsey took office in January 1994 preceded by a reputation for regard for NCAA regulations and a willingness to enforce them.

Dempsey had been athletic director at the University of Arizona, where his stint was an exercise in the types of problems the NCAA faces regularly. A former college basketball star, Dempsey was brought to Arizona in the wake of an athletic department slush-fund scandal, and Dempsey made his presence felt by assuring that the university stayed on the straight and narrow. He severely punished an assistant coach who had given a college athlete an airplane ticket, establishing himself as someone who was dedicated to enforcing NCAA regulations.

No stranger to the NCAA, Dempsey had served as the organization's secretary-treasurer since January 1993. Though his predecessor, Dick Schultz, resigned under the cloud of an NCAA investigation which concluded that Schultz had known about illicit loans to athletes at the University of Virginia, Schultz had been expected to strengthen the NCAA's enforcement efforts. If anything, Dempsey's reputation for strong enforcement and honesty is greater than Schultz's; if he can master the Byzantine bureaucracy, he may very well be the person to bring the NCAA into the modern age.

Donald Fehr (1948–   )

Executive director of the Major League Players' Association, Fehr worked with Marvin Miller in the early days of baseball player organization. Appointed in 1983, he is a strong advocate of the needs of his players. Although more willing than Miller was to deal with issues that are not specifically union related, Fehr is as dedicated as Miller in pursuing the players' rights to receive their fair share of the profits that major league baseball gets.

Althea Gibson (1927–   )

An enormously popular tennis player by the time of her retirement from the game in 1958, Gibson broke racial barriers in tennis by being the first black to compete in a major national tournament (Forest Hills, 1950). She was also the first black American to compete at Wimbledon (1951) and won both the Forest Hills and Wimbledon singles in 1957. Born to a poor family in South Carolina, her career in tennis began with winning play in various "Negro" tourneys including the New York State Negro girls' singles (1943) and the National Negro singles tournament in 1948.

Following her tennis career, Gibson tried professional golf, where she broke racial barriers in that sport with the assistance of Lenny Wirtz, Ladies Professional Golf Association director, who insisted that tournaments accept association players of all colors.[1]

"Shoeless" Joe Jackson (1887–1951)

One of the finest baseball players of the early twentieth century (and of all time), Jackson's career ended in discord following the

"Black Sox" scandal of 1920. He got his nickname after playing in his stocking feet in one game when his new shoes bothered him.

Jackson and seven other teammates on the White Sox were accused of taking bribes to throw the 1919 World Series. Although none of the players were convicted, they were banned for life from baseball by Commissioner Kenesaw Mountain Landis; Landis had been appointed commissioner specifically to help restore national confidence in the game.

Jackson had been a national hero. As the perhaps apocryphal story goes, during his trial a small boy came up to him and, tears in his eyes, begged Jackson to "Say it ain't so, Joe." Supposedly, Jackson could not respond.

In later years, Jackson denied that he had accepted a bribe. Feeling that baseball had turned away from him, he never petitioned to be reinstated; if he had been reinstated, he would surely have been ensconced in the Hall of Fame as one of the best batters and outfielders the game has ever known.

Billie Jean King (1943–   )

An incredibly powerful and successful tennis player during her professional career, King's name is recognized and respected even by those with no interest in tennis. Among her many achievements in both amateur and professional tennis is the world record number of Wimbledon titles—6 in singles competition, and 14 as a doubles partner.

Her win in the 1973 "Match of the Century" against 1939 Wimbledon men's champion Bobby Riggs, the "Clown Prince of Tennis," was a major advancement for women's rights in sports. Benjamin Rader has called King "one of the most important heroes of the revived feminist movement of the 1970's."[2] King established once and for all that women could play professional-level championship tennis, and have as much right as men to expect professional-level tournament purses and recognition. In retirement from tennis, King is active today in various social causes including discrimination against women and homosexuals.

Kenesaw Mountain Landis (1866–1944)

In the wake of the "Black Sox" scandal of 1919, in which eight baseball players were accused of accepting bribes to throw the World Series, team owners desperately searched for a way to restore the integrity of the game in the eyes of the public. Their solution, and one which worked, was to appoint an executive with tremendous administrative powers over all of baseball.

Judge Landis, appointed commissioner in January 1921, proved to be as forceful as any fan could desire; his banning of the players who had been involved in the scandal, including the popular "Shoeless" Joe Jackson, allowed organized baseball to look squeaky clean. In the interests of its public image, organized baseball was willing to accept the concept of the owners hiring a commissioner with almost unlimited powers—Landis's contract contained a clause loosely empowering him to act "in the best interests of baseball." This clause has remained in the contract of every baseball commissioner since Landis, including Fay Vincent, who resigned under fire for being a touch too vigorous in the pursuit of baseball's interests; the next commissioner will probably not have a similar clause in his or her contract.

Landis's contract did not reflect the power that he was allowed to exercise. Commissioners hired after Landis frequently found that they had less than total control over the major leagues, and could be both hired and fired without cause by the owners of the major league teams.

The history of the office of the baseball commissioner is dominated by power struggles between the owners and the commissioner. The last commissioner, Vincent, was removed by the owners for trying to exercise the power that, in the public mind if not in reality, the commissioner had always had. As of early 1994, no new commissioner had been appointed.

Though it is possible that organized baseball will continue to do business without a commissioner, it is more likely that it will eventually hire someone for the job. Regardless of who is hired, the new commissioner may well find him- or herself embroiled in controversy with the owners at one point or another, with the owners attempting to control an employee, and the commissioner trying to fulfill the demands of an office that, at least in theory, serves two masters—the team owners and the American public.

Branch Rickey (1881–1965)

Former owner of the Brooklyn Dodgers, Rickey decided that it was time to begin integrating blacks into the ranks of professional baseball players. In 1947, Rickey settled upon Jackie Robinson to be the first black to play professional ball.

Though his motives may have originally been economic, since he realized that blacks were an untapped segment of potential baseball fans, Rickey was also well aware that baseball's failure to field black players simply was not right. (Rickey was known, among other things, for not going to Sunday baseball games because of a promise he had made to his mother.)

His choice of Robinson was made carefully. Rickey needed someone who would be strong enough to take the abuse that the first black ballplayer was sure to receive without falling apart on the field. He chose well—Robinson became not only the first black to play in the major leagues, but also one of the finest ballplayers of all races, deserving of his Hall of Fame status.

Frank Robinson (1935–   )

The first black manager of a major-league baseball team, Robinson began his major-league playing career in 1956, playing with the Cincinnati Reds and earning the National League's Rookie-of-the-Year award. Although an appealing figure to the fans, Robinson was not always popular with management; though he had no incredibly major conflicts, he was traded several times in his career. His performance after each trade was exceptional, and Robinson was the first man ever to win the Most Valuable Player award in both the National and the American Leagues. Toward the end of his playing career, Robinson made it clear that he was interested in managing, and managed teams in the winter league in Puerto Rico for several years. In 1975 he was appointed player-manager for the Cleveland Indians, a position he held until 1977. He was manager of the San Francisco Giants and the Baltimore Orioles and had joined the Orioles executive staff in 1985. Still a member of the Orioles organization, he returned to coaching in 1988 to help the team break out of a slump.

Jackie Robinson (1919–1972)

The first black man to play professional baseball in modern times, Robinson was recruited by Branch Rickey both because of his outstanding baseball ability, and also because of his likely ability to control his temper when taunted by other players and fans. Robinson was the ideal choice. He managed to keep his temper in check while receiving the abuse and scorn from the racist world around him. He went on to become one of the finest baseball players of all time, regardless of race.

Following his baseball career, Robinson became a spokesman for the growing civil rights movement in the United States. According to Robert Lipsyte, "He funneled his competitive rage into politics, banking, housing, and civil rights, all with a strong racial thrust. . . . [T]he sporting press, according to Robinson, was put off by his complexity and his refusal to be a 'cringing handkerchief-head standing before you with his hat in his hand expressing eternal gratitude'."[3]

Pete Rose (1941–   )

Certainly one of the most aggressive and one of the best baseball players in recent years, Rose was known for his ability to wring the most out of each and every play in which he was involved, and quickly gained the nickname "Charlie Hustle." He set the record for most career hits (4,191), tied the 1897 record of Wee Willie Keeler for hitting safely in 44 straight games, and set or tied several other important records.

Following allegations of gambling misconduct, Rose was banished from baseball for life by Commissioner A. Bartlett Giamatti in August 1989; Giamatti's death several days after the banishment is widely attributed to the strain of the investigation. Rose never admitted to betting on baseball games (the charge that Giamatti was most concerned about), although he confessed he had gambled; shortly afterward, Rose was sentenced to prison for tax evasion.

As a banished player, Rose cannot be a member of the Baseball Hall of Fame, although his exploits on the field would have made any other ballplayer a legend in his own time. Whether he should have been banished and, especially, whether or not he should be in the Hall of Fame, are serious ethical issues which bear examination. To what extent should an athlete's off-field exploits affect the way he is seen by his peers in the game?

Rose has said that he will apply for reinstatement from the lifetime ban in order to permit his nomination to the Hall of Fame, but as of early 1994 he has not done so, perhaps waiting for a new baseball commissioner to be appointed. Applying the same energy to business that he did to baseball, Rose is involved in endorsements and other businesses designed to capitalize on his famous name.

Published information about Rose makes it impossible to gauge the extent of the bitterness he has regarding his suspension. Echoing earlier protestations, Rose told Ira Berkow in early 1993:

> What people don't understand is that I wasn't even suspended from baseball for betting on baseball games. I was suspended for admitting that I bet on football games with bookmakers. . . . And then at the press conference, Giamatti answers a question saying he believes I bet on baseball. But they could never prove it. . . . My only crime was picking the wrong friends.[4]

David Stern

The fourth commissioner of the National Basketball Association, who took office in February 1984, Stern has led the organization in an extremely successful international marketing effort which has brought the NBA countless millions of dollars. Respected by the players, Stern has been involved with the NBA since the mid-1970s, and, as one of the NBA's lawyers, worked on several important cases including the 1976 Oscar Robertson antitrust suit.

Actively involved in the important 1983 player negotiations, Stern was part of the group that established revenue sharing among the NBA teams.

Carl Stotz

Stotz, along with George and Bert Bebble, founded what became Little League Baseball in 1939, the world's largest youth sports organization. By soliciting local merchants, Stotz was able to provide his players in Williamsport, Pennsylvania, with uniforms and equipment. According to Jules Loh, Associated Press special correspondent, one of the reasons for the spread of Little League was the large number of former players who served throughout the world in World War II.[5]

In 1956, Stotz resigned from the Little League organization that he had built. Little League had grown too large and, Stotz felt, too commercial; it had gone way beyond his original intentions. Stotz retained the rights, however, to the name "Original Little League." Unlike the international organization, the Williamsport Original Little League allows only a few hundred children, boys and girls, to play baseball. And children throughout the world, playing baseball in both the original and the new Little League, owe a lot of their childhood pleasures to a man who was just beginning his career as a clerk in a lumberyard when he wanted to help some children have some fun.

Paul Tagliabue (1940–   )

The commissioner of the National Football League, Tagliabue was appointed to his position on 26 October 1989 to replace Pete Rozelle. As counsel to the NFL, Tagliabue had helped Rozelle bring professional football to its current status as a wealthy, attractive, and nationwide phenomenon. A former star in college basketball, Tagliabue has an understanding of what makes sports attractive to fans. As a longtime NFL insider, he is sensitive to the needs of the NFL organization and its relationship with the public.

Characterized as extremely smart, hardworking, and sincere, Tagliabue knows his business inside and out. Although, like all commissioners of professional sports, he is hired by the owners, Tagliabue seems to have the sincerity and the interest in both the organization and the players to keep football growing and to benefit the owners, the players, and the fans.

Jim Thorpe (1888–1953)

Jim Thorpe was one of the most impressive sports figures of the early twentieth century, if not of all time. Thorpe fell afoul of the problem of amateurism versus professionalism that plagued many American athletes until the U.S. Olympic Committee revised its rules and began to talk about eligibility rather than amateurism as a qualification for competing in the Olympics.

A mixed-blood American Indian, Thorpe was an almost instant star at the Carlisle Institute in Pennsylvania, an Indian school he attended during his high-school years. Although his forte was football, he excelled in several other sports including track and decathlon. With the sponsorship of the legendary coach "Pop" Warner, Thorpe trained for and competed in the 1912 Olympics, earning gold medals and setting world records for his achievements in the decathlon and the pentathlon.

Sadly, Thorpe was forced to return his medals after it was found that he had played baseball for money for a minor-league club during 1909–1911. Thorpe himself did not feel that he had done anything wrong. For a poor young man to participate in a sport other than his Olympic sport did not seem to be a problem. "How could I know," Thorpe asked, "that playing baseball for money [$25 a week] made me a pro in football and track?"[6]

Though Thorpe played baseball again, his life after 1930, when the United States fell into the Great Depression, was not very rewarding. Though his Olympic status was restored after his death, the period before his death in 1953 was extremely difficult.

Thorpe's example is the most striking, though not the only, instance of the problem that American athletes have had with the artificial division between professionalism and amateurism. It is unclear if Thorpe felt that, in addition to the amateur/professional question, he was discriminated against because of his Indian heritage. Today's Olympic organizations, in the United States and elsewhere, speak of eligibility, and the eligibility requirements are very clear. But for Jim Thorpe, being paid for doing anything athletic, even in a field that was not his area of competition, was a lifelong disaster.

Sonny Vaccaro

As top marketer for Nike shoes until 1992, Vaccaro was responsible for developing the idea of arranging court-shoe contracts with college basketball coaches. Operating at the limit (some would say the edge) of NCAA regulations, Vaccaro found a willing market for his endorsement contracts. Because he found it necessary to understand and perhaps even predict what was happening in college basketball, Vaccaro made it his business to know almost everyone in the basketball scene.

Fay Vincent (1927–   )

Vincent may have been "the last baseball commissioner," at least the last commissioner with any dream or intention of filling the shoes of Judge Landis (see entry above). A friend and aide of former commissioner Bart Giamatti, Vincent seemed like a good choice to replace the man who had died suddenly in office. But in trying to follow the mandate of ruling "in the best interests of baseball," Vincent managed to alienate a large number of the owners. Since Landis, there had always been a conflict between the reality of the commissioner being an employee of the owners (much as a corporate CEO is an employee of the board of trustees) and the theoretical responsibility of serving not only the owners, but also the players and the fans.

When Vincent resigned (following a no-confidence vote of the owners), the owners ostensibly began searching for a replacement.

As of early 1994, however, no replacement had been found. It seems unlikely that there will be a new commissioner until a new contract with the players is negotiated. If there ever is a new commissioner, that job will be substantially different than it has been heretofore.

Notes

1. *The Lincoln Library of Sport Champions,* Vol. VI, (Columbus, OH: Frontier Press, 1989): 100–105.

2. Benjamin Rader, *In Its Own Image: How Television Has Transformed Sport,* (New York: Macmillan, 1984).

3. Robert Lipsyte, "Where, Oh Where, Is Roar of the Athlete?" *New York Times,* 7 February 1993, VIII:8.

4. Ira Berkow, "Charlie Hustle's 2d Chance," *New York Times,* 28 February 1993, VIII:1.

5. Jules Loh, "Little League: At 50, League Still Suffers Growing Pains," *Richmond* (Virginia) *Times-Dispatch,* 4 June 1989, K:1.

6. *The Lincoln Library of Sports Champions,* Vol. VIII, (Columbus, OH: Frontier Press, 1989).

4

Documents

ALL ORGANIZATIONS HAVE DOCUMENTS—creeds, codes of conduct and deportment, reports and recommendations—that attempt to dictate ethical behavior, particularly those involved in the organized play of sport. Documents are an unbiased testament to the history, criticism, and continuing evolution of sports ethics. This chapter examines many types of documents dealing with sports ethics on all levels of organized play—childhood, college, Olympic, and professional. Excerpts from relevant court cases and laws, in addition to organization documents, are also included.

Children in Sports

Excerpt from Public Law 88-378; 78 Statue 325
An Act To Incorporate the Little League Baseball, Incorporated
(16 July 1964)

The United States Congress does not easily grant charters or recognition to just any organization. At the least, the organization needs to be in tune with what the Congress perceives as the national interest. Thus, a national law recognizing achievements (present, past, or future) is relatively rare, and an instance of unusual support for an organization or purpose. In 1964, the Little League, which had already begun to reach out to youngsters worldwide, was recognized as part of the American fabric.

OBJECTS AND PURPOSES OF CORPORATION

Sec 3. The objects and purposes of the corporation shall be—

    (1) To promote, develop, supervise, and voluntarily assist in all lawful ways the interest of boys who will participate in Little League baseball.

    (2) To help and voluntarily assist boys in developing qualities of citizenship, sportsmanship, and manhood.

    (3) Using the disciplines of the Native American game of baseball, to teach spirit and the competitive will to win, physical fitness through individual sacrifice, the values of team play and wholesome well-being through healthful and social association with other youngsters under proper leadership.

Excerpt from Public Law 93-551; 88 Statute. 1744
An Act To Amend the Act To Incorporate Little League Baseball To Provide that the League Shall Be Open to Girls as well as Boys (26 December 1974)

Following several lawsuits about the Little League's restrictions of girls and women (at least one of which had already been decided in their favor, Congress moved in 1974 to require access to the organization to members of both sexes. Little League could have refused the congressional mandate, choosing to go it alone and continue enrolling only boys. In enlarging its mission, Little League ensured its role as the largest youth sports organization in the United States, and in the world.

Section 3 of the Act of 16 July 1964, entitled "An Act to incorporate the Little League Baseball, Incorporated" (Public Law 88-378), is amended by striking out "boys" each place it appears and inserting in lieu thereof "young people" and by striking out "citizenship, sports-manship, and manhood" and inserting in lieu thereof "citizenship and sportsmanship."

Excerpt from the decision of Judge Philip Conford,
Superior Court of New Jersey, Appellate Division,
National Organization for Women v. Little League Baseball
(127 N.J. Super), argued 25 March 1974, decided 29 March 1974

In 1974, the National Organization for Women (NOW) challenged Little League regulations in the state of New Jersey which prohibited girls from playing youth baseball in their communities. By the end of March, after a court decision in favor of girls' play by the Appellate Division of Superior Court, nearly 2,000 Little League teams, representing 115,000 boys, temporarily suspended play rather than comply with the court's decision and an order of integration from the New Jersey Division on Civil Rights. The teams claimed that they would not be "intimidated" by NOW.

While the New Jersey teams took issue with what they saw as unwarranted meddling by the court in their business, the national Little League organization reacted with stoic, Eeyore-like pessimism. Commented Robert Stirrat, a national vice president, "Nothing's been going our way recently."

Although the court decision could be appealed to a higher state court, objective observers believed that the ruling of Judge Philip Conford of the State Superior Court would stand. As a "public accommodation" (i.e., a place or service paid for by all taxpayers from general funds), Little League could not allow sexual discrimination. Conford stated, in his majority (2-1) opinion, that

Little League is a public accommodation because the invitation is open to children in the community at large with no restriction whatever. It is public in the added sense that characteristically local governmental bodies make the playing area available to the local leagues, ordinarily without charge.

In June, national Little League officials announced that they would "defer to the changing social climate" and allow girls to play on their teams. Despite their earlier opposition, the national organization asserted on 12 June 1974 that they thought it "imprudent for an organization as large and universally respected as 35-year-old Little League baseball to allow itself to become embroiled in a public controversy."

The Little League Pledge

Most youth sports organizations are committed, at least nominally, to developing a spirit of good citizenship and a sound ethical background in their young players. Little League's commitment to its pledge, though occasionally neglected in the hurlyburly of everyday play, reflects a legitimate concern for the ethical well-being of its players, and is far from a *pro forma* statement that can be easily ignored.

I TRUST IN GOD
I LOVE MY COUNTRY
AND WILL RESPECT ITS LAWS
I WILL PLAY FAIR
AND STRIVE TO WIN
BUT WIN OR LOSE
I WILL ALWAYS
DO MY BEST

College Athletics

Excerpt from Title IX of the Education Amendments of 1972 (S659-PL-92-318) signed by President Richard M. Nixon 23 June 1972

The growing women's liberation movement in the United States had reached significant proportions by the early 1970s. Included in its growth was recognition that women and girls were being slighted in their access to all of the advantages of educational programs; men and boys enjoyed a disproportionate share of school financial outlays. Since federal assistance to education was (and is) of great import to colleges, universities, and even local school districts, the growing sentiment toward equal access for women and girls found its voice in the 1972 congressional regulations relating to funding of education from federal sources.

No person in the United States shall, on the basis of sex, be excluded from participation in, be denied the benefits of, or be subjected to discrimination under any educational program or activity receiving federal financial assistance.

Excerpt from 1979 Department of Health, Education, and Welfare compliance guidelines for 1972 Title IX

Despite the 1972 passage of Title IX, heartening to those seeking equal access to sports in education, the law had little meaning unless guidelines were established and enforced. In 1979, the

Department of Health, Education, and Welfare finally issued its interpretation of Title IX. Compliance was certainly not assured, but the possibility of equal access became a far more reachable goal than it had been in the years between 1972 and 1979.

1. The Regulation

The Regulation requires that recipients that operate or sponsor interscholastic, intercollegiate, club, or intramural athletics "provide equal athletic opportunities for members of both sexes." In determining whether an institution is providing equal opportunity in intercollegiate athletics, the regulation requires the Department to consider, among others, the following factors: . . .

(2) provision and maintenance of equipment and supplies;

(3) scheduling of game and practice times;

(4) travel and per diem expenses;

(5) opportunity to receive coaching and academic tutoring;

(6) assignment and compensation of coaches and tutors;

(7) provision of locker rooms, practice, and competitive facilities;

(8) provision of medical and training services and facilities;

(9) provision of housing and dining services and facilities; and

(10) publicity.

2. The Policy

The Department will assess compliance with both the recruitment and the general athletic program requirements of the regulation by comparing the availability, quality, and kinds of benefits, opportunities, and treatment afforded members of both sexes. Institutions will be in compliance if the compared program components are equivalent, that is, equal or equal in effect. Under the standard, identical benefits, opportunities, or treatment are not required, provided the overall effect of any differences is negligible.

If comparisons of program components reveal that treatment, benefits, or opportunities are not equivalent in kind, quality, or availability, a finding of compliance may still be justified if the differences are the result of nondiscriminatory factors. Some of the factors that may justify these differences are as follows:

(a) Some aspects of athletic programs may not be equivalent for men and women because of unique aspects of particular sports or athletic activities. . . .

Generally, these differences will be the result of factors that are inherent to the basic operation of specific sports. Such factors may include rules of play, nature/replacement of equipment, rates of injury resulting from participation, nature of facilities required for competition, and the maintenance/upkeep requirements of those facilities. For the most part, differences involving such factors will occur in programs offering football, and consequently these differences will favor men. If sport-specific needs are met equivalently in both men's and women's programs, however, differences in particular program components will be found to be justifiable.

(b) Some aspects of athletic programs may not be equivalent for men and women because of legitimately sex-neutral factors related to special circumstances of a temporary nature. For example, large disparities in recruitment activity for any particular year may be the result of annual fluctuation in team needs for first-year athletes. Such differences are justifiable to the extent that they do not reduce overall equality of opportunity.

(c) The activities directly associated with the operation of a competitive event in a single-sex sport may, under some circumstances, create unique demands or imbalances in particular program components. Provided that special demands associated with the activities of sports involving participants of the other sex are met to an equivalent degree, the resulting differences may be found nondiscriminatory. At many schools, for example, certain sports—notably football and men's basketball—traditionally draw large crowds. Since the costs of managing an athletic event increase with crowd size, the overall support made available for event management may differ in degree and kind. . . . if the recipient does not limit the potential for women's athletic events to rise in spectator appeal and if the levels of event management support available to both programs are based on sex-neutral criteria (e.g., facilities used, projected attendance, and staffing needs).

Excerpt from Article VI, Section 9, of NJCAA Constitution and Bylaws (1993–1994 handbook)

The National Junior College Athletic Association (NJCAA), like the NCAA, regulates the way junior and community colleges disburse scholarship funds to athletes, establishes standards for treatment of the athletes, and organizes the intramural tournaments in which junior colleges play.

Athletic Scholarship Guidelines For Divisional Play

Division I—A maximum of tuition and fees, room and board, book and course-related material and transportation costs one time per academic year to and from the college by direct route.

Division II—A maximum of tuition and fees OR tuition and books.

Division III—No athletic scholarship aid of any kind.

[Note: Divisional play is by sport not by college programs. The number of allowable scholarships for each sport in each division is listed in the sports procedures section of the *NJCAA Handbook.*]

The Sport Procedures section of the *NJCAA Handbook* is a chart (summarized below) listing requirements for the following items:

- Starting dates for practices and games
- Ending date for practices and games
- Number of contests allowed each season
- Number of scrimmages allowed per season
- Number of letters-of-intent per year
- Number of scholarships in the sport at any given time
- Signing date for each sport of the letter-of-intent
- Limiting number of allowable athletic financial scholarships to F1-Visa athletes (i.e, visiting athletes with a visa) to no more than one-quarter of the total athletic aid allowed by NJCAA rules in that particular sport

Excerpts from the *NCAA 1994 Manual*

Over five hundred pages in length, the *1994–1995 NCAA Manual* spells out in excruciating detail each and every policy and rule of the National Collegiate Athletic Association.

In fairness to the NCAA, it should be pointed out that many regulations (operating or administrative bylaws) are fine-tuned almost annually, the manual prints both the new and the old rules (for at least one year after superannuation), and there are many pages that contain both old and new bylaws. Additionally, the rules on playing seasons are broken down on a sport-by-sport basis, and take as many as 48 pages to describe each sport's season.

Among the criticisms the NCAA has been subjected to is the accusation that its regulations are so detailed that they take away members' desires to do more than the rules require. Many colleges and universities consequently feel the need to have an "enforcement officer" on staff whose primary responsibility is to know and interpret for the college the NCAA regulations. On the other hand, it is clear that the NCAA might well be criticized for not spelling out exactly what is required of its members. There can only be a certain number of instances when it is acceptable to discipline a member for failure to follow the spirit (and not the letter) of the bylaws.

The excerpts below are some of the NCAA's more interesting and more important statements and regulations. Some regulations have been highly criticized, such as article 32.7.5.8, which regulates the recording of disciplinary proceedings. The excerpts begin with parts of the NCAA Constitution, and are followed by Operating Bylaws (articles 10–23) and then Administrative Bylaws. Revision or adoption dates have been omitted; one of the significant regulations reprinted below (instituted in 1992) allows faculty members or athletic department members to give an athlete an occasional meal.

The NCAA uses a numerical heading system. In each main section, an article is numbered; further delineations of an article use the article's number, followed by a decimal point and an additional number. In some instances, there are as many as six numbers marking a regulation, as in article 16.1.4.2.4.1 (Eligibility for Bowl-Game Awards, which limits the award an athlete can receive from a sponsoring agency of a bowl game or a college to $300).

The following information is reprinted from the *1994–1995 NCAA Manual* by permission of the National Collegiate Athletic Association. The material is subject to annual review and change.

CONSTITUTION, ARTICLE 1

1.2 PURPOSES

The purposes of this Association are:

(a) To initiate, stimulate and improve intercollegiate athletics programs for student-athletes and to promote and develop educational leadership, physical fitness, athletics excellence, and athletics participation as a recreational pursuit;

(b) To uphold the principle of institutional control of, and responsibility for, all intercollegiate sports in conformity with the constitution and bylaws of this Association;

(c) To encourage its members to adopt eligibility rules to comply with satisfactory standards of scholarship, sportsmanship, and amateurism;

(d) To formulate, copyright and publish rules of play governing intercollegiate athletics;

(e) To preserve intercollegiate athletics records;

(f) To supervise the conduct of, and to establish eligibility standards for, regional and national athletics events under the auspices of this Association:

(g) To cooperate with other amateur athletic organizations in promoting and conducting national and international athletics events;

(h) To legislate, through bylaws or by resolutions of a Convention, upon any subject of general concern to the members related to the administration of intercollegiate athletics, and

(i) To study in general all phases of competitive intercollegiate athletics and establish standards whereby the colleges and universities of the United States can maintain their athletic programs on a high level.

1.3 FUNDAMENTAL POLICY

1.3.1 Basic Purpose. The competitive athletics programs of member institutions are designed to be a vital part of the educational system. A basic purpose of this Association is to maintain intercollegiate athletics as an integral part of the educational program and the athlete as an integral part of the student body and, by so doing, retain a clear line of demarcation between intercollegiate athletics and professional sports.

CONSTITUTION, ARTICLE 2

Principles for Conduct of Intercollegiate Athletics

2.1 THE PRINCIPLE OF INSTITUTIONAL CONTROL AND RESPONSIBILITY

2.1.1 Responsibility for Control. It is the responsibility of each member institution to control its intercollegiate athletics program in compliance with the rules and regulations of the Association. The institution's chief executive officer is responsible for the administration of all aspects of the athletics program, including approval of the budget and audit of all expenditures.
2.1.2 Scope of Responsibility. The institution's responsibility for the conduct of its intercollegiate athletics program includes responsibility for the actions of its staff members and for the actions of any other individual or organization engaged in activities promoting the athletics interest of the institution.

2.2 THE PRINCIPLE OF STUDENT–ATHLETE WELFARE

Intercollegiate athletics programs shall be conducted in a manner designed to protect and enhance the physical and educational welfare of student-athletes.

2.3 THE PRINCIPLE OF GENDER EQUITY

2.3.1 Compliance With Federal and State Legislation. It is the responsibility of each member institution to comply with federal and state laws regarding gender equity.
2.3.2 NCAA Legislation. The Association should not adopt legislation that would prevent member institutions from complying with applicable gender-equity laws, and should adopt legislation to enhance member institutions' compliance with applicable gender-equity laws.

2.3.3 Gender Bias. The activities of the Association should be conducted in a manner free of gender bias.

2.4 THE PRINCIPLE OF ETHICAL CONDUCT

Student-athletes of a member institution and individuals employed by, or associated with, that institution shall deport themselves with honesty and good sportsmanship. Their behavior shall at all times reflect the high standards of honor and dignity that characterize participation in competitive sports in the collegiate setting.

2.5 THE PRINCIPLE OF SOUND ACADEMIC STANDARDS

Intercollegiate athletics programs shall be maintained as a vital component of the educational program, and student-athletes shall be an integral part of the student body. The admission, academic standing, and academic progress of student-athletes shall be consistent with the policies and standards adopted by the institution for the student body in general.

2.6 THE PRINCIPLE OF NONDISCRIMINATION

The Association shall promote an atmosphere of respect for and sensitivity to the dignity of every person. It is the policy of the Association to refrain from discrimination with respect to its governance policies, educational programs, activities, and employment policies. [Adopted 1/16/93]

2.7 THE PRINCIPLE OF RULES COMPLIANCE

2.7.1 Responsibility of Institution. Each institution shall comply with all applicable rules and regulations of the Association in the conduct of its intercollegiate athletics programs. It shall monitor its programs to assure compliance and to identify and report to the Association instances in which compliance has not been achieved. In any such instance, the institution shall cooperate fully with the Association and shall take appropriate corrective actions. Members of an institution's staff, student-athletes, and other individuals and groups representing the institution's athletic interests shall comply with the applicable Association rules, and the member institution shall be responsible for such compliance.
2.7.3 Penalty for Noncompliance. An institution found to have violated the Association's rules shall be subject to such disciplinary and corrective actions as may be determined by the Association.

2.8 THE PRINCIPLE OF AMATEURISM

Student-athletes shall be amateurs in an intercollegiate sport, and their participation should be motivated primarily by education and by the physical, mental, and social benefits to be derived. Student participation in intercollegiate athletics is an avocation, and student-athletes should be protected from exploitation by professional and commercial enterprises.

2.12 THE PRINCIPLE GOVERNING FINANCIAL AID

A student-athlete may receive athletically related financial aid administered by the institution without violating the principle of amateurism, provided the amount does not exceed the cost of education authorized by the Association. Any other financial assistance, except that received from one upon whom the student-athlete is naturally or legally dependent, shall be prohibited unless specifically authorized by the Association.

2.13 THE PRINCIPLE GOVERNING PLAYING AND PRACTICE SEASONS

The time required of student-athletes for participation in inter-collegiate athletics shall be regulated to minimize interference with their opportunities for acquiring a quality education in a manner consistent with that afforded the general student body.

11.2.2 Athletically Related Income. Contractual agreements, including letters of appointment, between a full-time or part-time athletics department staff member. . . . and an institution shall include the stipulation that the staff member is required to receive annually prior written approval from the chief executive officer for all athletically related income and benefits from sources outside the institution. The staff member's request for approval shall be in writing and shall include the amount and the source of the income. Sources of such income shall include, but are not limited to, the following

(a) Income from annuities;

(b) Sports camps;

(c) Housing benefits (including preferential housing arrangements);

(d) Country club memberships;

(e) Complimentary ticket sales;

(f) Television and radio programs, and

(g) Endorsement or consultation contracts with athletics shoe, apparel or equipment manufacturers.

11.3.2.8 Compensation in Exchange for Use of Merchandise. Staff members of a member institution's athletics department shall not accept, prior to receiving approval (in writing in Divisions I and II) from the institution's chief executive officer, compensation or gratuities (excluding institutionally administered funds) from an athletic shoe, apparel, or equipment manufacturer in exchange for the use of such merchandise during practice or competition by the institution's student-athletes. [see 11.2.2]; [revised 1/10/92].

12.01.3 "Individual" vs. "Student-Athlete." NCAA amateur status may be lost as a result of activities prior to enrollment in college. If NCAA rules specify that an "individual" may or may not participate in certain activities, this term refers to a person prior to and subsequent to enrollment by a member institution. If NCAA rules specify a "student-athlete," the legislation applies only to that person's activities subsequent to enrollment.

13.15.4 Slush Funds. An institution shall not permit any outside organization, agency or group of individuals to utilize, administer or expend funds for recruiting prospects, including the transportation and entertainment of, and the giving of gifts or services to, prospects or their relatives or friends.

14.2.1 Five-Year Rule—Division 1. The student-athlete shall complete his or her seasons of participation within five calendar years from the beginning of the semester or quarter in which the student-athlete first registered for a minimum full-time program of studies in a collegiate institution. . . .

14.2.1.3 Pregnancy Exception. A member institution may approve a one-year extension of the five-year period of eligibility for a female student-athlete for reasons of pregnancy.

14.4 SATISFACTORY-PROGRESS REQUIREMENTS

14.4.1 Satisfactory-Progress Requirements—All Divisions. To be eligible to represent an institution in intercollegiate athletics competition, a student-athlete shall maintain satisfactory progress toward a baccalaureate or equivalent degree at that institution as determined by the regulations of that institution. As a general requirement, "satisfactory progress" is to be interpreted at each member institution by the academic authorities who determine the meaning of such phrases for all students, subject to controlling legislation of the conference(s) or similar association of which the institution is a member. . . .

14.4.3.3.1 Division 1. A student-athlete who is entering his or her third year of collegiate enrollment shall present a cumulative minimum grade-point average (based upon a maximum of 4.000) that equals at least 90 percent of the institution's overall cumulative minimum grade-point average required for graduation. A student-athlete who is entering his or her fourth or subsequent year of collegiate enrollment shall present a cumulative minimum grade-point average (based upon a minimum of 4.000) that equals 95 percent of the institution's overall cumulative minimum grade-point average required for graduation. . . .

15.4.8 Athletics Funds or Endowments. No part of an institution's financial aid budget shall be set aside either for particular sports or for athletics in general, nor may an institution establish athletically related quotas of financial aid recipients. . . .

15.4.9 Consistent Financial Aid Package. The composition of the financial aid package offered to a student-athlete shall be consistent with the established policy of the institution's financial aid office for all students and shall meet all of the following criteria:

(a) A member institution shall not consider athletics ability as a criterion in the formulation of the financial aid package;

(b) The financial aid procedures used for a student-athlete are the same as the existing official financial aid policies of the institution;

(c) The financial aid package for a particular student-athlete cannot be clearly distinguishable from the general pattern of all financial aid for all recipients at the institution, and

(d) The percentage of the total dollar value of institutionally administered grants awarded to student-athletes shall be closely equivalent to the percentage of student-athletes within the student body. . . .

16.1.4.2.1 Number and Value of Awards. The total value of any single award to any one student-athlete for a special event many not exceed $300, except awards presented by the Association to student-athletes for participation in NCAA championship events. . . .

16.1.4.2.2 NCAA Championships Participation. Awards presented by the Association to student-athletes for participation in any NCAA championship event are not subject to any limitation on the value of the award. . . .

16.12.1.6 Occasional Meals. A student-athlete or the entire team in a sport may receive an occasional family home meal from an institutional staff member or representative of athletics interest under the following conditions:

(a) The meal must be provided in an individual's home (as opposed to a restaurant) and may be catered;

(b) Meals must be restricted to infrequent and special occasions, and,

(c) The institution (or a representative of its athletics interests) may not provide transportation to student-athletes to attend the meal function.

16.12.2.3 Other Prohibited Benefits. An institutional employee or representatives of the institution's athletics interests may not provide a student-athlete with extra benefits or service, including, but not limited to:

(a) A loan of money;

(b) A guarantee of bond;

(c) The use of an automobile, or,

(d) Signing or cosigning a note with an outside agency to arrange a loan.

ADMINISTRATIVE BYLAW, ARTICLE 32
ENFORCEMENT POLICIES AND PROCEDURES

32.2.2.4 Notice to Institution. The enforcement staff shall submit a letter to the chief executive officer to notify a member institution of preliminary inquiries into its athletics polices and practices when information has been developed to indicate that violations of the Association's governing legislation may have occurred that will require further in-person investigation. Such a letter shall advise the chief executive officer that the enforcement staff will be undertaking a preliminary investigation, that the investigation will be conducted under the direction of the assistant executive director for enforcement and that members of the enforcement staff wish to meet with the chief executive officer to discuss the nature of the investigation and to deliver a more complete notice of preliminary inquiry in person. The notice shall state that in the event the allegations appear to be of a substantial nature, an official inquiry may be filed in accordance with the provisions of 32.5 or, in the alternative, the institution will be notified that the matter has been closed. Whenever possible, the notice also shall contain the following information regarding the nature of the potential violations:

(a) The involved sport;

(b) The approximate time period during which the alleged violations occurred;

(c) The identity of involved individuals;

(d) An approximate time frame for the investigation;

(e) A statement indicating that the institution and involved individuals may be represented by legal counsel at all stages of the proceedings;

(f) A statement requesting that individuals associated with the institution not discuss the case prior to interviews by the enforcement staff and institution except for reasonable campus communications not intended to impede the investigation of the allegations and except for consultation with legal counsel;

(g) A statement indicating that other facts may be developed during the course of the investigation that may relate to additional violations, and

(h) A statement regarding the obligation of the institution to cooperate in the case.

32.3.6 Disclosure of Purpose of Interview. When an enforcement representative requests information that could be detrimental to the interests of the student-athlete or institutional employee being interviewed, that individual shall be advised that the purpose of the interview is to determine whether the individual has been involved directly or indirectly in any violation of NCAA legislation. Prior to alleging that a student-athlete or staff member has violated NCAA ethical-conduct legislation, the individual shall be advised that such an allegation may be forthcoming based upon the individual's:

(a) Involvement in violations;

(b) Refusal to furnish information relevant to investigation of a possible violation when requested by the NCAA or by the institution, or,

(c) Provision of false or misleading information to the NCAA, conference or institution concerning the individual's knowledge of or involvement in a violation.

32.5 OFFICIAL INQUIRY

32.5.1 Letter to Chief Executive officer. If the enforcement staff determines that an allegation or complaint warrants an official inquiry, the staff shall determine its scope and thrust and direct a letter to the chief executive officer of the member involved (with copies to the faculty athletics representative and the athletics director of the member and the executive officer of the conference of which the institution is a member), fully informing the chief executive of the matter under inquiry and requesting cooperation to the end that the facts may be discovered.

32.5.1.1 Request for Disclosure/Appearance. By this letter, the chief executive officer of the member involved shall be requested to disclose all relevant information, and the letter may require the appearance of the chief executive or a designated representative before the committee at a time and place that are mutually convenient, if such appearance is deemed necessary. If a member declines to meet with the committee after having been requested to do so, the member shall not have the right to appeal either the committee's findings of facts and violations or the resultant penalty.

32.5.9 Obligation to Provide Full Information. A member that is subject to official inquiry shall collect all information available to it concerning the allegations set forth in the inquiry. At any appearance before the committee, the member and the enforcement staff shall have the obligation of providing full information concerning each allegation (i.e., information that would corroborate or refute each allegation).

32.7.5 Hearing Procedures. The exact procedure to be followed in the conduct of the hearing will be determined by the committee.

32.7.5.8 Recording of Proceedings. The proceedings of institutional hearings shall be recorded by a court reporter (unless otherwise agreed) and shall be tape-recorded by the committee. No additional verbatim recording of these proceedings will be permitted by the committee. The Committee on Infractions shall maintain custody of the tape recordings and any transcriptions. Reasonable access to review the tape recordings shall be provided at the NCAA national office or at custodial sites reasonably near the institution and involved individuals. In the event a transcript is necessary for use in an appeal, the relevant material shall be reproduced at the direction of the Committee on Infractions for submission to the appellate body and for review at the NCAA national office or at custodial sites reasonably near the institution and involved individuals. If an appeal is not sustained, the institution or individuals who file the appeal shall be responsible for the cost of the transcript, as well as the cost related to the use of the appropriate custodial office; except that the involved institution or individuals may be granted a waiver of responsibility for such costs by the Committee on Infractions.

Excerpts from *NCAA v. Board of Regents of University of Oklahoma* (83-271), argued 20 March 1984, decided 27 June 1984

One of the battles which the NCAA has fought has been over television rights to NCAA football games. In 1981, the NCAA entered into an agreement which would allow the NCAA to regulate the televising of football games, and would also make the NCAA a financial partner to most televising arrangements.

The College Football Association (CFA) objected to the plan, and made its own arrangements which would have netted more money for the schools involved, and allowed greater television coverage, than would have happened under NCAA regulation. When the NCAA attempted to discipline the schools involved, a lawsuit was filed on behalf of the CFA against the NCAA, and the case eventually was heard in 1983 in the U.S. Supreme Court, as an appeal by the NCAA of the U.S. Court of Appeal's decision in favor of the CFA.

The excerpt below is from two parts of the published opinion. The first part, called a syllabus, is a summary of the case, prepared by the Reporter of Decisions, explaining the details of the case. The second part is an excerpt from the majority decision, written by Mr. Justice Stevens. Both parts are interesting and important for what they say about the history of organized college sports, the relationships of colleges to the NCAA, and the court's attitude toward the economically fertile area of televised college sports.

1. Excerpt from the Syllabus

In 1981, petitioner National Collegiate Athletic Association (NCAA) adopted a plan for the televising of college football games of its member institutions for the 1982–1985 seasons. The plan recites that it is intended to reduce the adverse effect of live television upon football game attendance. The plan limits the total amount of televised intercollegiate football games that any one college may televise, and no member of the NCAA is permitted to make any sale of television rights except in accordance with the plan. The NCAA has separate agreements with the two carrying networks, the American Broadcasting Co. and the Columbia Broadcasting System, granting each network the right to telecast the live "exposure" described in the plan. Each network agreed to pay a specified "minimum aggregate compensation" to the participating NCAA members, and was authorized to negotiate directly with the members for the right to televise their games. Respondent universities, in addition to being NCAA members, are members of the College Football Association (CFA), which was originally organized to promote the interests of major football-playing colleges within the NCAA structure, but whose members eventually claimed that they should have a greater voice in the formulation of football television policy than they had in the NCAA. The CFA accordingly negotiated a contract with the National Broadcasting Co. that would have allowed a more liberal number of television appearances for each college and would have increased the revenues realized by CFA members. In response, the NCAA announced that it would take disciplinary action against any CFA member that complied with the CFA-NBC contract. . . .

2. Excerpt from the opinion of Mr. Justice Stevens

Since its inception in 1905, the NCAA has played an important role in the regulation of amateur collegiate sports. It has adopted and promulgated playing rules, standards of amateurism, standards for academic eligibility, regulations concerning recruitment of athletes, and rules governing the size of athletic squads and coaching staffs. In some sports, such as baseball, swimming, basketball, wrestling, and track, it has sponsored and conducted national tournaments. It has not done so in the sport of football, however. With the exception of football, the NCAA has not undertaken any regulation of the televising of athletic events. . . .

In 1938, the University of Pennsylvania televised one of its home games [Stevens' note— According to the NCAA football television committee's 1981 briefing book: "As far as is known, there were [then] six television sets in Philadelphia; and all were tuned to the game."] From 1940 through the 1950 season all of Pennsylvania's home games were televised. That was the beginning of the relationship between television and college football. . . .

A television committee was developed . . . to develop an NCAA television plan for 1951.

The committee's 1951 plan provided that only one game a week could be telecast in each area, with a total blackout on 3 of the 10 Saturdays during the season. . . . The plan received the virtually unanimous support of the NCAA membership; only the University of Pennsylvania challenged it. Pennsylvania announced that it would televise all its home games. The council of the NCAA thereafter declared Pennsylvania a member in bad standing and the four institutions scheduled to play at Pennsylvania in 1951 refused to do so. Pennsylvania then reconsidered its decision and abided by the NCAA plan. . . .

The plan adopted in 1981 for the 1982–1983 seasons is at issue in this case. This plan, like each of its predecessors, recites that it is intended to reduce, insofar as possible, the adverse effects of live television upon football game attendance. It provides that "all forms of television of the football games of NCAA member institutions during the Plan control periods shall be in accordance with this Plan. . . ."

In separate agreements with each of the carrying networks, ABC and the Columbia Broadcasting System (CBS), the NCAA granted each the right to telecast the 14 live "exposures" described in the plan, in accordance with the "ground rules" set forth therein. Each of the networks agreed to pay a specified "minimum aggregate compensation to the participating NCAA member institutions" during the 4-year period in an amount that totaled $131,750,000. . . .

Because it restrains price and output, the NCAA's television plan has a significant potential for anticompetitive effects. The findings of the District Court indicate that this potential has been realized. The District Court found that if member institutions were free to sell television rights, many more games would be shown on television, and that the NCAA's output restriction has the effect of raising the price the networks pay for television rights. Moreover, the court found that by fixing a price for television rights to all games, the NCAA creates a price structure that is unresponsive to viewer demand and unrelated to the prices that would prevail in a competitive market. And, of course, since as a practical matter all member institutions need NCAA approval, members have no real choice but to adhere to the NCAA's television controls.

The anticompetitive consequences of this arrangement are apparent. Individual competitors lose their freedom to compete. Prices are higher and output lower than they would otherwise be, and both are unresponsive to consumer preference. . . .

Thus, the NCAA television plan on its face constitutes a restraint upon the operation of a free market, and the findings of the District Court establish that it has operated to raise prices and reduce output. . . .

. . . . The NCAA's argument that its television plan is necessary to protect live attendance is not based on a desire to maintain the integrity of college football as a distinct and attractive product, but rather on a fear that the product will not prove sufficiently attractive to draw live attendance when faced with competition from televised games. At bottom the NCAA's position is that ticket sales for most college games are unable to compete in a free market. The television plan protects ticket sales by limiting output—just as any monopolist increases revenues by reducing output. By seeking to insulate live ticket sales from the full spectrum of competition because of its assumption that the product itself is insufficiently attractive to consumers, petitioner forwards a justification that is inconsistent with the basic policy of the Sherman Act.

. . . . The plan simply imposes a restriction on the source of revenue that is more important to some colleges than to others. . . .

The NCAA plays a critical role in the maintenance of a revered tradition of amateurism in college sports. There can be no question but that it needs ample latitude to play that role, or that the preservation of the student-athlete in higher education adds richness and diversity to intercollegiate athletics. . . . Today we hold only that the record supports the District Court's conclusion that by curtailing output and blunting the ability of member institutions to respond to consumer preference, the NCAA has restricted rather than enhanced the place of intercollegiate athletics in the nation's life. Accordingly, the judgment of the Court of Appeals is Affirmed.

The Knight Commission Reports

In October 1989 the Knight Commission, established by the Trustees of the Knight Foundation at the request of the NCAA, undertook an examination of intercollegiate athletics, designed to provide a framework of reform from within the NCAA. The three reports that the commission produced, in 1991, 1992, and 1993, are startling evidence of both the problems within college sports and the desire of many in the college community to correct them. Many of the recommendations and evaluations made by the commission have been adapted by the NCAA; the commission's recognition that the NCAA is, in actuality, the likely governing body for college sports into the foreseeable future, makes the recommendations of special significance.

In August 1994, former members of the Knight Commission were disturbed by suggestions that the NCAA would roll back some of its academic reforms, including Initial Eligibility Standards for college athletes. According to a 5 August 1994 Knight Foundation press release, Creed C. Black, president and CEO of the Knight Foundation, and William C. Friday and Reverend Theodore M. Hesburgh, former co-chairs of the Knight Commission, wrote to the NCAA to suggest that if reforms are rolled back, "its leadership will reconvene the Commission if it appears necessary to 'rejoin the battle for academic integrity in college sports.' "

The excerpts from the three documents that follow are extensive, because the Knight Commission's evaluations are so often to the mark; they recognize both the strengths and the weaknesses of college sports. Though all of the commission's recommendations may not be carried out, the recommendations that are made are drawn with a solid sense of *realpolitik* in mind. The following excerpts are reprinted, with permission, from the Knight Foundation.

Excerpt from the first report of the Knight Commission,
Keeping Faith With the Student-Athlete, *March 1991*

At their best, which is most of the time, intercollegiate athletics provide millions of people—athletes, undergraduates, alumni and the general public—with great pleasure, the spectacle of extraordinary effort and physical grace, the excitement of an outcome in doubt, and a shared unifying experience. Thousands of men and women in the United States are stronger adults because of the challenges they mastered as young athletes.

But at their worst, big-time college athletics appear to have lost their bearings. With increasing frequency they threaten to overwhelm the universities in whose name they were established and to undermine the integrity of one of our fundamental national institutions: higher education.

The Knight Commission believes that intercollegiate athletics, kept in perspective, are an important part of college life. We are encouraged by the energy of the reform movement now under way. But the clamor for reform and the disturbing signals of government intrusion confirm the need to rethink the management and fundamental premises of intercollegiate athletics.

The Commission's bedrock conviction is that university presidents are the key to successful reform. They must be in charge—and must be *understood* to be in charge—on campuses, in conferences and in the decision-making councils of the NCAA.

We propose what we call the "one-plus-three" model, a new structure of reform in which the "one"—presidential control—is directed toward the "three"—academic integrity, financial integrity, and independent certification. . . . Without such a model, athletics reform will continue in fits and starts, its energy squandered on symptoms, the underlying problems ignored.

This is how these recommendations can help change college sport:

PRESIDENTIAL CONTROL

1. Trustees will delegate to the president—not reserve for the board or individual members of the board—the administrative authority to govern the athletics program.
2. Presidents will have the same degree of control over athletics that they exercise elsewhere in the university, including the authority to hire, evaluate, and terminate athletics directors and coaches, and to oversee all financial matters in their athletics departments.
3. The policy role of presidents will be enhanced throughout the decision-making structures of the NCAA.
4. Trustees, alumni, and local boosters will defer to presidential control.

ACADEMIC INTEGRITY

1. Cutting academic corners in order to admit athletes will not be tolerated. Student-athletes will not be admitted unless they are likely, in the judgment of academic officials, to graduate. Junior college transfers will be given no leeway in fulfilling eligibility requirements.
2. "No Pass, No Play" will be the byword of college sports in admissions, academic progress, and graduation rates.
3. An athlete's eligibility each year, and each academic term, will be based on continuous progress toward graduation within five years of enrollment.
4. Graduation rates of student-athletes in each sport will be similar to the graduation rates of other students who have spent comparable time as full-time students.

FINANCIAL INTEGRITY

1. Athletic departments will not operate as independent subsidiaries of the university. All funds raised and spent for athletics will go through

the university's central financial controls and will be subject to the same oversight and scrutiny as funds in other departments. Athletics foundations and booster clubs will not be permitted to provide support for athletics programs outside the administration's direct control.

2. Contracts for athletics-related outside income of coaches and administrators, including shoe and equipment contracts, will be negotiated through the university.

3. Institutional funds can be spent on athletic programs. This will affirm the legitimate role of athletics on campus and can relieve some of the pressure on revenue-producing teams to support non-revenue sports.

CERTIFICATION

1. Each year, every NCAA institution will undergo a thorough, independent audit of all academic and financial matters related to athletics.

2. Universities will have to withstand the scrutiny of their peers. Each NCAA institution awarding athletics aid will be required to participate in a comprehensive certification program. This program will verify that the athletics department follows institutional goals, that its fiscal controls are sound, and that athletes in each sport resemble the rest of the student body in admissions, academic progress, and graduation rates.

The reforms proposed above are designed to strengthen the bonds that connect student, sport, and higher learning. Student-athletes should compete successfully in the classroom as well as on the playing field and, insofar as possible, should be indistinguishable from other undergraduates. All athletes—men or women, majority or minority, in revenue-producing and non-revenue sports—should be treated equitably....

Excerpt from "The Need For Reform," in first report of the Knight Commission, Keeping Faith With the Student-Athlete, *March 1991*

Games and sports are educational in the best sense of that word because they teach the participant and the observer new truths about testing oneself and others, about the enduring values of challenge and response, about teamwork, discipline and perseverance. Above all, intercollegiate contests—at any level of skill—drive home a fundamental lesson: Goals worth achieving will be attained only through effort, hard work, and sacrifice, and sometimes even these will not be enough to overcome the obstacles life places in our path.

The value and successes of college sport should not be overlooked. They are the foundation of our optimism for the future.

At the 828 colleges and universities which comprise the National Collegiate Athletic Association (NCAA), over 254,000 young men and women participate in 21 different sports each year in about one quarter of a million contests. At the huge majority of these institutions, virtually all of these young athletes participate in these contests without any evidence of scandal or academic abuse. This record is one in which student-athletes and university administrators can take pride. . . .

All of these positive contributions that sports make to higher education, however, are threatened by disturbing patterns of abuse, particularly in some big-time programs. These patterns are grounded in institutional indifference, presidential neglect, and the growing commercialization of sport combined with the urge to win at all costs. The sad truth is that on too many campuses big-time-revenue sports are out of control. . . .

. . . . Judging by the tone of recent NCAA conventions, concern for the university's good name and the welfare of the student-athlete— irrespective of gender, race, or sport—will be the centerpiece of athletics administration as we approach a new century. We do not want to interfere with that agenda. We hope to advance it.

THE PROBLEM

The problems described to the Commission—in more than a year of meetings and discussions with athletics directors, faculty representatives, coaches, athletes, conference leaders, television officials, and accrediting associations—are widespread. They are not entirely confined to big schools . . . or to football or basketball . . . or to men's sports. But they are most apparent within major athletics programs and are concentrated most strongly in those sports for which collegiate participation serves the talented few as an apprenticeship for professional careers.

Recruiting, the bane of the college coach's life, is one area particularly susceptible to abuse. While most institutions and coaches recruit ethically and within the rules, some clearly do not. Recruiting abuses are the most frequent cause of punitive action by the NCAA. Even the most scrupulous coaching staffs are trapped on a recruiting treadmill, running through an interminable sequence of letters, telephone calls, and visits. The cost of recruiting a handful of basketball players each year exceeds, on some campuses, the cost of recruiting the rest of the freshman class.

Athletics programs are given special, often unique, status within the university; the best coaches receive an income many times that of most full professors; some coaches succumb to the pressure to win with recruiting violations and even the abuse of players; boosters respond to athletic performance with gifts and under-the-table payments; faculty members, presidents, and other administrators, unable to control the enterprise, stand by as it undermines the institution's goals in the name of values alien to the best the university represents.

These programs appear to promise a quick route to revenue, recognition, and renown for the university. But along that road, big-time athletics programs often take on a life of their own. Their intrinsic educational value, easily lost in their use to promote extra-institutional goals, becomes engulfed by the revenue stream they generate and overwhelmed by the accompanying publicity. Now, instead of the institution alone having a stake in a given team or sport, the circle of involvement includes the television networks and local stations that sell advertising time, the corporations and local businesses buying the time, the boosters living vicariously through the team's success, the local economies critically dependent on the big game, and the burgeoning population of fans who live and die with the team's fortunes. . . .

The athletic director can become the CEO of a fair-sized corporation with a significant impact on the local economy. The "power coach," often enjoying greater recognition throughout the state than most elected officials, becomes chief operating officer of a multi-million-dollar business.

Within the last decade, big-time athletics programs have taken on all of the trappings of a major entertainment enterprise. . . . But the promise of easy access to renown and revenue often represents fool's gold. Recognition on the athletic field counts for little in the academic community. Expenses are driven by the search for revenues and the revenue stream is consumed, at most institutions, in building up the program to maintain the revenue. Renown for athletic exploits can be a two-edged sword if the university is forced to endure the public humiliation of sanctions brought on by rules violations. . . .

At the root of the problem is a great reversal of ends and means. Increasingly, the team, the game, the season, and "the program"—all intended as expressions of the university's larger purposes—gain ascendancy over the ends that created and nurtured them. Non-revenue sports receive little attention and women's programs take a back seat. As the educational context for collegiate athletics competition is pushed aside, what remains is, too often, a self-justifying enterprise whose connection with learning is tainted by commercialism and incipient cynicism.

In the short term, the human price for this lack of direction is exacted from the athletes whose talents give meaning to the system. But the ultimate cost is paid by the university and by society itself. If the university is not itself a model of ethical behavior, why should we expect such behavior from students or from the larger society? . . . .

... One recent analysis indicates that fully one-half of all Division I-A institutions (the 106 colleges and universities with the most competitive and expensive football programs) were the object of sanctions of varying severity from the NCAA during the 1980s. Other institutions, unsanctioned, graduate very few student-athletes in revenue-producing sports.

The problems are so deep-rooted and longstanding that they must be understood to be systemic. They can no longer be swept under the rug or kept under control by tinkering around the edges. Because these problems are so widespread, nothing short of a new structure holds much promise for restoring intercollegiate athletics to their proper place in the university. . . . We believe college sports face three possible futures:

- higher education will put its athletics house in order from within;
- athletics order will be imposed from without and college sports will be regulated by government; or,
- abuse, unchecked, will spread, destroying not only the intrinsic value of intercollegiate athletics but higher education's claim to the higher moral ground it should occupy. . . .

FOCUS ON STUDENTS

Even clearer, in the Commission's view, is the need to start with the student-athlete. The reforms we deem essential start with respect for the dignity of the young men and women who compete and the conviction that they occupy a legitimate place as students on our campuses. . . .

Regulations governing the recruitment of student-athletes— including letters-of-intent, and how and under what conditions coaches may contact athletes—take up 30 pages of the *NCAA Manual.*. But there is no requirement that the prospective student-athlete be found academically admissible before accepting a paid campus visit. A prospective player can very easily agree to attend an institution even though the admissions office does not know of the student's existence. Similarly, student-athletes deemed eligible in the fall can compete throughout the year, generally regardless of their academic performance in the first term.

It is hard to avoid the conclusion that there are few academic constraints on the student-athlete. Non-academic prohibitions, on the other hand, are remarkable. Athletics personnel are not permitted to offer rides to student-athletes. University officials are not permitted to invite a student-athlete home for dinner on the spot of the moment. Alumni are not allowed to encourage an athlete to attend their alma mater.

Each of these prohibitions—and the many others in the *NCAA Manual*—can be understood individually as a response to a specific abuse. But they add up to a series of checks and balances on the *student-athlete as an athlete* that have nothing to do with the *student-athlete as a student*. Some rules have been developed to manage potential abuse in particular sports, at particular schools, or in response to the particular circumstances of individual athletes. Whatever the origin of these regulations, the administration of intercollegiate athletics is now so overburdened with legalism and detail that the *NCAA Manual* more nearly resembles the IRS Code than it does a guide to action.

It is time to get back to first principles. Intercollegiate athletics exist first and foremost for the student-athletes who participate, whether male or female, majority or minority, whether they play football in front of 50,000 or field hockey in front of their friends. It is the university's obligation to educate all of them, an obligation perhaps more serious because the demands we place on them are so much more severe. Real reform must begin here.

A NEW MODEL: "ONE-PLUS-THREE"

The reform we seek takes shape around what the Commission calls the "one-plus-three" model. It consists of the "one"—presidential control—directed toward the "three"—academic integrity, financial integrity and accountability through certification. This model is fully consistent with the university as a context for vigorous and exciting intercollegiate competition. It also serves to bond athletes to the purposes of the university in a way that provides a new framework for their conduct.

THE "ONE": PRESIDENTIAL CONTROL

Presidents are accountable for the major elements in the university's life. The burden of leadership falls on them for the conduct of the institution, whether in the classroom or on the playing field. The president cannot be a figurehead whose leadership applies elsewhere in the university but not in the athletics department.

The following recommendations are designed to advance presidential control:

1. **Trustees should explicitly endorse and reaffirm presidential authority in all matters of athletic governance. . . .** We recommend that governing boards:

   • Delegate to the president administrative authority over financial matters in the athletics program.

- Work with the president to develop common principles for hiring, evaluating, and terminating all athletics administrators, and affirm the president's role and ultimate authority in this central aspect of university administration.
- Advise each new president of its expectations about athletics administration and annually review the athletics program.
- Work with the president to define the faculty's role, which should be focused on academic issues in athletics.

2. **Presidents should act on their obligation to control conferences.** We believe that presidents of institutions affiliated with athletics conferences should exercise effective voting control of these organizations. . . .

3. **Presidents should control the NCAA. . . .** The Commission recommends that:

- Presidents make informed use of the ultimate NCAA authority—their votes on the NCAA Convention floor. . . .
- The Presidents Commission follow up its recent success with additional reform measures, beginning with the legislation on academic requirements it proposes to sponsor in 1992. . . .
- Presidents stay the course. Opponents of progress have owed they will be back to reverse recent reform legislation. Presidents must challenge these defenders of the status quo. . . .

4. **Presidents should commit their institutions to equity in all aspects of intercollegiate athletics.** The Commission emphasizes that continued inattention to the requirements of Title IX (mandating equitable treatment of women in educational programs) represents a major stain on institutional integrity. . . . We recommend that presidents:

- Annually review participation opportunities in intercollegiate programs by gender.
- Develop procedures to insure more opportunities for women's participation and promote equity for women's teams in terms of schedules, facilities, travel arrangements, and coaching.

5. **Presidents should control their institution's involvement with commercial television.** The lure of television dollars has clearly exacerbated the problems of intercollegiate athletics. . . . Clearly, something must be done to mitigate the growing public perception that the quest for television dollars

is turning college sports into an entertainment enterprise. . . .
Greater care must be given to the needs and obligations of the
student-athlete and the primacy of the academic calendar over
the scheduling requirements of the networks.

THE "THREE": ACADEMIC INTEGRITY

The first consideration on a university campus must be academic
integrity. The fundamental premise must be that athletes are students
as well. They should not be considered for enrollment at a college or
university unless they give reasonable promise of being successful at
that institution in a course of study leading to an academic degree.
Student-athletes should undertake the same course of study offered
to other students and graduate in the same proportions as those
who spend comparable time as full-time students. Their academic
performance should be measured by the same criteria applied to
other students.

Admissions—At some Division I institutions, according to NCAA
data, every football and basketball player admitted in the 1988–89
academic year met the university's regular admissions standards. At
others, according to the same data, not a single football or basketball
player met the regular requirements. At half of all Division I-A
institutions, about 20 percent or more of football and basketball
players are "special admits," i.e. admitted with special consideration.
That rate is about 10 times as high as the rate for the total student
body. . . .

Academic Progress—The most recent NCAA data indicate
that in one-half of all Division I institutions about 90 percent of
all football and basketball players are meeting "satisfactory"
progress requirements and are, therefore, eligible for intercollegiate
competition. Under current regulations, however, it is possible for a
student-athlete to remain eligible each year but still be far from
a degree after five years as a full-time student. The 1991 NCAA
convention began to address this issue in enacting provisions requiring
that at the end of the third year of enrollment, student-athletes should
have completed 50 percent of their degree requirements.

The 1991 convention also made significant headway in reducing
the excessive time demands athletic participation places on student
athletes. Throughout the 1980s . . . football and basketball players at
Division I-A institutions spent approximately 30 hours a week on their
sports in season, more time than they spent attending or preparing
for class. Football and basketball are far from the only sinners.
Baseball, golf, and tennis players report the most time spent on sport.
Many other sports for both men and women, including swimming and
gymnastics, demand year-round conditioning if athletes are to
compete successfully. . . .

Graduation Rates—At some Division I institutions, 100 percent of the basketball players or the football players graduate within five years of enrolling. At others, none of the basketball or football players graduate within five years. In the typical Division I college or university, only 33 percent of basketball players and 37.5 percent of football players graduate within five years. Overall graduation rates for all student-athletes (men and women) in Division I approach graduation rates for all students in Division I according to the NCAA—47 percent of all student-athletes in Division I graduate in five years.

Dreadful anecdotal evidence about academic progress and graduation rates is readily available. But the anecdotes merely illustrate what the NCAA data confirm: About two-thirds of the student-athletes in big-time, revenue-producing sports have not received a college degree within five years of enrolling at their institution.

The Commission's recommendations on academic integrity can be encapsulated in a very simple concept—"No Pass, No Play.". . . . The following recommendations are designed to advance academic integrity:

1. **The NCAA should strengthen initial eligibility requirements.** Proposition 48 has served intercollegiate athletics well. It has helped insure that more student-athletes are prepared for the rigors of undergraduate study. It is time to build on and extend its success. We recommend that:

   - By 1995, prospective student-athletes should present 15 units of high-school academic work in order to be eligible to play in their first year.
   - A high-school student-athlete should be *ineligible* for reimbursed campus visits or for signing a letter-of-intent until the admissions office indicates he or she shows reasonable promise of being able to meet the requirements for a degree.
   - Student-athletes transferring from junior college should meet the admissions requirements applied to other junior college students. Moreover, junior college transfers who did not meet NCAA Proposition 48 requirements when they graduated from high school should be required to sit out a year of competition after transfer.
   - Finally, we propose an NCAA study of the conditions under which colleges and universities admit athletes. The study should be designed to see if it is feasible to put in place admissions requirements to insure that the range of academic ability for incoming athletes, by sport, would

approximate the range of abilities for the institution's freshman class.

2. **The letter-of-intent should serve the student as well as the athletics department.** Incoming freshmen who have signed a letter-of-intent to attend a particular institution should be released from that obligation if the head coach who recruited them leaves the institution, or if the institution is put on probation by the NCAA, before they enroll. . . . Currently, student-athletes are locked into the institution no matter how its athletics program changes—a restriction that applies to no other student.

3. **Athletics scholarships should be offered for a five-year period.** In light of the time demands of athletics competition, we believe that eligibility should continue to be limited to a period of four years, but athletics scholarship assistance routinely should cover the time required to complete a degree, up to a maximum of five years. Moreover, the initial offer to the student-athlete should be for the length of time required to earn a degree up to five years, not the single year now mandated by NCAA rules. The only athletic condition under which the five-year commitment could be broken would be if the student refused to participate in the sport for which the grant-in-aid was offered. . . .

4. **Athletics eligibility should depend on progress toward a degree.** In order to retain eligibility, enrolled athletes should be able to graduate within five years and to demonstrate progress toward that goal each semester. . . .

5. **Graduation rates of athletes should be a criterion for NCAA certification.** The Commission believes that no university should countenance lower graduation rates for its student-athletes, in any sport, than it is willing to accept in the full-time student body at large. . . .

THE "THREE": FINANCIAL INTEGRITY

An institution of higher education has an abiding obligation to be a responsible steward of all the resources that support its activities— whether in the form of taxpayers' dollars, the hard-earned payments of students and their parents, the contributions of alumni, or the revenue stream generated by athletics programs. . . . The Commission therefore recommends that:

1. **Athletics costs must be reduced.** The Commission applauds the cost control measures—including reductions in coaching

staff sizes, recruiting activities, and the number of athletic scholarships—approved at the 1991 NCAA convention. . . .

2. **Athletics grants-in-aid should cover the full cost of attendance for the very *needy*.** . . . [W]e believe existing grants-in-aid (tuition, fees, books, and room and board) fail to adequately address the needs of some student-athletes. . . . [W]e recommend that grants-in-aid for low-income athletes be expanded to the "full cost of attendance," including personal and miscellaneous expenses, as determined by federal guidelines.

3. **The independence of athletics foundations and booster clubs must be curbed.** Some booster clubs have contributed generously to overall athletics revenues. But too many of these organizations seem to have been created either in response to state laws prohibiting the expenditure of public funds on athletics or to avoid institutional oversight of athletic expenditures. . . .

4. **The NCAA formula for sharing television revenue from the national basketball championship must be reviewed by university presidents.** . . .

5. **All athletics-related coaches' income should be reviewed and approved by the university.** . . . [W]e recommend that the NCAA ban shoe and equipment contracts with individual coaches. If a company is eager to have an institution's athletes using its product, it should approach the institution not the coach.

6. **Coaches should be offered long-term contracts.** Academic tenure is not appropriate for most coaches, unless they are *bona fide* members of the faculty. But greater security in an insecure field is clearly reasonable. . . .

7. **Institutional support should be available for intercollegiate athletics.** The Commission starts from the premise that properly administered intercollegiate athletics programs have legitimate standing in the university community. In that light, general funds can appropriately be used when needed to reduce the pressure on revenue sports to support the entire athletics program. There is an inherent contradiction in insisting on the one hand that athletics are an important part of the university while arguing, on the other, that spending institutional funds for them is somehow improper.

THE "THREE": CERTIFICATION

The third leg of our triangle calls for independent authentication by an outside body of the integrity of each institution's athletics program.

It seems clear that the health of most college athletics programs, like the health of most individuals, depends on periodic checkups. . . . Regarding independent certification, the Commission therefore recommends:

1. **The NCAA should extend the certification process to all institutions granting athletics aid.** The NCAA is now in the midst of a pilot effort to develop a certification program. . . . We recommend that this pilot certification process be extended on a mandatory basis to all institutions granting athletics aid. . . . [C]ertification will depend, in large measure, on the comparison of student-athletes, by sport, with the rest of the student body in terms of admissions, academic progress and graduation rates. . . .
2. **Universities should undertake comprehensive annual policy audits of their athletic program.** . . . The new annual review should examine student-athletes' admission records, academic progress and graduation rates, as well as the athletics department's management and budget. . . .
3. **The certification program should include the major themes put forth in this document.** . . .

Excerpt from the second report of the Knight Commission,
A Solid Start, *March 1992.*

The second report recaps the progress made in the year since the first report was issued. Although concluding that much had been done, the commission also noted that there was still plenty of room for reform.

As an indicator of what had been done right, the Knight Commission cited two Louis Harris public opinion polls sketching the public's attitude toward intercollegiate athletics. In 1989, 78 percent of Americans "believed big-time intercollegiate sports were out of control." In February 1992, however, only 47 percent of the public held that view.

The Knight Commission lauded the 1992 NCAA convention for its passing of reform measures. Excerpts from the Commission's summary of reforms and its comments on the measures follow.

1. Effective this year:

   • **Satisfactory Progress in Degree Requirements.** "Majoring in eligibility" is a thing of the past. Division I student-athletes must have completed 25 percent, 50 percent, and 75 percent of the program course requirements for their specific degree in order to compete in their third, fourth, and firth years of enrollment, respectively.

- **Satisfactory Progress in Grade Point Average.**
- **Satisfactory Progress in School Year.** Division I and II student-athletes will have to take three-quarters of their courses during the regular academic year instead of relying on summer school to make up credits.
- **Coaches' Income.** It is clear who employs the coaches. All coaches in Division I and II are now required to obtain prior, annual, written approval from university presidents for all athletically related income, the use of the institution's name, and outside compensation from shoe and apparel companies.
- **Official Visits.** [Restricts visits to a recruiting college according to time and high-school grades and SAT/ACT scores.]
- **Transfer Students.** Mid-year transfer students . . . at all Division I and II institutions must meet satisfactory requirements the following fall, not one year later.

2. Effective by 1993:

- **Presidential Control.**
- **Certification.** The proposals of the NCAA Subcommittee on Certification, which encompass the "one-plus-three" model, will be considered at the 1993 convention.
- **Gender Equity.** A study of gender equity in intercollegiate athletics will be completed, including consideration of equity in grants-in-aid for women's sports.
- **Cost Containment.** Grants-in-aid for Division II programs will be reduced by 10 percent, matching cost reductions enacted in 1991 for Division I.

3. Effective by 1994:

- **Financial Integrity.** University presidents and the NCAA Council will have access to a comprehensive examination of financial issues. . . .

4. Effective by 1995:

- **Initial Eligibility.** New initial-eligibility rules will insure that prospective student-athletes have a reasonable chance of completing college. By August 1995, prospects will be required to present a 2.5 grade point average (out of a possible 4.0) in

13 core high-school units, along with a combined SAT score of 700 (ACT score of 17) in order to compete in their first year of enrollment. . . .

Excerpt from the third report of the Knight Commission,
A New Beginning for a New Century, *March 1993.*

In this third and final report, the commission again reviews some of the reforms that have been made, and strongly urges the NCAA to continue the reform process. In addition, the commission sums up what it sees as the challenges for the future. The report concludes with the commission's "Principles for Action," a statement of principles that the commission has urged upon the NCAA's member colleges since the first report, and which is stated in each of the three reports.

CHALLENGES AHEAD

The progress is encouraging, but the struggle for reform is far from won. Winning that struggle is what the "one-plus-three" model is all about. Academic and athletics officials now possess a new framework within which to tackle the many problems of college sports:

- Abuses in recruiting, the bane of the college coach's life;
- The compulsion of boosters to meddle in athletics decision-making;
- The search for television revenues and the influence of the entertainment industry on intercollegiate athletics;
- The relationship among high school, junior college, college, and professional sports;
- The need to respect the dignity of the young men and women who represent the university on the playing field;
- The obligation to further strengthen academic standards so that the profile of student-athletes matches that of other full-time undergraduates in admissions, academic progress and graduation rates; and,
- The imperative to meet the needs of minority student-athletes, particularly those from backgrounds of inner-city or rural poverty.

. . . [T]wo great issues, cost containment and gender equity, dominate athletics policy discussions. . . . Costs should not be controlled at the price of rebuffing women's aspirations. Opportunities for women must be provided in the context of controlling outlays for athletics programs that already cost too much. The cost control and equity dilemmas have to be addressed together.

The Cost Explosion. Despite recent modest reductions in athletic expenses, the hard work of cost reduction lies ahead. . . . All institutions . . . are in the midst of harrowing financial reductions. . . . In this environment, athletics programs can expect no special immunity from the financial hardships facing the institutions they represent.

NCAA figures indicate that throughout the 1980s, athletics programs engaged in a financial arms race. . . . The urge to be nationally competitive, no matter the expense, assumed its own dynamic. Despite conventional wisdom, about 70 percent of Division I programs now lose money, many of them operating deeply in the red. . . . On most campuses, athletics operating costs can be reduced substantially. . . .

Gender Equity. Against the backdrop of the imperative for cost reduction, the unfinished agenda of equity for women also demands attention. . . . In general . . . Title IX regulations call for accommodating the athletics interests of enrolled women, allocating financial assistance in proportion to the number of male and female participants, and making other benefits equivalent. Slowly, often in the face of opposition, opportunity for women to participate in intercollegiate athletics has become a reality.

But the opportunity is not truly equal. On many campuses, fans would be outraged if revenue-generating teams were expected to make do with the resources available to women. Even leaving out of the equation the major revenue-generating sports—football and men's basketball—women's programs generally operate on smaller budgets than men's. No matter the cause, the situation carries with it the threat of continued legal and Congressional scrutiny into whether young women are denied the benefits of participation in college sports.

The equity issue transcends athletics politics because it goes to the heart of what higher education is all about. . . .

Statement of Principles

Each of the three Knight Commission reports concludes with the same "Statement of Principles" which it recommends as the basis of discussion within member institutions and especially with the governing bodies of the institutions.

Preamble: This institution is committed to a philosophy of firm institutional control of athletics, to the unquestioned academic and financial integrity of our athletics program, and to the accountability of the athletics department to the values and goals befitting higher education. In support of that commitment, the board, officers, faculty, and staff of this institution have examined and agreed to the following general principles as a guide to our participation in intercollegiate athletics:

I. The educational values, practices, and mission of this institution determine the standards by which we conduct our intercollegiate athletics program.

II. The responsibility and authority for the administration of the athletics department, including all basic policies, personnel, and finances, are vested in the president.

III. The welfare, health, and safety of student-athletes are primary concerns of athletics administration on this campus. This institution will provide student-athletes with the opportunity for academic experiences as close as possible to the experiences of their classmates.

IV. Every student-athlete—male and female, majority and minority, in all sports—will receive equitable and fair treatment.

V. The admission of student-athletes—including junior college transfers—will be based on their showing reasonable promise of being successful in a course of study leading to an academic degree. That judgment will be made by admissions officials.

VI. Continuing eligibility to participate in intercollegiate athletics will be based on students being able to demonstrate each academic term that they will graduate within five years of their enrolling. Students who do not pass this test will not play.

VII. Student-athletes, in each sport, will be graduated in at least the same proportion as non-athletes who have spent comparable time as full-time students.

VIII. All funds raised and spent in connection with intercollegiate athletics programs will be channeled through the institution's general treasury, not through independent groups, whether internal or external. The athletics department budget will be developed and monitored in accordance with general budgeting procedures on campus.

IX. All athletics-related income from non-university sources for coaches and athletics administrators will be reviewed and approved by the university. In cases where the income involves the university's functions, facilities, or name, contracts will be negotiated with the institution.

X. Annual academic and fiscal audits of the athletics program will be conducted. Moreover, this institution intends to seek NCAA certification that its athletics program complies with the principles herein. This institution will promptly correct any deficiencies and will conduct its athletics program in a manner worthy of this distinction.

The Olympic Athlete and the International Olympic Committee

Excerpt from the Amateur Sports Act of 1978 (Public Law 95-606 [S. 2727]), 8 November 1978

Although the United States Olympic Committee (USOC) and its predecessors had been involved in the United States' planning for the International Olympics since the turn of the century, the USOC and Congress both felt it was necessary to formalize the status of the USOC. The Amateur Sports Act of 1978 spelled out, on a broad scale, what the responsibilities of the USOC were to be, along with its rights as a congressionally chartered organization. There is an interesting tension between the congressional charge to the USOC to best represent the United States and the international organization's commitment to international sports without politics.

In March 1994, following the Lillehammer Olympics, the USOC board of directors determined to discuss with Congress the possibility of changing and revising the act. Of special concern was the USOC's responsibility for enforcing ethical standards involving American athletes, and how these standards conflict with or complement the legal rights of athletes.

The issue arose specifically because of two attempts of the United States Figure Skating Association (USFSA) to suspend skater Tonya Harding following her public admission that she had known about, but failed to report to the police or other authorities, information implicating her associates and her husband in the January attack on skater Nancy Kerrigan. (Excerpts from USOC publications are reprinted below with permissions).

At its regular meeting in mid-March, USOC Executive Director Harvey Schiller reported that awareness of the Olympic Movement and the USOC is at an all-time high. This is a critical opportunity for us—we are at a crossroads—and must decide where we go from here.

We are facing a double-edged sword. The American public has high expectations, and our athletes are also held in high esteem. The skating controversy shows us just what's expected by the general public, which weighs the morality and personal conduct of our athletes, and from all of America, which demands the very, very best of our athletes.

None of us looked for or expected this in the Amateur Sports Act in 1978. We face new, unexpected challenges before us and we need to make sure we're on top of every subject or we'll suffer.

USOC Press Release, 19 March 1994

Amateur Sports Act of 1978 (Public Law 95-606 [S.2727])
8 November 1978

An Act to promote and coordinate amateur athletic activity in the United States to recognize certain rights for United States amateur athletes, to provide for the resolution of disputes involving national governing bodies, and for other purposes.

Title I, Sec. 104:

The objects and purposes of this Corporation shall be to—

(1) Establish national goals for amateur athletic activities and encourage the attainment of these goals;

(2) Coordinate and develop amateur athletic activity in the United States directly relating to international amateur athletic competition, so as to foster productive working relationships among sports-related organizations;

(3) Exercise exclusive jurisdiction, either directly or through its constituent members or committees, over all matters pertaining to the participation of the United States in the Olympic Games and in the Pan-American Games, including the representation of the United States in such games, and over the organization of the Olympic Games and the Pan-American Games when held in the United States;

(4) Obtain for the United States, either directly or by delegation to the appropriate national governing body, the most competent amateur representation possible in each competition and event of the Olympic Games and of the Pan-American Games;

(5) Promote and encourage physical fitness and public participation in amateur athletic activities;

(6) Promote and encourage physical fitness and public participation in amateur athletic competition;

(7) Assist organizations and persons concerned with sports in the development of amateur athletic programs for amateur athletes;
(8) Provide for the swift resolution of conflicts and disputes involving amateur athletes, national governing bodies, and amateur sports organizations, and protect the opportunity of any amateur athlete, coach, trainer, manager, administrator, or official to participate in amateur athletic competition;
(9) Foster the development of amateur athletic facilities for use by amateur athletes and assist in making existing amateur athletic facilities available for use by amateur athletes;
(10) Provide and coordinate technical information on physical training, equipment design, coaching, and performance analysis;
(11) Encourage and support research, development, and dissemination of information in the areas of sports medicine and sports safety;
(12) Encourage and provide assistance to amateur athletic activities for women;
(13) Encourage and provide assistance to amateur athletic programs and competition for handicapped individuals, including, where feasible, the expansion of opportunities for meaningful participation by handicapped individuals in programs of athletic competition for able-bodied individuals; and,
(14) Encourage and provide assistance to amateur athletes of racial and ethnic minorities for the purpose of eliciting the participation of such minorities in amateur athletic activities in which they are underrepresented.

The Olympic Oath

There is a place in our world for simple clarity. Before and after one of the Olympic Games, the athletes, who are, after all, only human, carry the same weight of nationalism, prejudices, and biases that most of us do. In theory, the Games are free of such feelings. Though clearly not all athletes are moved by and committed to the Olympic ideal, many are, and there are many who continue the Olympic ideal away from the Games in their everyday lives. The Olympic Oath has been sworn each year since 1920 by an athlete who is deemed representative of all of the athletes at an Olympics.

In the name of all competitors, I promise that we will take part in these Olympic Games, respecting and abiding by the rules which govern them, in the true spirit of sportsmanship, for the glory of sport and the honour of our teams.

Excerpts from the *United States Olympic Committee 1994 Fact Book*

The *Fact Book* describes many of the programs and efforts of the United States Olympic Committee, and reinforces the USOC's mission.

Purpose And Goals

The USOC is dedicated to providing opportunities for American Athletes at all age and skill levels, and to preparing and training those athletes for their challenges that range from domestic competitions to the Olympic Games themselves.

Athletic Support

The USOC Athletic Support Department administers three distinct program areas—athlete grants, employment opportunities, and career and educational assistance. . . .

Athlete Grants

During the four-year period leading up to the 1996 Olympic Games in Atlanta, the USOC will award close to 10,000 grants in direct aid to athletes, totaling $26 million.

The USOC administers five types of athlete grants—Basic, Special Assistance, Tuition, Olympic Job Opportunities Program (OJOP), and Operation Gold.

In any grant year, an athlete may not receive more than $5,000 in Special Assistance or Tuition Grants, either alone or in combination, unless the athlete also receives an OJOP Grant, in which case the combined total cannot exceed $8,500.

Basic Grant: The Basic Grant is designed to help defray basic living and training expenses of elite-level athletes, as determined by the national governing boards (NGBs). The USOC allocates a sum of money to each NGB, based on the number of athletes on the U.S. Olympic Team, multiplied by $2,500. For sports not on the program of the Olympic Games (i.e. Pan-American Games only), the allocation is based on the size of the U.S., Pan-American Team, multiplied by $1,250.

Each NGB then disburses the funds to its top athletes, based on a proposal submitted to and approved by the USOC, with the minimum award being $1,250. Basic Grant recipients must be eligible to represent the United States in the next Olympic and/or Pan-American Games, and meet all eligibility requirements of the respective NGB and international sports federation.

Special Assistance Grants: Special Assistance Grants are available only to those athletes who qualified for and received a Basic Grant. Up to $5,000 may be awarded to an athlete based on demonstrable need and meritorious circumstances.

Tuition Grant: Tuition Grants of up to $5,000 may be awarded, based on a showing of financial need, to athletes who are enrolled in a degree- or certificate-granting program of study. The USOC believes strongly in encouraging athletes to further their formal education in preparation for a worthwhile career upon retirement from competitive athletics.

Olympic Job Opportunities Grant: Olympic Job Opportunities Grants of up to $6,000 are available to athletes who have been accepted into the Olympic Job Opportunities Program, and who are employed by a non-profit organization. Based on need, this grant is intended to supplement an OJOP athlete's salary, and also serves as an incentive to nonprofit employers to hire OJOP athletes.

Operation Gold Grant: Operation Gold Grants of about $1,000 to $15,000, based on performances at the Olympic Games and World Championships or an equivalent competition, are available to athletes who achieve top performances at these events.

An enhanced Operation Gold program for the 1993–1996 quadrennium offers $15,000 for a gold medal, $10,000 for a silver, $7,500 for a bronze, and $5,000 for a fourth-place finish to each individual or team member in the 1994 Olympic Winter Games in Lillehammer and the 1996 Summer Olympic Games in Atlanta.

In non-Olympic years, the plan pays up to $6,000 for a gold medal, $5,000 for a silver, $4,000 for a bronze, $3,000 for a fourth place, $2,500 for a fifth or sixth place, and $2,000 for a seventh or eighth place in a sport's most significant competition.

Bonuses are also available for athletes that compete only in the Pan-American sports. The USOC will also pay athletes $1,000 for significant improvement in performances at the Olympic Games, World Championships or other international competitions, even if an athlete does not win a medal or finish high enough to qualify for the bonuses.

Olympic Job Opportunities Program: The Olympic Job Opportunities Program seeks to place athletes in jobs that provide a degree of financial security and an opportunity to progress toward a productive career, as well as work-schedule flexibility that allows athletes the necessary time off to train and compete.

Since 1989, the professional services firm of Ernst & Young has been a sponsor of the OJOP. During the 1993–1996 quadrennium, Ernst & Young will once again support athletes through program sponsorship, along with a new sponsor, The Olsten Corporation, a leader in the supplemental staffing industry.

The USOC, in partnership with Ernst & Young and Olsten, actively solicits the participation of corporations and other entities as prospective OJOP employers, with the objective of providing athletes with a wide array of employment opportunities throughout the country.

Each athlete who applies for the OJOP must first be endorsed by his or her NGB. Only those athletes determined to be potential Olympic or Pan-American Team members can be endorsed. During the 1989–1992 quadrennium, nearly 450 athletes found employment through the OJOP.

Excerpts from the *Guide to Banned Medications,*
published by the United States Olympic Committee Drug Education
and Doping Control Program, 27 May 1993

The International Olympic Committee (IOC) describes "doping" as

the administration of or any use by a competing athlete of any substance foreign to the body or any physiological substance taken in abnormal quantity or taken by an abnormal route of entry into the body with the sole intention of increasing in an artificial and unfair manner his/her performance in competition. When necessity demands medical treatment with any substance which because of its nature, dosage, or application is able to boost the athlete's performance in competition in an artificial and unfair manner, this too is regarded by the IOC as doping.

To deter doping and other drug abuse, the IOC has prepared a fairly comprehensive list of banned substances and a testing program at the Olympics and related competitions. The following excerpt clarifies the IOC's position about the drugs on the list.

An athlete's misuse of drugs on the IOC-banned list threatens the health of the athlete, the dignity of amateur sport, and public support of the Olympic Movement. Drug education and positions on the ethics of sport, especially with respect to anabolic steroids, have not been effective deterrents to abuse unless accompanied by the threat of public disclosure and punitive action via drug testing. The complexities of implementing a credible drug-testing program require a merging of commitment and operations of the USOC and the NGBs that is mutually feasible and agreeable.

The USOC agrees to keep operational a complete drug-testing program for NGBs that is equivalent to the IOC program, to distribute the official banned list, and to provide a confidential toll-free hotline for accurate clarification of any related questions. Essentially, the USOC observes the IOC list of banned drugs for its drug control program. Before taking any medication prior to competition have it verified by the head physician for the event or a knowledgeable USOC medical staff member or call the USOC Hotline. In addition, always declare every drug or substance that you are taking to the officials at drug testing.

Excerpt from the Olympic Charter of the International Olympic Committee in force as of 24 September 1993

The International Olympic Committee (IOC) is the largest international organization dedicated to the furtherance of international sport competition. Both the Summer Olympics and the Winter Olympics are showcases for athletes and, despite the IOC's efforts, for national exhibitionism.

Despite criticism, occasionally severe, of its ways of dealing with such issues as drug abuse, there is no doubt that the IOC has furthered its goals of internationalism, and provided an opportunity, albeit fleeting, for the premiere athletes of the world to gather and compete in an atmosphere of cooperation and good sport.

Considering the political and social tensions that plague any international organization, it is incredible that the Olympics has managed to do what it does, and do it well. Almost consistently led by an array of strong-minded, committed individuals, it's worthwhile to understand as much as possible about how the IOC defines itself and its mission.

The Olympic Charter is designed to define the Olympic Movement, and also to carefully define the most important aspects of the Olympic events. On first blush, the delineation of such details as the exact words to be spoken by the president of the IOC at the end of his closing remarks is overly cautious and restrictive. However, considering that the organization of the Olympics is of such international importance, and that a high level of coordination is necessary for the Olympics to run as smoothly as possible, the detail is, more than likely, a very good thing.

Most important in the charter are the fundamental principles of the Olympic Movement, its treatment of such important problems as drug abuse, nationalism, and advertising and publicity in relation to the Olympic ideal.

FUNDAMENTAL PRINCIPLES

1. Modern Olympism was conceived by Pierre de Coubertin, on whose initiative the International Athletic Congress of Paris was held in June 1894. The International Olympic Committee (IOC) constituted itself on 23 June 1894.

2. Olympism is a philosophy of life, exalting and combining in a balanced whole the qualities of body, will, and mind. Blending sport with culture and education, Olympism seeks to create a way of life based on the joy found in effort, the educational value of good example, and respect for universal, fundamental ethical principles.

3. The goal of Olympism is to place sport everywhere at the service of the harmonious development of man, with a view to encouraging the establishment of a peaceful society concerned with the preservation of human dignity.

4. The Olympic Movement, led by the IOC, stems from modern Olympism.

5. Under the supreme authority of the IOC, the Olympic Movement encompasses organizations, athletes, and the persons who agree to be guided by the Olympic Charter. The criterion for belonging to the Olympic Movement is recognition by the IOC.

6. The goal of the Olympic Movement is to contribute to building a peaceful and better world by educating youth through sport practiced without discrimination of any kind and in the Olympic spirit, which requires mutual understanding with a spirit of friendship, solidarity, and fair play.

7. The activity of the Olympic Movement is permanent and universal. It reaches its peak with the bringing together of the athletes of the world at the great sport festival, the Olympic Games.

8. The Olympic Charter is the codification of the Fundamental Principles, Rules and Bye-laws adopted by the IOC. It governs the organization and operation of the Olympic Movement and stipulates the conditions for the celebration of the Olympic Games.

CHAPTER 2-20-1.3

Oath of membership for individual members of the IOC:

> Granted the honour of becoming a member of the International Olympic Committee and of representing it in my country . . . , and declaring myself aware of my responsibilities in such capacity, I undertake to serve the Olympic Movement to the very best of my ability, to respect and ensure the respect of all the provisions of the Olympic Charter and the decisions of the IOC, which I consider as not subject to appeal on my part, to keep myself free from any

political or commercial influence and from any racial or religious consideration, and to defend in all circumstances the interests of the IOC and those of the Olympic Movement.

CHAPTER 5-61-1,2

Propaganda and Advertising
1. No kind of demonstration or political, religious, or racial propaganda is permitted in the Olympic areas. No form of publicity shall be allowed in and above the stadia and other competition areas which are considered as part of the Olympic sites. Commercial installations and advertising signs shall not be allowed in the stadia, nor in the other sports grounds.
2. The IOC Executive Board alone has the competence to determine the principles and conditions under which any form of publicity may be authorized.

BYLAW TO RULE 61

No form of publicity or propaganda, commercial or otherwise, may appear on sportswear, accessories or, more generally, on any article of clothing or equipment whatsoever worn or used by the athletes or other participants in the Olympic Games, except for the identification—as defined in paragraph 8 below—of the manufacturer of the article or equipment concerned, provided that such identification shall not be marked conspicuously for advertising purposes. . . .

[The regulations that finish this document are specific in nature, explaining that, for example, the limit on identification on headgear such as hats and helmets cannot be more than 6 cm high, no greater than 10% of the equipment displayed, etc.]

Professional Sports Organizations

Excerpt from *Federal Base Ball Club of Baltimore v. National League of Professional Base Ball Clubs et al.*, decided 29 May 1922. Excerpt from the opinion of the Court by Mr. Justice Holmes.

It is practically a cliché that Major League Baseball enjoys an antitrust exemption. The exemption, however, is not a legislated one; it was enunciated in the 1922 Supreme Court case cited above. The Court invited Congress to legislate an explicit law that would make clear that baseball was included in the cluster of antitrust laws which govern other businesses. Other court decisions, in the Supreme Court and elsewhere, have also made the same invitation to Congress. Unless a decision is grievously wrong, the Supreme Court would prefer not to overturn a precedent. There have been occasional attempts to create a law eliminating the exemption, and in 1994 Senator Howard Metzenbaum of Ohio chaired a committee to explore such legislation. As of mid-1994, however, such legislation has not been passed, and baseball maintains its exemption from antitrust attack.

[T]he fact that in order to give the exhibitions the League must induce free persons to cross state lines and must arrange and pay for their doing so is not enough to change the character of the business. . . . [T]he transport is a mere incident, not the essential thing. That to which it is incident, the exhibition, although made for money would not be called trade or commerce in the commonly accepted use of those words. As it is put by the defendant, personal effort, not related to production, is not a subject of commerce. That which in its consummation is not commerce does not become commerce among the States because the transportation that we have mentioned takes place. To repeat the illustrations given in the court below [the appellate court of the District of Columbia], a firm of lawyers sending out a member to argue a case, or the Chautauqua lecture bureau sending out lecturers, does not engage in such commerce because the lawyer or lecturer goes to another State.
      . . . [I]f we are right the plaintiff's business is to be described in the same way and the restrictions by contract that prevented the plaintiff from getting players to break their bargains and the other conduct charged against the defendants were not an interference with commerce among the States.

The Baseball Reserve Clause and Free Agency

Curt Flood, a major-league baseball player, refused to accept the dictates of the long-accepted Reserve Clause under which his services could be transferred to any other major-league baseball club, at a dictated salary, without his agreement. When his "owners" tried to enforce the Reserve Clause, Flood sued. Although Flood lost his case in the Supreme Court in June 1972, the publicity surrounding the case, the awareness of the Reserve Clause, and the growing power of the Major League Baseball Players' Association, soon led to the elimination of the Reserve Clause and the institution of free agency.

In free agency, once a contract with a player expires, it is not automatically renewed (except for certain clear instances, such as in the case of a player beginning his second year in the major leagues). Owners had insisted that free agency would be the downfall of professional baseball. In fact, free agency allows for greater competition among clubs for talented ballplayers. If anything, free agency lowers the likelihood that a single club will become a dynasty, dominating its league year after year after year:

Reserve Clause

On or before February 1st (or if a Sunday then the next preceding business day) of the year next following the last playing season covered by this contract, the Club may tender to the Player a contract for the term of that year by mailing the same to the Player at the address following his signature hereto. . . . If prior to March 1 next succeeding said February 1, the Player and the Club have not agreed upon the terms of such contract, then on or before 10 days after said March 1, the Club shall have the right by written notice to the Player . . . to renew this contract for the period of one year on the same terms, except that the amount payable to the Player shall be such as the Club shall fix in said notice; provided, however, that said amount, if fixed by a Major League Club, shall be an amount payable at a rate not less than 75 percent of the rate stipulated for the preceding year.

Excerpts from the National Baseball League's Uniform Player's Contract

Restrictions on unethical behavior are standard parts of every major-league baseball player's contract, and clauses similar to those below are in almost all other professional sports contracts.

Loyalty

3(a). The player agrees to perform his services hereunder diligently and faithfully, to keep himself in first-class physical condition and to obey the Club's training rules, and pledges himself to the American public and to the Club to conform to high standards of personal conduct, fair play and good sportsmanship.

Baseball Promotion

3(b). In addition to his services in connection with the actual playing of baseball, the Player agrees to cooperate with the Club and participate in any and all reasonable promotional activities of the Club and its League, which, in the opinion of the Club, will promote the welfare of the Club or professional baseball, and to observe and comply with all reasonable requirements of the Club respecting conduct and service of its team and its players, at all times whether on or off the field.

Pictures and Public Appearances

3(c) The Player agrees that his picture may be taken for still photographs, motion pictures, or television at such times as the Club may designate and agrees that all rights in such pictures shall belong to the Club and may be used by the Club for publicity purposes in any manner it desires. The Player further agrees that during the playing season he will not make public appearances, participate in radio or television programs, or permit his picture to be taken or write or sponsor newspaper or magazine articles or sponsor commercial products without the written consent of the Club, which shall not be withheld except in the reasonable interests of the Club or professional baseball.

Excerpt from the "Major League Baseball Community Relations Report," December 1993

As a major-league spectator sport, baseball is committed to providing its fans with family entertainment and lasting sports memories. However, as a business enterprise, Major League Baseball and its teams are also committed to being responsible citizens that make positive contributions to the community.

Each year, Major League Baseball teams contribute more than 35 million dollars combined to a diverse range of programs and organizations, including homeless shelters, health organizations, national disaster relief, education programs, youth athletic/social centers, child/family advocacy organizations, drug/alcohol education/ rehabilitation, civil rights organizations, summer camps for children, and baseball field rehabilitation and construction.

In addition to outright monetary contributions, clubs make substantial in-kind donations of tickets, memorabilia, and equipment to community organizations and encourage their corporate sponsors to make similar contributions.

One of the finest examples of Major League Baseball's community involvement is in the development of youth baseball programs. More than 500,000 children participate in baseball programs sponsored by Major League Baseball, and more than 10,000 children participate annually in team-sponsored baseball clinics. Major League Baseball teams spend millions of dollars each year to purchase uniforms and equipment and to build and maintain fields. This year, six of MLB's teams contributed at least $100,000 each to youth baseball programs. Additionally, teams contribute hundreds of thousands of tickets to youth baseball programs each season for fund-raising activities and team outings. Major League Baseball has also joined with corporate sponsor Coca-Cola in an effort to support youth baseball. Now completing its second year, Homers for America is a long-term, collaborative effort by Coca-Cola, Major League Baseball, and the National Association of Professional Baseball Leagues to build and renovate baseball parks, primarily in the inner cities.

To encourage kids to participate in the National Pastime, Major League Baseball endorses and funds two youth baseball programs — Reviving Baseball in the Inner-City (RBI) for kids ages 13–17, and Rookie League for children 12 and under. By emphasizing academic as well as athletic achievement, RBI teaches inner-city children that it is important to excel in the classroom as well as on the playing field. Rookie League, through its use of modified equipment and playing rules, offers young children the opportunity to learn baseball fundamentals in a safe, supportive atmosphere.

While many teams sponsor alcohol and drug education programs locally, Major League Baseball participates in the fight against alcohol abuse as a member of TEAM, which stands for Techniques for Effective Alcohol Management. TEAM is a coalition representing professional sports, federal and state agencies and private sector organizations that promotes responsible alcohol use at stadiums and other facilities.

MLB joined the TEAM coalition for two reasons:

1. To assist stadiums in the evaluation and implementation of alcohol sales and consumption policies.
2. To conduct public service campaigns that reinforce public awareness of the dangers associated with drinking and driving. These campaigns promote use of "designated drivers" and encourage responsible drinking.

As a result of MLB's participation in TEAM, clubs have reviewed and altered their alcohol policies, including the serving sizes and number of beers available for purchase. Many clubs now cut off beer sales before the game ends and nearly half do not vend beer in the stands. Alcohol-free sections are also commonplace in most stadiums. . . .

The History of Reviving Baseball in the Inner-City (RBI)

Reviving Baseball in the Inner-City was introduced in Los Angeles in 1989 to give inner-city youth the opportunity to learn and enjoy the game of baseball.

The concept of RBI was developed by John Young, a former professional baseball player and current major league scout who had grown up in South Central Los Angeles at a time when the area developed many professional baseball players. However, by the late 1970s, Young noted a significant decrease in the number of skilled athletes emerging from his childhood home.

. . . . Young discovered that the drop-off was due to many factors, including a lack of funding, organization/marketing and community support for youth baseball, as well as an overall deterioration of the social climate in many inner-city areas. . . .

Young decided that the best way to revive baseball in South Central Los Angeles would be to introduce a comprehensive youth baseball program for 13–16 year olds. Not only would this program encourage participation in baseball and expand the pool of talented scouting prospects, but, more importantly, it would provide these young adults with a positive, team-oriented activity that would keep them off the streets while challenging their bodies and minds.

With the help of Roland Hemond, the current Baltimore Orioles General Manager . . . Young was able to secure Major League Baseball's endorsement for his program. The first RBI program was introduced in South Central Los Angeles in the summer of 1989.

The only requirements Young had for his program were that it cost nothing to participate and that every child play in every game. Consisting of 12 teams, the league was financed primarily with a grant from the Amateur Athletic Foundation and private donations. . . .

Although Young had developed RBI to replenish the pool of draft-worthy baseball players in South Central Los Angeles, he knew that many American baseball players signed to professional contracts come from college programs. Simply teaching kids to play the game would not be enough. With that in mind, he set a plan in motion to make RBI an academic, as well as athletic, program.

Bob Adams, a Little League teammate and friend of Young's from childhood, was the Dean of Santa Monica College. Having been a college baseball player himself, Adams was willing to help Young create what became the Academy of Excellence Program.

The Academy of Excellence Program at Santa Monica College is a service that assesses the academic status of the Los Angeles RBI participants and provides educational programs to address their needs. The Academy includes individual tutoring, college prep classes and SAT preparation courses. . . .

Young had intended to keep the RBI program local for five years before launching it nationally. However, due to the success of the program in Los Angeles, the Matthews Dickey Boys Club in St. Louis adopted RBI in 1990, and Kansas City and New York followed with the formation of RBI leagues in 1992. This year, Boston, Chicago, Cleveland, Miami, and Philadelphia introduced RBI programs. Several other cities, including Atlanta (Georgia), Richmond (Virginia), and San Juan (Puerto Rico), have youth baseball programs that are affiliated with RBI.

More than anything else, RBI stresses that a good education is vital in any career, including sports. Most RBI leagues support educational programs similar to the Los Angeles RBI Academy of Excellence that motivates participants to stay in school and pursue postsecondary education. School attendance/performance is also a requirement for joining and remaining on many RBI-sponsored teams.

A girl's softball program will be added to RBI in 1994 and Major League Baseball hopes to expand the entire RBI program to every major league market and other large urban areas in the future.

Excerpt from an 11 February 1994 Press Release from Major League Baseball Announcing A Restructuring of the Commissioner's Office

In the wake of the resignation of Commissioner Fay Vincent on 17 September 1992, it became apparent to organized baseball that a redefinition of the commissioner's office was necessary if further debacles were to be avoided. Regardless of the correctness of Vincent's actions while in office, the conflicts between Vincent and the owners arose in good part from the divergence of opinion about the commissioner's responsibility to act "in the best interests of baseball."

The excerpt below, taken from the press release announcing the restructuring, and the restructuring document itself, claim that the reorganization gives the commissioner's office even more power than before. Additionally, Major League Baseball took the opportunity to smooth out some plainly administrative details (such as the role of the commissioner's office in certain standing committees).

Although Bud Selig and others from Major League Baseball insisted in front of Congress that the restructuring made the commissioner's office more powerful, it was difficult for Senator

Metzenbaum and others on his committee to understand how removing the commissioner from the important matter of labor negotiations represented an increase in power.

RESTRUCTURING REPORT ENHANCES COMMISSIONER'S AUTHORITY

Major League Baseball owners have enhanced the authority and independence of the Baseball Commissioner under a restructuring agreement released today.

In its report, MLB's Restructuring Committee reaffirmed Baseball's need for a strong commissioner and noted its changes affecting the governance of baseball will achieve the following goals:

1. To preserve the strength and independence of the Commissioner.
2. To centralize the administration of Baseball within the Office of the Commissioner.
3. To clarify the scope of the Commissioner's "best interests" power.

In addition to retaining his traditional powers pursuant to the Major League Agreement [MLA], particularly the Commissioner's primary and long-established role of protecting the integrity of, and public confidence in, Baseball, the Commissioner will also be responsible for the coordination of certain matters currently handled by the two leagues.

With respect to labor matters, the Committee recommended and the owners approved that the Commissioner will have executive responsibility for labor, with the ultimate legal obligations belonging to the Clubs, as employers of the players, under federal law. As a result, the Player Relations Committee will be dissolved and the Commissioner will serve as chairman of a new labor committee to manage all players relations matters, including collective bargaining. The Commissioner will appoint owners to serve as members of the committee and form a Labor Department within the Office of the Commissioner. He will be responsible for hiring appropriate labor experts and staff to handle the day-to-day duties of this department and to support the new Labor Committee.

In order to expand and reinforce the Commissioner's authority, in matters of central governance, the league presidents will report directly to the Commissioner. Furthermore, the election or re-election of a League President will require the approval of the Commissioner as well as a majority vote of the clubs in the affected league. . . .

Excerpt from the Report of the Restructuring Committee

The Restructuring Committee was appointed at a meeting of the Major League Executive Council held in St. Louis on 9 September 1992. The Committee was directed to consider all aspects of the governance of Major League Baseball (MLB) and was requested to report to the Council with any recommendations. . . . In order to facilitate MLB's search for a new Commissioner, we have focused our efforts to date on clarifying and strengthening the continuing role of the Commissioner within MLB. . . .

. . . . The Committee determined that the need for preserving the integrity of, and public confidence in, Baseball is as compelling today as it was in 1921. Further, after thorough consideration and study of the historical role of the Commissioner and the exercise of his powers, the Committee concluded not only that the office of the Commissioner has successfully served MLB and Baseball fans in this vital role, but also that such success has been due to the continued strength and independence of the office.

The role of the Commissioner in protecting the public interest has long distinguished MLB from all other professional sports and has justified the special status of Baseball as the national game. In order to reinforce the Commissioner's authority and responsibility to protect the integrity of the game for present and future generations of fans, and to foster their continued confidence in MLB, the Committee recommends that the strength and independence of the Commissioner in this role be preserved. . . .

. . . . The Commissioner's role in labor has historically been ambiguous as a result of the absence of any express authority for him to act in this area. . . . .The Committee concluded that the uncertain role occupied by the Commissioner with respect to labor issues served only to impede collective bargaining. . . .

III. CLARIFICATION OF COMMISSIONER'S "BEST INTERESTS" POWERS

Both the historical uncertainly regarding the role of the Commissioner in collective bargaining matters and the recent litigation between the Commissioner and the Chicago Cubs regarding National League realignment have highlighted the confusion that exists with respect to the scope of the Commissioner's "best interests" powers under the MLA [Major League Agreement]. . . .

In order to ensure that the MLA accurately reflects both the historical and present intentions of the parties thereto with respect to the scope of the Commissioner's best interests powers and to prevent any further confusion or disputes in this area that could impede the effective governance of Baseball, the Committee recommends that the MLA be amended to clarify that:

(a) The scope of the Commissioner's best interests powers . . . is not in any way limited by any other provision of the MLA or of either League constitution. . . .
(b) The best interest powers . . . are inapplicable to the subject of collective bargaining between the Clubs and the Major League Baseball Players Association. . . .
(c) Unless such matters involve the integrity of, or public confidence in, the national game of Baseball, the Commissioner is not authorized to exercise his best interest powers. . . .

Excerpts from the *1993 National Football League Substance Abuse Policies*

The NFL has an extensive set of policies regarding abuse of anabolic steroids and related substances, and abuse of drugs and alcohol. Negotiated with the Players' Association and part of the collective bargaining agreement, the policies spell out various testing procedures (random and reasonable-cause), penalties for positive tests, treatment methods, and appeal methods for reinstatement. The following are from overviews that accompany the full policies, and from a brochure given to NFL players, "The NFL Drug Program and You."

AN OVERVIEW OF NFL STEROID POLICY

WHAT SUBSTANCES ARE PROHIBITED?

• Anabolic Steroids and Related Substances.
• Growth Hormones and Clenbuterol.
• Diuretics and Other Masking Agents.
• Dietary "Supplements" Containing Prohibited Substances.

WHO IS TESTED?

• All players in preseason.
• Weekly preseason, regular season, and postseason tests, and periodic off-season tests with players selected by computer on a coded or "blind" basis.
• Reasonable-cause testing for players with prior steroid involvement or where medical or behavioral evidence warrants.

WHAT IF I VIOLATE THE POLICY?

- First positive test—Medical evaluation and suspension for four regular and/or postseason games.
- Second positive test—Medical evaluation and suspension for six regular and/or postseason games.
- Third positive test—Minimum one-year suspension.
- Players will not be paid during suspensions.
- Players are subject to discipline for positive tests during the off season, as well as during the remainder of the year.

WHAT IF I FAIL OR REFUSE TO TAKE A TEST?

- Failure or refusal to take a test will warrant disciplinary action by the Commissioner, as will efforts to evade or distort test results.

HOW CAN I APPEAL A TEST RESULT?

- Players may appeal test results and/or discipline to the Commissioner. You will receive a hearing and may be represented by counsel.

AN OVERVIEW OF NFL DRUGS OF ABUSE POLICY

WHAT SUBSTANCES ARE PROHIBITED?

- Amphetamines and Related Substances, Cocaine, Marijuana, Heroin, Opiates, and PCP. The abuse of alcohol and prescription drugs is also prohibited.

WHO IS TESTED?

- All players in preseason or when they report.
- Players subject to reasonable cause testing as medically determined, in-season and off-season.

WHAT IS REASONABLE CAUSE?

- Reasonable cause includes prior established drug use, prior substance abuse treatment, drug- or alcohol-related involvement with the criminal justice system, or other medical or behavioral evidence of substance abuse.

HOW CAN I GET HELP FOR A DRUG OR ALCOHOL PROBLEM?

• Any player may contact the Drug Advisor for confidential help. If you have not previously sought help from the Advisor, you will not be disciplined and your treatment will be confidential.

WHAT IS A SUBSTANCE ABUSE EVALUATION?

• Players testing positive, or otherwise involved in drug-related misconduct, are required to obtain a substance abuse evaluation to evaluate the extent and effects of any chemical dependency, and to assist in formulating a treatment program. Players subject to reasonable-cause testing will be evaluated at least annually.

WHAT IF I USE DRUGS OF ABUSE IN VIOLATION OF THE POLICY?

• First positive test—notice, and evaluation and treatment as directed by physicians.
• Second positive test—removal from active roster for six games without pay. Treatment as directed by physicians.
• Third positive test—banned from further NFL play for at least one year; may then petition the Commissioner for reinstatement.
• Drug-related misconduct other than positive tests also brings disciplinary action.
• Players are subject to discipline for positive tests or other drug-related misconduct during the off-season, as well as during the remainder of the year.

HOW IS ALCOHOL TREATED UNDER THE POLICY?

• Players with established alcohol-related misconduct, such as driving while intoxicated, will have their cases individually reviewed by the Commissioner, who may impose a fine or suspend the player.

WHAT IF I FAIL OR REFUSE TO TAKE A TEST?

• Failure or refusal to take a preseason or reasonable-cause test is equivalent to a positive test and may result in disciplinary action by the Commissioner.

HOW CAN I APPEAL A TEST RESULT?

• Players may appeal test results and/or discipline to the Commissioner. You will receive a hearing and may be represented by counsel.

Excerpts from "The NFL Drug Program and You"

Dear NFL Player:

The integrity of National Football League games and the health and public esteem of NFL players are vitally important. The League's drug policies are designed to promote these objectives. . . .

I am also convinced that our policies have been effective, that drug and steroid use among NFL players has sharply decreased, and that players can obtain effective and confidential treatment and other assistance for substance abuse problems. . . .

Paul Tagliabue,
Commissioner

The primary aims of the NFL Policy on Substance Abuse are to protect the health of the players, the respect they receive from NFL fans, and the fairness of competition among teams. These points are essential to protecting the integrity of professional football and maintaining public confidence in the NFL. . . .

5

Organizations

Amateur Athletic Foundation of Los Angeles (AAF)
2141 West Adams Boulevard
Los Angeles, CA 90018
(213) 730-9600
FAX: (213) 730-9637
Barry Zepel, Communications Director

Headed by Anita DeFrantz, the well-known former Olympics star and member of the United States Olympic Congress, the AAF was formed for the purpose of serving sports and athletics in Southern California. It was originally funded by an endowment of about $90 million dollars, Southern California's share of surplus funds after the 1984 Olympic Games in Los Angeles.

Although its grants (more than $27 million) are restricted to the eight southern-most counties of California, many of its programs and studies (especially its coaching education program) are of national interest or have national implications.

AAF also operates the Paul Ziffren Sports Resource Center, which is the largest sports library in North America, with resources open to scholars, coaches, athletes, and others from all over the world. In addition to books, articles, photographs, videotapes, and archival Olympic publications, the center sponsors conferences, seminars, workshops, and special speakers.

American Legion Baseball
700 N. Pennsylvania Street
Indianapolis, IN 46204
(317) 635-8411
James R. Quinlan, Coordinator

American Legion Baseball for youngsters is an extremely popular program, rivaled only by Little League Baseball in popularity. The organization's stated purposes are:

1. To inculcate in our American youth a better understanding of the American way of life and to promote 100 percent Americanism.
2. To instill in our Nation's youth a sincere desire to develop within themselves a feeling of citizenship, sportsmanship, loyalty, and team spirit.
3. To aid in the improvement and development of the physical fitness of our country's youth.
4. To build for the Nation's future through our youth.

Atlanta Paralympics Organizing Committee
One Atlantic Center, Suite 2500
1201 West Peachtree Street, N.E.
Atlanta, GA 30303
(404) 588-1996
FAX: (404) 877-7012
Lisa Cape, Public Relations Manager

The fundamental philosophy guiding the Paralympic Movement is that world-class disabled athletes should have opportunities and experiences equivalent to those afforded nondisabled athletes. In order to compete in the Paralympics, each athlete must meet strict qualifying standards and be selected to his or her national team. Competitors include: "Elite athletes with physical or visual impairments, representing four international federations: the blind, paraplegics and quadriplegics, people with cerebral palsy, amputees and others (including dwarfs)."

The organization traces its roots to the International Wheelchair Games held in London, England, in 1948. Sir Ludwig Guttman, a neurosurgeon, planned the Wheelchair Games to coincide with the 1948 London Olympics. In 1960, the first Paralympic Games were held in Rome, shortly after the completion of the Rome Olympics. Since then, the Paralymic Games have shared cities and years with the Olympic Games four times, including those planned for Atlanta, Georgia, in 1996.

The 1988 Paralympic Games in Seoul, South Korea, drew more than 1.5 million spectators. The 1996 games are expected to draw 4,000 athletes from 102 nations. Competition over ten days will include 16 sports (14 of which are Olympics-sanctioned sports).

Boys and Girls Clubs of America

771 First Avenue
New York, NY 10017
(212) 351-5900
FAX: (212) 351-5972
Tim Richardson, Assistant Director of Program Services

Tracing its roots to the Hartford, Connecticut, creation of the Dashaway Club in 1860, the Boys and Girls Club Movement of America "is a nationwide affiliation of local, autonomous organizations and Boys and Girls Clubs of America working to help youth of all backgrounds, with special concern for those from disadvantaged circumstances, develop the qualities needed to become responsible citizen and leaders."

The organization serves roughly two million youths in various ways including local sports and fitness programs. The clubs offer activities in six areas: "Personal and educational development, citizenship and leadership development, cultural enrichment, health and physical education, social recreation, and outdoor and environmental education."

The clubs' principles are that Boys and Girls Clubs

> are for boys and girls. They have a girl and boy membership and satisfy the age-old desire of boys and girls to have a "club" of their own. . . . have full-time professional leadership, supplemented by part-time workers and volunteers. . . . require no proof of good character. They help and guide girls and boys who may be in danger of acquiring, or who already have acquired, unacceptable habits and attitudes, as well as boys and girls of good character. . . . make sure that all girls and boys can afford to belong. Membership dues are kept low so that all boys and girls can afford to belong and even the least interested will not be deterred from joining. . . . are for all girls and boys. Boys and girls of all races, religions and ethnic cultures are eligible to become members. . . . are building centered. Activities are carried on in the warm, friendly atmosphere of buildings especially designed to conduct programs. . . . are non-sectarian. . . . have an open door policy. Clubs are open to all members at any time during hours of operation. . . . have a varied and diversified program that recognizes and responds to the collective and individual needs of girls and boys. . . . are guidance oriented. Clubs emphasize values inherent in the relationship between the boys and girls and their peers, and girls and boys and adult leaders. They help boys and girls to make appropriate and satisfying choices in their physical, educational, personal, social, emotional, vocational and spiritual lives.

Clubs can award, annually, the Sir Thomas J. Lipton Sportsmanship Award, given for "exhibiting integrity, perseverance, sportsmanship and depth of character on and off the field of play." Local winners are eligible for the national award. Lipton, who tried unsuccessfully to gain the America's Cup for yacht racing was, according to the organization, enormously popular in the United States and was given a gold "loving cup" despite his failure to win the America's cup.

The club also coordinates a Player of the Week award in a program called NBAHOOPS; recognized players in local participating clubs receive packages of SkyBox brand basketball cards and albums.

The Federation of Gay Games, Inc.
584 Castro Street
San Francisco, CA 94114
(415) 648-4931
Susan Kennedy, Co-President

Gay Games IV Organizing Committee
19 West 21st Street, Suite 1202
New York, NY 10010
(212) 633-9494
FAX: (212) 633-9488
Jay Hill, Executive Director

The Gay Games was conceived in 1980 by Dr. Tom Waddell, a decathlon athlete from the 1968 Mexico City Olympics. Under Waddell's leadership, the first games were held in San Francisco in 1982. Gay Games II was held in 1986, also in San Francisco, and was "the largest international amateur sporting event held in North America that year." 3,482 women and men from 16 nations participated in 17 sports. The 1990 games were held in Vancouver, British Columbia, and the Gay Games IV were played in New York City from June 18–25, 1994. The Games are organized under the direction of The Federation of Gay Games.

The purpose of The Federation of Gay Games, Inc. is "to foster and augment the self-respect of gay women and men throughout the world and to engender respect and understanding from the non-gay world through the medium of organized, non-competitive cultural/artistic and athletic activities . . ."

Institute for the Study of Youth Sports (ISYS)
IM Sports Circle, Room 213
Michigan State University
East Lansing, MI 48824–1049
(517) 353-6689
FAX: (517) 353-5363
Vern Seefeltd, Ph.D., Professor and Director

Vern Seefeldt is a nationally recognized expert on youth sports and the physical effects of youth athletic competition. Although ISYS was established by the Michigan legislature in 1978, its mission is national in scope. It's mandates are to: (1) "Determine the beneficial and detrimental effects of participation in youth sports through on-campus and field-based research programs"; (2) "produce educational materials for parents, coaches, officials, and administrators"; and (3) "provide educational programs for coaches, officials, administrators and parents."

International Olympic Committee (IOC)—Comite International Olympique
Chateau de Vidy
1007 Lausanne
Switzerland
(41-21) 621-6111
FAX: (41-21) 621-6216
Michele Verdier, Information Director

The IOC has the ultimate responsibility for the organization of both the summer and the winter Olympic Games. In addition to assisting various National Olympic Committees (NOCs) organize the Games in their country, the IOC sets all rules and policies for the Games, and meets with representatives of the NOCs on a regular basis to determine international policies and regulations.

John S. and James L. Knight Foundation
One Biscayne Tower, Suite 3800
2 South Biscayne Boulevard
Miami, FL 33131-1803
(305) 539-0009
Virginia L. Henke, Communications Director

The Knight Foundation, while not a sports organization, is a private institution committed to higher education. They were chosen by the NCAA to form a commission to evaluate and report on the NCAA's academic policies and to make recommendations regarding these policies.

Little League Baseball, Incorporated
P.O. Box 3485
Williamsport, PA 17701
(717) 326-1921;
FAX: (717) 326-1074
Dennis M. Sullivan, Communications Director

Founded by Carl Stotz in 1939, Little League is the largest youth sports organization in the world, serving approximately 2,700,000 youngsters throughout the world, although its largest group of participants are in the United States. It is dedicated to "promote, develop, supervise, and voluntarily assist in all lawful ways the interests of those who will participate in Little League Baseball."

Under the auspices of the national organization, local teams are organized into leagues, and a tournament schedule established under a variety of rules established to ensure safety and fairness on the field. Teams that win in their local leagues can progress through a variety of tournaments operated on larger geographical bases, through state tournaments to regional tournaments. The eventual winners of the tournaments face off in an international Little League World Series, held at headquarters in Williamsport each year.

The organization originally served preadolescent American boys, but has now grown to an international organization which has no discriminatory barriers for girls and women. Additionally, the national organization coordinates a wider variety of ball games including softball and Tee-Ball (which utilizes a batting tee instead of a pitched ball) for six- and seven-year-olds. Among its special programs is its Challenger Division. Challenger currently enrolls 20,000 disabled youths in the United States and operates with special rules that allow the physically and mentally handicapped to participate in Little League programs at their own level.

National Association of Intercollegiate Athletics (NAIA)
6120 South Yale Avenue, Suite 1450
Tulsa, OK 74136
(918) 494-8828
FAX: (918) 494-8841
Wallace H. Schwartz, Vice President for Administrative Services

Formed in 1940, the NAIA was the result of an effort in 1937 to organize a college basketball tournament. One of the movers behind this tournament was James Naismith, the founder-inventor of basketball. Now comprising approximately four hundred colleges, the NAIA offers regulation and coordination of tournaments in fields such as basketball, football, baseball, volleyball, track and field, and swimming. In 1988, the NAIA adopted athlete eligibility rules that required successful participation in academics; other rules, adopted at the same time, regulate member colleges' recruiting and scholarship-granting activities.

The NAIA statement of philosophy asserts that "the purpose of the NAIA is to promote the education and development of students through intercollegiate athletic participation . . . [and to] share a common commitment to high standards and the principle that athletics serve as an integral part of education."

National Collegiate Athletic Association (NCAA)
6201 College Boulevard
Overland Park, KS 66211–2422
(913) 339-1906
FAX: (913) 339-1950
Cedric Dempsey, Executive Director

As mentioned throughout this book, the NCAA is the major organization controlling four-year college and university sports activities. It regulates all aspects of sports scholarship, including recruitment through national competitions.

National Junior College Athletic Association (NJCAA)
P.O. Box 7305
Colorado Springs, CO 80933–7305
(719) 590-9788
FAX: (719) 590-7324
George Killian, Executive Director

The NJCAA is the organization which controls the intramural tournament activities of two-year and junior colleges. Member schools in any of 24 regions compete in a variety of sports, including basketball, football, soccer, swimming, tennis, etc.

Member schools are rated as Division I, II, or III schools, according to the type of recruiting the school does and its rules for awarding scholarships. As in the NCAA, Division I schools can award full scholarships. All schools must abide by NJCAA recruiting regulations which include such requirements as limits to the number and length of time a possible recruit may visit a campus, and to the amount of money that may be spent on food for the recruit.

The Northeastern University Center for the Study of Sport in Society (CSSS)
360 Huntington Avenue
Northeastern University, 244HN
Boston, MA 02115
(617) 373-4025
Jeffrey P. Brown, Communications Coordinator

The CSSS is the most active organization directly involved in the area of sports ethics. In addition to coordinating the activities of 22 other groups, CSSS runs several programs of its own. Its mission statement says, "The mission of the Northeastern University's Center for the Study of Sport in Society is to increase the awareness of sport and its relation to society, and to develop programs that identify problems, offer solutions, and promote the benefits of sport."

Among its programs are the Mentors in Violence Prevention (MVP) program, which analyzes sexual violence issues on campuses, and the "TEAMWORK—SOUTH AFRICA" program, designed to "teach young people to be more sensitive to human rights, racial and ethnic issues, and . . . how the principles of teamwork can help them to develop greater respect and harmony in these areas. . . . In exchange for free access to expanded sports facilities and intramural activities, young people [are] required to commit to the principles of TEAMWORK: to keep off the streets, to stay in school, to avoid drugs and alcohol use, to be racially sensitive and to eschew gang violence."

CSSS also has an outreach program to integrate efforts of athletes and athletic department staffers in Boston area colleges and universities in visiting junior and senior high schools, community centers, churches, and hospitals in their areas. A "pro sports unit" headed by Tom Kowalski at DePaul University, Chicago, runs educational programs designed to encourage athletes to return to college to complete their studies.

The Philosophic Society for the Study of Sport
Department of Physical Education, Recreation, and Health
Kean College of New Jersey
Union, NJ 07083-9982

The society holds regular conferences and publishes *Journal of the Philosophy of Sport*, edited by Klaus V. Meier (University of Western Ontario, Canada). The *Journal* publishes articles about sports and an annual brief bibliography on the philosophy of sport. Information about the journal can be obtained from its publisher, Human Kinetics Publishers, Inc., Box 5067, Champaign, IL 61825-5076.

Pop Warner Little Scholars, Incorporated
920 Towne Center Drive
Langhorne, PA 19407
(215) 752-2591
FAX: (215) 752-2879
John Butler, Executive Director

Almost 200,000 boys and girls participate in football programs organized by Pop Warner. Named for the legendary football coach, the program began in the late 1920s in Philadelphia as a program for wayward boys. Pop Warner is dedicated to having all of its members participate, and also emphasizes satisfactory achievement in school as part of the requirements for participation. Among the league rules: every player plays in at least eight plays per game; teams pick their own captains; there are no "all-star" or "most valuable player" teams. Participation depends on satisfactory academic progress.

Special Olympics International
1350 New York Avenue N.W.
Suite 500
Washington, DC 20005
(202) 628-3630

Special Olympics is an international program of sports training and athletic competition for children and adults with mental retardation. The first games were held in 1968, and founded by Eunice Kennedy Shriver. World Games, which alternate between summer and winter sports, are held every two years. The organization holds or sanctions more than 15,000 games, meets, and tournaments worldwide. In addition to its regular games, the international organization has several other programs, including the Unified Sports Program, which teams people of comparable age and skills with and without mental retardation on the same teams; the Motor Activities Training Program, which "provides comprehensive motor activity training of individuals with severe and profound limitations;" and a Model Schools District Program to encourage sports curricula and activities in elementary and secondary schools.

The mission of the Special Olympics is "to provide year-round sports training and athletic competition in a variety of sports for children and adults with mental retardation in order to create continuing opportunities for them to develop physical fitness, demonstrate courage, experience the joy of achievement, be included in the community, build skills and make friends."

Special Olympics involves 500,000 volunteers in capacities ranging from coaches to drivers. The next World Games, to be held in Connecticut in July 1995, will involve more than 6,500 athletes from more than 130 countries.

U.S. National Senior Sport Organization (USNSO)
14323 South Outer 40 Road, Suite N-300
Chesterfield, MO 63017
(314) 878-4900
FAX: (314) 878-9957
Douglas Corderman, President

A member of the United States Olympic Committee, USNSO held the first U.S. National Senior Olympics in St. Louis in 1987. Organized senior sports competition began in 1969. More than 250,000 persons over the age of 55 are involved in USNSO games. Competition is in five age groups ranging from age 55 to 100-and-over, with both men's and women's divisions. A biennial event is held—The U.S. National Senior Sports Classic, also known as "The Senior Olympics." The May 1995 event is scheduled for San Antonio, Texas.

Seventy-two hundred athletes from 48 states participated in the 1993 event in Baton Rouge, Louisiana. An off-year competition, the 1994 USNSO Track and Field Senior Open was held in St. Louis, Missouri, on 17–19 June, 1994. Competition at the Senior Olympics is in 18 sport categories: archery, badminton, basketball, bowling, cycling, golf, horseshoes, shuffleboard, softball, swimming, table tennis, tennis, track and field, triathlon, racewalk, racquetball, road race, and volleyball.

The stated mission of the USNSO is "to promote fitness and excellence of health of senior adults. An active advocate of senior fitness through competition, the USNSO is in constant contact with the public, other sports organizations, the media, and potential sponsors to help raise the national image, interest, and support of senior games and fitness."

United States Olympic Committee (USOC)
Olympic House (USOC Headquarters)
One Olympic Plaza
Colorado Springs, CO 80909–5760
(719) 578-4529
FAX: (719) 578-4677
Mike Moran, Director, Public Information and Media Relations

The USOC organizes and works toward the development of Olympic sport in the United States. Designated by act of Congress as the organization to work with and develop the United States' sporting efforts, the USOC both represents the United States as a member of the International Olympic Committee, and operates a variety of important programs in the United States, including recognition of individual sport associations and full coordination of the American effort in the Olympics.

YMCA of the USA
Mid-America Field Office
37 West Field Street, Suite 600
Columbus, OH 43215
(614) 621-1231
Dick Jones, Associate Director of Sports

Despite its Christian mission statement, "to put Christian principles into practice through programs that build healthy body, mind, and spirit for all," the YMCA is open to people of all faiths. Included in the YMCA philosophy is the belief that "its sports programs can help people to grow personally, clarify values, improve relationships, appreciate diversity, develop leadership skills, and have fun. . . ." It is for the development of such virtues that the YMCA promotes its sports programs.

In 1992, there were a total of 954 member YMCAs which operated 1,150 branches, units, and camps, totaling 2,104 centers. Internationally, the YMCA serves approximately 30 million people in more than a hundred countries around the world.

The "Y" was founded in London, England, in 1844 by George Williams and a group of friends dedicated to saving fellow live-in clerks from "the wicked world on the London streets." In the United States, the first YMCA was opened in 1851 by Thomas Sullivan, a lay missionary and retired sea captain. After World War II, women and girls were admitted to full membership and participation in the U.S. YMCA. Half of the people the "Y" serves in the United States are 18 years of age or under.

6

Selected Print and Nonprint Resources

Selected Articles

SOME OF THE BEST AND MOST INFORMATIVE writing about sports and the issues of sports ethics appears in newspapers and sports magazines, as well as in professional and academic journals and books. While ten years ago sports ethics issues were barely considered by the popular press, they are now perceived to be extremely relevant, if not essential, to proper sports coverage. The reader, fan, or ethicist in search of such coverage can easily find him- or herself overwhelmed by an "embarrassment of riches." The articles selected below both deal with important issues, and represent some of the best writing available today.

Associated Press Newsfeatures. **"Baseball Official Replies: We Rate Better Than a 'C'."** *Ft. Lauderdale Sun-Sentinel.* (23 July 1991): 5C.

Responding to a report that characterized baseball's efforts on behalf of achieving equality for minorities in both playing and management assignments, Major League Baseball claimed that it had, indeed, done much achieve racial equality. According to a December 1990 report by Clifford Alexander, a baseball consultant quoted in this article, 15 percent of front office jobs were held by minorities in 1990 (as opposed to 2 percent in 1987): 1 percent Asian, 9 percent black, and 5 percent Hispanic. On-field jobs had decreased in 1990 to 19 percent from 20 percent the year before.

Associated Press Newsfeatures. **"Pro Basketball Ranked Best in Minority Study."** *Ft. Lauderdale Sun-Sentinel* (23 July 1991): 1C.

According to a "report card" issued by the Center for the Study of Sport in Society (CSSS), opportunities for minority advancement in professional sport are best in basketball where, in 1991, 72 percent of its players were black, there were black general managers in five cities, and there were black head coaches in six cities. In the National Football League (NFL), which earned a B+ (for improvement), blacks hold 6 percent of management positions in the NFL, including "key roles with Chicago, New England, San Diego, and Philadelphia." The NFL was also praised for commissioner Paul Tagliabue's decision to move the Super Bowl from Phoenix after state voters rejected a bid to make Martin Luther King's birthday a state holiday. The report also made note of NFL counseling programs for retired players.

Professional baseball received the lowest grade of "C." According to the Associated Press, the CSSS felt that the movement to put minorities into management jobs in baseball had died down after the original furor caused by L.A. Dodger executive Al Campanis' remark that blacks did not have the "necessities" to work in baseball management.

Blum, Debra. **"College Sports' L-Word."** *Chronicle of Higher Education* XL, no. 27 (9 March 1994): 34.

Debra Blum writes regularly in the weekly sports pages of the *Chronicle*, reviewing the prevalent prejudices against female homosexuality in sports. Not only is there fear of lesbianism, but the fear is so widespread that one woman was able to successfully sue a college that she claimed had spread a rumor that she was a lesbian.

Despite a growing acceptance of gay people in other areas, Blum indicates that sports lags behind, though that attitude may be changing. Sue Rankin, perhaps the only openly gay female head coach at a major university, reported to Blum that "coming out" has had positive benefits because it allows her to be "seen as a positive role model for her athletes, regardless of her sexuality."

————. **"Defending College Sports."** *Chronicle of Higher Education* XL, no. 25 (23 February 1994): A41.

This article is a brief review of the work of Russell W. Gough, an assistant professor of philosophy at Pepperdine University. Among his academic responsibilities, Gough teaches an annual course for first-year athletes which examines "the relationship between sports and ethics." Gough believes that "college sports, in particular college coaches, have had a bad rap," and feels "as if we have forgotten the purpose and value of sports. . . . It is perceived as stuck in a moral abyss, when there is a whole lot of good going on that is not given enough credit." Gough believes that sport builds character and that athletic programs should be recognized as playing a notable role in higher education and moral development.

————. **"Rumbles on the Court."** *Chronicle of Higher Education* XL, no. 26 (2 March 1994): 34, 36.

Blum examines what seems to be a season of excessive outbursts by college basketball coaches on the court. In one regrettably notable incident, one basketball coach threatened to kill another coach after a one-point loss. The coach later apologized, and he was suspended by his college for one game. One coach who had been involved in a lesser interchange at another game believes that things on the court haven't changed as much as our perceptions of on-court behavior have changed: "We all play every game on TV, so now everyone sees what happens."

————. **"Top Players Produce Up to $1 Million of Revenue for Their Universities."** *Chronicle of Higher Education* XL, no. 32 (13 April 1994): 33–34.

This article reports on a study by economist Robert W. Brown (University of North Texas) of the real financial worth of college star athletes. He concludes that an athlete who becomes a draft pick for the NFL is worth $500,000 a year for his school, and a basketball player who will be drafted by the NBA is worth about $1 million per year. In addition, he alleges that for each .124 drop in required grade point average, a college has a chance to recruit "one more premium football player," possibly encouraging schools to lower admission standards in order to reach a larger pool of athletes. In comparison, an athlete's educational compensation is worth, on average, approximately $20,000.

————. **"The Undaunted 'Kook'."** *Chronicle of Higher Education* XL, no. 32 (13 April 1994): 33–34.

Dick Devenzio is a sportswriter who, for several years, has been arguing that college athletes are not getting their full financial rights from the colleges and universities for which they play. According to Blum, the argument for paying college athletes is becoming "more convincing" and Devenzio is being seen as less of a ridiculous rebel than a person with a serious point to make.

Brown, Curt. **"Playing Hurt: Injuries in Youth Sports."** *Minneapolis Star Tribune* (1 November 1992): 1S+.

In this article surveying the area of youth sports injuries, Brown capably summarizes many of the hazards to which young athletes are subjected. While our perceptions may be that physical injury in youth sports, both organized and casual, is minimal, Brown shows otherwise. Four million children in the United States are treated in emergency rooms each year for sports-related injuries, the second largest cause of ER treatment. Obviously, not all of these cases are major but there is evidence that the problem is quite real. At least 55 high-school football players have died in the past ten years; in a three-year period, Brown estimates that there have been approximately three dozen deaths among basketball players between the ages of 11 and 20. In youth baseball, there were 51 deaths between 1973 and 1983.

This is a very important article, and should be read by anyone with any involvement is youth sports. Injury can be minimized, easily and quickly. That more is not being done to prevent sport-induced injury and death among our young people comes close to being a national disgrace. Brown puts forth an extensive, but reasonable, list of preventative measures to minimize injuries in youth sports. .

Brubaker. Bill. **"The Sneaker Phenomenon: In Shoe Companies' Competition, The Coaches Are the Key Players."** *Washington Post* (11 March 1991): A1+.

In this careful and important examination of the relationship between coaches and the various athletic shoe companies and equipment makers, Brubaker records the history of the efforts to secure coaches' endorsements of athletic shoes and sports clothing, and demonstrates convincingly how closely connected the two have become. Brubaker's article was stimulated by the announcement that L.A. Gear had hired "a sports agent, David Spencer, to negotiate contracts with 15 college coaches and youth basketball programs in 36 states."

Though shoe endorsements of one type or another were made after World War I, the person who is most responsible for the current wave of endorsement seeking is the well-known Sonny Vaccaro, an executive with Nike shoes. Under Vaccarro's guidance, large numbers of coaches have signed agreements with Nike, and, as of 1991, some were receiving payments of as much as $200,000.

Deitch, Joseph. **"New Jersey Q & A: Larry Hazzard: Commissioner Keeps His Eye on Boxing."** *New York Times* (24 October 1993): 11

New Jersey is one of the most important states in the boxing business. Large numbers of important matches are staged each year in Atlantic City. Because of its importance, New Jersey's regulation of boxing, along with Nevada's, should be expected to be the most forward-looking and the most protective of the boxer's health. In this interview with New Jersey Commissioner Larry Hazzard, one gets the impression that, though boxing is acknowledged to be "a very dangerous sport," the control that the New Jersey State Athletic Control Board exercises is aimed at, at least, minimizing the danger to boxers and making contests as much of a sporting event as possible.

Grady, Denise. **"Sex Test of Champions."** *Discover* (June 1992): 78–82.

Distinguishing between a female and a male athlete is not a simple or clear-cut matter, according to Grady. The IOC performs sex tests on a cell scraping of the lining of the mouth; this and other tests may give false results or even turn up one of several genetic or hormonal conditions which make a legitimate male or female athlete ineligible for competition. A small but significant number of females do have the "Y" chromosome which genetically marks them as male. The IAAF has dropped chromosome testing in favor of physical examination (IOC officials are opposed to the physical examination because it is "offensive").

Grady notes that sex testing *seems* reasonable because men are "usually bigger and stronger and faster than women, and a man masquerading as a woman would have a significant advantage over his rivals in almost any athletic event." However, Grady points out, "The problem is that the testing is based on an oversimplified notion of what determines a human being's sex."

Hahn, Cindy. **"Surviving Stardom."** *Tennis* 28, no. 6 (October 1992): 30–37; and **"Teen Turmoil, Part II: Taming the Tour."** *Tennis* 28, no. 7 (November 1992): 45–48.

These two articles discuss the tremendous psychological and physical strain on current, past, and future young tennis stars including Jennifer Capriati, Chris Evert, Monica Sabatini, Venus Williams (an up-and-coming star at the age of 12), and others. After reviewing the many difficulties that these child stars have (such as physical overexertion, the loss of privacy and, perhaps, their chance to have a normal childhood), Hahn makes several recommendations to make life better for these children.

Helyar, John. **"Sen. Mitchell, Do You Really Want This Job?; How Fay Vincent Was Ejected from the Game."** *Wall Street Journal* (15 April 1994): B1, B6.

In September 1992, Fay Vincent, Commissioner of Baseball, was removed from office by a vote of the major-league team owners (formally, his contract was paid to the end of its time period so that another commissioner could be appointed at the owners' convenience). Clearly, Vincent had alienated a substantial number of the owners; a two-thirds vote of the owners was needed before his removal could be accomplished. In mid-April 1994, the job still stood open, though the rumor of the week of April 15th was that Senator George Mitchell had declined to consider appointment to the United States Supreme Court by President Clinton, opting to negotiate quietly with baseball's owners for appointment as commissioner.

Helyar's article, an excerpt from a forthcoming book, is certain to arouse attention, argument, and bitterness. Helyar presents his version of the events leading up to Vincent's firing, beginning with the regal summoning of Yankee's management to Vincent's office only hours before an important game. Though Helyar does not name his sources, the conversations between Yankee's management and Vincent on 1 July 1992 are mostly presented as verbatim quotations.

Henry III, William A. **"The Last Bastions of Bigotry."** *Time* (22 July 1991): 66–67.

This article reviews the status of discrimination in American golf clubs one year after the Professional Golfers Association (PGA) announced that it would not hold tournaments at clubs that discriminated against members on the basis of race. At the time, 17 of its 39 tour courses were private clubs with no black members. Since then, some clubs have admitted a very few blacks, Hispanics, and women. Other clubs, in fact, have declined to be a part of the tour, although those that did cited "other reasons" for skipping the tour, such as renovation of their greens.

Huntingford, Felicity, and Angela Turner. **"Aggression: A Biological Imperative?"** *New Scientist* (London, England) (4 August 1988): 44–47.

Huntingford and Turner briefly examine the theories of violence and their connection to human society proposed by the ethnologist Konrad Lorenz in his 1963 book, published in 1967 as *On Violence*. Huntingford is an academic specializing in animal aggression. While an urge to aggression and/or violence may indeed be normal, one of Lorenz's points—that the aggressive urge is safely released through both taking part in and watching aggressive sports—is not a valid conclusion. This article is not primarily about sports, but about how accurate or inaccurate Lorenz's ideas are. Though the authors of this article are interested in humans, they are also interested in nature, and they provide a rapid review of some interesting nonhuman instances of biologically based aggressive inclinations modified by other factors. If there is a link between aggressive behavior and our taste for aggressive sports, it is far from being a hopelessly deterministic one. The authors point out that aggressive behavior in society increases if condoned or justified by peers, and that even behavior dictated by biology can be mediated by society.

Klein, Frederick. **"Leisure & Arts: Letter of Indenture for Student Jocks."** *Wall Street Journal* (15 April 1994): A7.

Frederick Klein has written the sports column for the *Wall Street Journal* for several years, and his columns have consistently shown an awareness of ethical problems in sports and that the sports world, both professional and amateur, is frequently less than deserving of idolatry.

In this column, Klein considers the "National Letter of Intent," which student-athletes recruited into most NCAA Division I schools are usually required to sign. The letter-of-intent is a standardized document created for colleges by the Collegiate Commissioners Association. Klein details some of the restrictions that student-athletes are put under by the contract, and suggests strongly that "almost all of its obligations, and all of its possible penalties, fall upon the youngster. A more one-sided agreement can hardly be imagined."

Miller, Marvin. **"Baseball Revenue-Sharing: Brother, Can You Spare A Dime?"** *Sport* 85, no. 5 (May 1994): 12, 94.

Revenue-sharing, in which wealthier professional teams share their earnings with relatively poorer teams, is becoming *de rigeur* in professional sports. In 1994, it seems likely to be one of the items on the bargaining table for the next baseball collective bargaining agreement. In order for revenue-sharing to work, owners must have the permission of the players.

Miller, who turned the Major League Baseball Players' Association (MLBPA) into the modern labor union that it is, believes the idea of revenue-sharing is ridiculous for several reasons, not the least of which is that it is anticompetitive because it would allow uncompetitive franchises to receive funds from those that are successful. Miller states that it is "stupid to remove from some club owners an incentive to win by subsidizing their failures to be competitive." Additionally, the players would also have to approve a concomitant salary cap. Miller points out that a salary cap simply does not make sense, in his view, as something a union could even consider, and which might actually be illegal.

Miller's love for a good fight, as well as his dedication to the union cause, is obvious, both from this article and from his book, *A Whole New Ballgame*. It seems unlikely that this article is an attempt to either guide or second-guess Don Fehr, current head of the MLBPA. Perhaps Miller is assisting the association by firing off the first shot of what may be a long labor-management war in 1994–1995.

Norman, Geoffrey. **"Smart Ball."** *Sports Illustrated* 73, no. 10 (3 September 1990): 114–125.

This is an absorbing and valuable portrait of football life at several Division III schools—colleges that don't give athletic scholarships and at which football (and indeed, all other sports) are given a lower priority than studies. At M I T , Swarthmore, and the University of Chicago, for example, sports are an extracurricular activity; students are in school to learn, and learning comes first. The players' enthusiasm for winning is just as strong here as in Division I schools, but is coupled with the desire do well academically. Above all else, the players and coaches that Norman describes adhere to an intellectual ideal that demands that the college/university's role is to educate its students.

Romano, John. **"Athletes and Rape: Is There a Link?"** *St. Petersburg Times (28 June 1992).*

This article reviews the possibility that athletes are responsible for a greater proportion of sexual assaults than the general male population. No fully satisfactory statistical evidence has either proven or disproven the possibility. Confusing the issue is that cases involving athletes, especially well-known athletes, are reported by the media more frequently than others. Those who believe that athletes are involved more than their nonathletic peers cite several likely reasons, including an acceptance of violence carried into their lives from the playing field, and a sense that they are entitled to whatever they wish to take.

Rubin, Jeff. **"Safe Equipment a Tough Sell."** *Palm Beach Post* (17 August 1990): 3C.

Rubin suggests that the reason that youth sports equipment is not popular is that it is unfamiliar to those involved in administering youth sports. Although he doesn't detail this plausible explanation, Rubin does review two areas of possible equipment reform in youth baseball, safety balls and breakaway bases. In both cases, there is evidence that injury to young players can be reduced by using the newer equipment. Of three safety baseballs, the 'Reduced Injury Factor' ball made by Worth Sports reduced the chances of head injury when a batter was hit by a pitched ball. The other two types of balls also show appreciable possibility of preventing injury. Runners sliding into bases improperly can suffer leg and ankle injuries, and breakaway bases might reduce those injuries. One type of the new bases is being used now by the Toronto Blue Jays during spring training in Florida.

Salter, David. **"Playing Ball with Colleges."** *USA Weekend* (21–23 January 1994): 8.

Salter is assistant public relations director at Ramapo College in New Jersey, and author of *Blueprint for Success: An In-Depth Analysis of NCAA Division III Athletics, and Why It Should Be the Model for Intercollegiate Reform* (Francis Merrick, 1994). This article sums up some of the salient points of his book.

Salter argues that the less-competitive NCAA Division III schools are able to do more, academically and socially, for their athletes than other schools that are more concerned about making money and achieving prestige through their sports programs. Salter asserts several advantages to Division III athletics: Presidents, not athletic departments, control the schools' athletic budgets, thus reducing the "lust for revenue;" coaches have a role in educating athletes, and their educational performances are so important to the schools they are "not evaluated solely on win-loss records;" and, Division III players do not receive athletic scholarships, and are thus not subject to their financial tyranny. As a result, Salter contends, using Division III athletic regulations as a model for Division I and Division II schools will result in better-educated college athletes.

Sandomir, Richard. **"TV Sports: Death Is Cheap: Maybe It's Just $14.95."** *New York Times* (8 March 1994): 13B.

On 11 March 1994, Pay-Per-View cable television showed "The Ultimate Fighting Championship II," a fight event that would be, as Sandomir characterized it, "a no-rules war among martial artists that could conclude in rigor mortis." Sandomir was clearly opposed to the idea of the exhibition, and after reading this column, it's difficult not to agree with him. Certain to be more brutal and violent than any boxing match or other martial arts performance, the affair was held "in Denver, situated in the only state lacking a boxing commission, making it the only place in the country able to stage such an event." In the following week's column, Sandomir remarked that the organizers of the event had actually thanked him for his negative preview; apparently any publicity is considered better than none.

Saporito, Bill. **"The Owners' New Game Is Managing."** *Fortune* 124, no. 1 (1 July 1991): 86–91.

As a result of increased costs, especially in player salaries, the management of professional clubs in four sports—baseball, football, basketball, and hockey—have been forced to deal with the same financial issues with which owners of any other large business grapple as a matter of course. More and more, owners are beginning to sound like managers of large national corporations: "The buzzwords in sports biz are now 'additional revenue streams,' 'extending the arena,' and even 'customer service.' "

Schrof, Joanie M. **"Pumped Up."** *U.S. News & World Report* (1 June 1992): 54–63.

This article is a good popular survey of the status of steroid abuse in the United States, and of the efforts (relatively feeble by some standards) to deal with the problem. Schrof discusses why both adolescents and adults take steroids, reviews the problems that are caused by steroids, including outbursts of irritability known as "roid rages," and the pressures to take and continue taking steroids. Schrof cites her magazine's investigation, coupled with other research sources, in her startling conclusions.

Telander, Rick. **"The Face of Sweeping Change."** *Sports Illustrated* 73, no. 11 (10 September 1990): 38–44.

An appreciative but objective biographical sketch of Paul Tagliabue, written several weeks after he assumed the position of commissioner of the National Football League. Telander predicts that Tagliabue is the right man to lead the NFL in the 1990s, dealing with the problems and the successes that the former commissioner, Pete Rozelle (with Tagliabue's assistance as Chief Counsel), engineered in the 1970s and the 1980s. Though Tagliabue has his detractors, he has largely achieved the success and leadership strength that Telander predicted.

Weinstock, Jeff. **"Rebel Yell."** *Sport* (February 1993): 26–29, 33.

This is an interesting interview with Charles Barkley, the star basketball athlete who has been at the center of one of the many controversies about an athlete's position as a role model. The quotable and intelligent Barkley is unquestionably an attractive figure with a propensity for forwardness: "One can't help but love him for it, because there is something terribly appealing about someone brazen enough to, as Barkley did last year, deny having read or written parts of his own autobiography, although he did stop short of denying having lived them."

In addition to being flamboyant, however, Barkley has been involved in several incidents which are, at best, public-relations disasters. Although he has an explanation for how various incidents have been misread, Barkley has, at minimum, acquired a reputation for being capable of blowups as well as PR coups. Weinstock notes that Barkley is accepted, at least as long as he delivers top-quality performance on the basketball court.

Weistart, John. **"The 90's University: Reading, Writing, and Shoe Contracts."** *New York Times* (28 November 1993): VIII, 9.

In response to serious difficulties with individual coaches signing "shoe contracts" with manufacturers, new NCAA regulations in 1993 required that the contracts be made with the college or university. Weistart, a well-known expert in sports law, points out that even the new arrangement is fraught with difficulties.

Monographs, Reports, and Papers

The Amateur Athletic Foundation of Los Angeles. **Coverage of Women's Sports in Four Daily Newspapers.** (January 1991).

This study analyzes the coverage of women's sports in comparison to men's sports and overall sports coverage in four highly rated American newspapers for a three-month period in 1990. Among the conclusions cited in the report's summary: "Stories focusing exclusively on men's sports outnumbered stories addressing only women's sports by a ratio of 23 : 1." When men's baseball and football stories were eliminated from the count, the ratio of men's sports stories to women's fell to 8.7 : 1.

The Amateur Athletic Foundation of Los Angeles. **Gender Stereotyping in Televised Sports.** (August 1990).

This study analyzes and compares the treatment of women and men in televised sports coverage during an important six-week period of games and tournaments which included large numbers of sports activities in which both men and women were involved (including the 1989 U.S. Open mixed-doubles tennis tournament). Among the conclusions: In televised sports news, "women are humorous sex objects in the stands, but missing as athletes;" men's sports received 92 percent of the air time, women's sports 5 percent; and television sports news did focus regularly on women, but rarely on women athletes. More common were portrayals of women as comical targets of the newscasters' jokes and/or as sexual objects (e.g., women spectators in bikinis).

American Medical Association. **"Council Report: Medical and Non-medical Uses of Anabolic-Androgenic Steroids."** *Journal of the American Medical Association* 264, no. 22 (12 December 1990).

An American Medical Association (AMA) Council on Scientific Affairs report was adopted by the House of Delegates in December 1989. Stimulated by a resolution to "identify current prevention activities, urge the development of steroid treatment programs, and support stricter laws and legislation to limit use," the report represents as definitive a statement as the AMA can make on steroids. The report states that the AMA is opposed to drug use to "enhance or sustain athletic performance," and recommends:

- Support of increased criminal penalties for steroid abuse.
- Making educational materials relating to steroids available to doctors and to the public.

- Encouraging further research of the effects of steroids and accurate reporting of "suspected adverse effects to the FDA (Food and Drug Administration)."
- Working with "sports organizations to increase understanding of health effects" of steroids and "to discourage the use of steroids."

Anderson, W.A., et al. **"National Survey of Alcohol and Drug Use by College Athletes."** *Physician and Sports Medicine* 19, no. 2 (1991): 91–104.

Replicating an earlier study performed in 1985, the study reports a survey taken in 1989. Using a 58-page questionnaire, the survey extensively measured attitudes about and use of alcohol, cocaine, crack, amphetamines, steroids, and other drugs. According to an abstract of the article, "fewer athletes reported use of cocaine and marijuana/hashish in 1989 than in 1985. Use of smokeless tobacco and major pain medications had increased. Use of alcohol and anabolic steroids had not changed significantly. The data did not support the idea that college athletes use alcohol and drugs more than their non-athletic peers."

Blackwell, J. **"Discourses on Drug Use: Social Construction of a Steroid Scandal."** *The Journal of Drug Issues* 21, no. 1 (1991): 147–164.

In this article, a sociologist examines the reaction to the Ben Johnson steroid abuse scandal of 1988, and its implications for dealing with abuse in general. Blackwell finds that the Canadian examination of drug abuse (the "Dubin Report") focused so much attention on athletes' use of steroids that it de-emphasized parallel problems with drugs on the street and drugs in medicine.

Carr, C.N., S.R. Kennedy, and K.M. Dimick. **"Alcohol Use Among High School Athletes: A Comparison of Alcohol Use and Intoxication in Male and Female High School Athletes and Non-Athletes."** *Journal of Alcohol and Drug Education* 36, no. 1 (1990): 39–43.

According to an abstract of this article, the authors found that "male athletes consume alcohol significantly more than male non-athletes and that male athletes drink alcohol to intoxication at a significantly greater difference than female athletes."

Though the results of this study appear to conflict with Ringwalt's (see below), the differences may be due to differences in survey method, statistical analysis, or even in local attitudes toward drinking. Regardless of the exact results, there can be no denying that alcohol abuse among both high-school students and athletes is a major problem that needs to be addressed by society.

The Final Report of the President's Commission on Olympic Sports, 1975–1977. U.S. Government Printing Office, Stock no. 641-000-00002-3.

This extensive report examines why the United States "does not nearly approach achieving its full potential in sports." While recognizing that the federal government has not and should not attempt to direct amateur athletics, the report makes several recommendations to make the American athletes more competitive without compromising their ethical integrity. Of special interest is the report's discussion of "amateurism."

Goldberg, L., et al. **"Anabolic Steroid Education and Adolescents: Do Scare Tactics Work?"** *Pediatrics* 87, no. 3 (1991): 283–286.

Finding an appropriate way to deliver ethical and/or health messages to youngsters is problematic. In the 1980s, for example, an anticrime program called "Scared Stiff" was introduced in several places in the United States. The program took students into jails where they were lectured by convicts in an effort to convince them that crime and its consequent jail time would be a totally unpleasant experience, and one that they should avoid. Though the program legitimately claimed some success in lowering teen crime, other evaluations showed that balanced discussions of values as well as discussions of the consequences of crime, were equally effective.

In this study, Goldberg and his associates compared the effects on high-school football players of two different education programs about steroids. One program was a balanced presentation about steroids, discussing both risks and benefits. The second program was a "risks-only" program, emphasizing only the drawbacks of steroid abuse. The authors show that the balanced program is much more likely than a scare-tactic approach to be effective in changing attitudes toward steroid use, at least in the short term.

Gough, Russell. **"When Rules Strangle Ethics: What We Can Learn from the NCAA."** Paper presented at The National Conference on Ethics in America, California State University, Long Beach, 9–11 March 1994. This paper will be reprinted in the "Book of Proceedings" of the conference.

Gough is an assistant professor of philosophy at Pepperdine University in California. He has written extensively, and astutely, on the NCAA and other issues in both the popular press and in academic articles. This paper addresses the incredible length and detail of the *NCAA Manual,* and the effect such an overwhelmingly large work is likely to have upon NCAA members.

In this paper, Gough observes that "any institution or enterprise which attempts, as the NCAA has attempted, to legislate behavior comprehensively runs the serious risk of strangling—even to the point of precluding—the ethical development of its members or employees." There are two main reasons why this occurs.

The first reason is that "attempts to legislate behavior comprehensively can foster myopic, legalistic attitudes that harm and hinder thoughtful ethical judgment." Gough believes that the response to the gigantic size of the *NCAA Manual* leads to an attitude in which only those rules that are explicitly stated are observed, provoking an attitude that says that if "it's not against the rules, it's okay."

Second, Gough contends that the promulgation of meaningless or unimportant rules cheapens the important ones: "[A]ttempts to legislate behavior comprehensively can undermine the ethical importance of rules. . . . [U]nenforceable rules and petty rules . . . are not ethically innocuous, especially when they are many. . . . If . . . an enterprise creates rules that are unenforceable and petty, then that enterprise may ultimately divest all institutional rules of their ethical import."

Lin, Geraline C., and Lynda Erinoff, eds. **Anabolic Steroid Abuse.** Research Monograph 102. U.S. Department of Health and Human Services. U.S. Government Printing Office (1990). DHHS publication number (ADM)90-1720.

This monograph is the result of papers and discussions from a meeting on anabolic steroid abuse, 6–7 March 1989, in Rockville, Maryland, at the National Institute on Drug Abuse. Although these are generally highly technical papers by and for chemists, biologists, medical doctors, and others in related fields, there is much that the interested layman can find in this survey of the state of steroid-abuse study. In one interesting article, Paul J. Goldstein reviews briefly the history of anabolic steroid use, reviews how and where steroids are used, and concludes with important recommendations for further research.

The history of performance-enhancing drugs as detailed by Goldstein is an interesting one. Athletes have used performance-enhancing concoctions of caffeine, sugar, alcohol, cocaine, and even nitroglycerine, since Greek times. Muscle-men and body builders have enthralled the public throughout this century in such roles as Tarzan and Conan the Barbarian, played by increasingly mega-pectoralled actors from Victor Mature to Arnold Schwartzenegger. Unfortunately, this enthrallment has led young athletes and Superman wannabe's to seek the dangerous help of steroids and other chemical additives.

Among the most interesting articles is "Incidence of the Nonmedical Use of Anabolic-androgenic Steroids" by Charles E. Yesalis and William A. Anderson, et al. This article presents a brief but comprehensive survey of the history of steroid abuse and some important observations on the current state of abuse. Dr. Yesalis is one of the leading scholars in the study of steroid abuse in the United States.

The Miller Lite Report on Women in Sports. In cooperation with the Women's Sports Foundation. (December 1985).

The result of a survey of 1,682 respondents to an opinion poll, this report details how sports are becoming commonplace among girls and women. A variety of other important conclusions arise from the survey's results, including the feeling among women that men are often threatened by losing to women. Younger women, however, are more likely than older ones to seek sports partners of equal ability. Older women are likely to accept the idea that the sexes should be kept separate in sports. Another very interesting finding of the survey was that involvement in sport is motivated most by the choice of childhood playmates. Women who played with mixed groups or with boys are far more likely to "view their adolescent body images positively, participate and attain leadership positions in organized sports at every level, and participate more actively in sports/fitness activities as adults. . . ."

The survey does not represent a random sampling of women; it was sent to members of the Women's Sports Foundation. As an evaluation of the characteristics of this selected group, however, it is an important contribution to understanding the needs and desires of athletic women.

Minorities in Sport: The Effect of Varsity Sports Participation on the Social, Educational, and Career Mobility of Minority Students. Executive summary. (15 August 1989).

This report evaluates the supposition that participation in sports at the pre-high-school level enhances the likelihood that a child will continue his or her education after high school. It concludes that "athletic participation enhanced involvement in school and community, heightened popularity among peers, and inspired leadership aspirations." But it also found that "high school sports have been oversold as a vehicle for upward mobility among minorities. . . . [I]t was mainly whites, not Hispanics or African-Americans, for whom athletic participation proved to be related to upward mobility after high school."

Ringwalt, Chris. **"Student Athletes and Non-Athletes: Do Their Use of and Beliefs about Alcohol and Other Drugs Differ?"** *Special Research Report.* North Carolina State Department of Public Instruction, Alcohol and Drug Defense Program, Raleigh, NC (1988).

This is the report of a study of 10,259 students in grades 7 through 12, including 3,328 athletes. The study analyzed differences in the use of and beliefs about drugs by young athletes and nonathletes. According to an abstract of the article, Ringwalt found that there were "no significant differences between athletes and non-athletes in the use of and beliefs related to drugs." Although athletes used smokeless tobacco more than non-athletes, athletes were less likely to smoke cigarettes. Though neither group varied in their rate of intoxication, athletes were more likely to have been intoxicated in the 30 days preceding the study.

Stehlin, D. **"For Athletes and Dealers, Black Market Steroids Are Risky Business."** In *Anabolic Steroids: A Review of Current Literature and Research.* Tempe, Arizona: DIN Publications, 1991. 10–11.

This article addresses some of the dangers of using black-market steroids (as opposed to misusing prescribed steroids or steroids diverted from a legitimate source). In addition to the problems associated with steroid use, users who buy on the black market may be getting drugs that are improperly made, possibly impure, and sometimes counterfeit non-steroids. Problems with impure and improperly made drugs, especially, constitute a major health risk for black-market steroid users.

Terney, R., and L.G. Mclain. **"Use of Anabolic Steroids in High School Children."** *American Journal of Diseases of Children* 144, no. 1 (1990): 99–103.

The extent of anabolic steroid abuse, although recognized as a major problem, is not very well documented. Steroid use among children, especially, is difficult to assess for several reasons, not the least of which is reluctance to talk about the use of a substance that is known to be generally prohibited and/or illegal. Thus, the results of a survey about steroids is likely to produce conservative results. The authors found that among 2,113 high school students, 4.4 percent of the students surveyed (94 students—6.5 percent of the males and 2.5 percent of the females) admitted to using anabolic steroids. Athletes had a higher rate of steroid use by a margin of 5.5 percent versus 2.4 percent for nonathletes.

The authors conclude that steroid abuse represents a "serious, as yet unappreciated drug problem in our adolescents."

The Wilson Report: Moms, Dads, Daughters, and Sports. In cooperation with the Women's Sports Foundation. (7 June 1988).

The result of more than 1,500 telephone interviews with a randomly selected group of mothers, fathers, and daughters, this evaluation of interest in sports among the general population discloses that an overwhelming number of parents (87 percent) accept the idea that sports are as important for girls as for boys, and that almost as large a percentage of girls (82 percent) participate in sports or plan to participate in the future.

Among the general population sampled, parental attitude toward sports is a determining factor in the girls' participation. Only 27 percent of the younger girls said that it was their fathers' interests and examples which encouraged them; for older girls, the figure nearly doubles to 44 percent. For the others, the mother is cited as the major influencing factor.

Book-Length Nonfiction

Andre, Judith, and David N. James, eds. **Rethinking College Athletics.** Philadelphia: Temple University Press, 1991. ISBN 0-87722-716-0.

This is an excellent collection of academic articles and talks, about half of which were presented at a March 1988 conference on ethical issues in sports at Old Dominion University in Virginia, and a subsequent speaker's program at the same school. While some of the articles are probably of interest only to academics in specialized fields, other articles address many of the same concerns written about in other books and newspapers aimed at the nonacademic with an interest in sports.

Several of the articles are extremely provocative, such as Norman Fost's "Banning Drugs in Sports: A Skeptical View," in which Fost holds that our usual negative reaction to drug use is not a matter of ethics, but derives from a "moralism" in which restrictive rules are made to deal with "vaguely undesirable activities, such as pornography." Fost does not advocate drug use. Rather, he sees it as one of several responses to the athlete's desire to gain a competitive edge.

This collection is well worth looking at by those who are not disturbed by academic language and structure.

Ashe, Arthur A., Jr. **A Hard Road To Glory: A History of the African American Athlete.** 3 volumes. New York: Warner Books, 1988. ISBN 0-446-71008-3.

This is an incredibly detailed and well-written encyclopedic work, describing the achievements of black athletes between 1619 and 1984; an addendum brings some of the information up to the beginning of 1987 when the book went to press.

Despite the extensive coverage of both the well known (especially in recent history) and the obscure, the three volumes of this definitive work are written smoothly and carefully. Although this is the first source one should go to in order to learn about the history of blacks in sport, it's also possible to browse through the volumes for pleasure. In addition to the usual scholarly apparatuses of notes, index, and bibliography, each volume has a large reference section that sums up the achievements of various athletes on a sport-by-sport basis.

Atyeo, Don. **Violence in Sports.** New York: Van Nostrand Reinhold Company, 1981. ISBN 0-442-20865-0.

Previously published by Paddington Press, Ltd., as *Blood & Guts* in 1979, this work is somewhat dated in the examples presented, although one is immediately struck by the realization that, though the names have changed, the situations described have not. Sports, as defined in the United States, Europe, and most other areas of the world, remain, in Atyeo's view, as a reflection of desires for mastery of the environment, and as a replacement for the aggressive instinct and generally uncivilized violence.

Atyeo's position on violence may not yet be a majority one, but it seems to be gaining credence. He points to such examples as riots at soccer games and the aggressive spirit of American football as examples of aggression that, in any other situation, would be totally unacceptable. But he certainly recognizes that those who engage in such activities are fully aware of what they are doing. The players share a spiritual link with the gladiators of the early Roman Empire. Nowhere is this more visible than in professional boxing, where the clear objective of the activity is to beat one's opponent senseless.

Even when competition is nonviolent (as in such sports as skating, skiing, and running), we surround the events with the nationalistic trappings of war. The drumbeats of nationalism that surround even the modern Olympics are not new. The early Greek Olympians were taught that they were defending the honor of their nation-states, and modern Olympians seem quite willing to mouth the truism that the glory of their countries, as well as their own personal glory, is the function of the Olympics.

Atyeo notes that, following the publication of Konrad Lorenz's *On Aggression,* there was some imaginable justification for violent sports. Lorenz proposed, and Atyeo reiterates, that "the main function of sport today lies in the cathartic discharge of aggressive urge. . . ." Though Lorenz's view of the social usefulness of sport is disproved by the violence and aggression that take place off the field and after sporting events, the need or even the attraction of such events remains a secret hidden behind a door that, to date, no psychologist or sociologist has completely opened.

Bissinger, H.G. **Friday Night Lights; A Town, a Team, and a Dream.** Reading, MA: Addison-Wesley Publishing Company, 1990. ISBN 0-201-19677-8.

In 1988, Bissinger, a Pulitzer Prize–winning author, moved himself and his family into the small, west-Texas town of Odessa in order to spend the next several months following the trials and triumphs of the local high school football team and the ebb and flow of the local community around that team and its members. Though Odessa is a real place, it's also an archetypal town, typical of hundreds if not thousands of places in America where the life of the community is largely defined by its high school football program. When there is success, the world is bright and full of joy; when there is loss, the world turns gray and chilly, and the loss is perceived as failure.

Bissinger documents both the good and the bad about the player's and the town's fascination with football. The highly touted benefits of the game—personal fame and glory, discipline, a ticket to an education, and so on—are all apparent, as are the more destructive aspects of the game—high personal standards of success, disappointment and depression in the face of failure, the staking of a lifetime's hopes and desires on a few chance encounters on the way to the goal post.

Bissinger's experiences after the book was published show how important high school football and the sport culture is in some places. After the book was published, the Odessa football team was investigated by local authorities for violations of training rules; though Bissinger could not have been the sole source to inspire an investigation, he received angry letters and phone calls from people upset about what was happening to the team. Threats of violence and death are not the type of accompaniments one usually associates with high school sports (or with book publishing). The linkage between the two is worth extensive consideration.

Chandler, Joan. **Television and National Sport: The United States and Britain.** Urbana and Chicago: University of Illinois Press, 1988.

This is a carefully researched, well thought-out, and exuberantly written work. Chandler, a University of Chicago professor, is a self-described television sports fan. Though her comparisons between sports in the United States and Britain are apt and important, the American sports ethicist will be more interested in Chandler's take on the effects of television on baseball, football, and other sports.

Chandler contends that television neither created nor effected attitudes toward sports in the United States, but rather reflected changes in our society born of other cultural and technological developments such as transportation and an increasingly more extravagant life-style. If anything, television, according to Chandler, allows us to see how sport mirrors the society in which it exists. Professional ballplayers, for example, have always worked for both a love of their sport and for the salaries it brings them, although Major League Baseball wanted the fans to believe that players played only for the fun and challenge of the sport. That television has made possible the observation of players' personal lives, union activities, salary negotiations, and the like, is not the fault of television.

Chandler's evaluations into sport in either country make the book a gold mine of insight into sport's relationship with television, and into sport as a reflection of our society.

Cosell, Howard, with Shelby Whitfield. **What's Wrong With Sports.** New York: Simon & Schuster, 1991. ISBN 0-671-70840-6.

Writing in the pugnacious style that made him a highly successful sports journalist, Cosell describes what he characterizes as the utter lack of regard for ethics and morality in sports today. His targets include National Football League franchise relocations ("carpet-bagging"), pro boxing, and college athletics. Though his history seems to be accurate, Cosell's interpretations are relentlessly pessimistic. When boxer Sugar Ray Leonard wanted to come out of retirement after treatment for a detached retina, he easily got his license; Cosell is adamant that the licensing showed a callous disregard for human values by the authorities. An argument could be made that Leonard was entitled to do as he wished, especially since the retina had been repaired. However, many of the incidents Cosell relates are decidedly unsavory, like that of Boxer Benny Harjo (billed by his manager as "Bionic Benny"), who was licensed for a professional match even though he had a surgically implanted pacemaker.

Edwards, Harry. **The Revolt of the Black Athlete.** New York: The Macmillan Company, The Free Press, 1969.

Now a professor of sociology, Edwards was the prime mover of the 1968 Olympic boycott movement (the Olympic Committee For Human Rights), asserting that blacks should not participate in the Mexico City games because treatment of American blacks in both the Olympic movement and in college and professional sports was racist. The Olympic Games was not the only issue; Edwards demonstrated convincingly that racism in American amateur sports was pervasive.

As a result of the efforts of the Committee for Human Rights, Tommie Smith and Juan Carlos, two black athletes who had won a gold and a silver medal, made headlines by raising their fists in a "black power demonstration" during the Olympics award ceremonies. In an astounding overreaction, the two athletes were suspended from further competition by the Olympic Committee which insisted that there was no room for politics in the Olympics.

Although Edwards own voice is heard clearly enough, a large portion of the book is given over to various documents such as news reports of black unrest at colleges and the responses of college administrators, athletic departments, and others. One does not have to agree that confrontation is the way to solve problems in order to be appalled by the racist conditions these documents reveal—de facto segregated housing, lack of jobs and scholarships for black athletes, failure to provide adequate housing even for scholarship black athletes, and the minuscule numbers of black coaches, athletic directors, and other key college personnel—the list goes on and on.

Some of the goals of the Committee for Human Rights have been achieved since the late 1960s, but there can be no doubt that a racist spirit still stalks today's black athletes. Edwards is aware that the problems of sports in America are a reflection of the entire society. Solving the problems of sports racism is no guarantee that racism in society is solved.

Espy, Richard. **The Politics of the Olympic Games.** Berkeley: University of California Press, 1979. ISBN 0-520-03777-4.

This is a very detailed explication, for the period 1944–1979, of the relationship between international politics and the Olympic Games. Although the IOC has frequently insisted that international politics has no place in the Games, the nature of our modern world means that international politics is inevitably reflected in such major events as the Olympics. Espy shows how the shifting tides of political interests are filtered through the Olympic games. The attempt by the former Soviet Union, for example, to capture the 1980 Olympics for Moscow is detailed, along with the cross-currents of the Soviet's treatment of Israeli athletes and of its own Jewish athletes during the University Games, a world-class event. Espy makes clear how intimately the Olympics are connected with major world events. Such a connection is inevitable, given the attractiveness of the Games, the attention they are paid, and the nationalism inherent in Oympic competition. As Espy points out, "The propaganda value became readily apparent when the prowess of an athletic feat was rewarded under a national banner while a national anthem played. . . ."

Fine, Gary Alan. **With the Boys: Little League Baseball and Preadolescent Culture.** Chicago: The University of Chicago Press, 1987. ISBN 0-2262-4936-0.

This is an excellent observational study of five local Little League organizations, backed up with an extensive grasp of the professional literature; as a sociologist, Fine, who did field research for three years, is concerned with defining the social structures that Little Leagues impose upon their localities, and with examining their effects.

The benefits and drawbacks of the Little League system (and, by implication, other organized youth sports), are not Fine's main concern. He does, however, address benefit-drawback concerns in Appendix 1, "The Effects of Little League Baseball;" Fine's low-key summary of the impact of Little League is reassuring to the concerned observer, emphasizing as it does that the Leagues generally reduce delinquency, promote tolerance, teach baseball skills, provide regular programs of exercise, and promote leadership and self-esteem.

Fleisher, Arthur A., Brian L. Goff, and Robert D. Tollison. **The National Collegiate Athletic Association: A Study in Cartel Behavior.** Chicago and London: The University of Chicago Press, 1992. ISBN 0-226-25326-0.

In this superb economic analysis of the NCAA, the authors, all economists, analyze the activities of the NCAA and the college sports world in comparison to a hypothetical model of cartel behavior. This is an important book, both for sports-minded economists and for those interested in the behavioral ethics of the college athletic world.

Cartels occur when there is collusion among producers and/or suppliers in an effort to control the market for the goods in which they trade, and reach benefits in excess of what competition would bring them (as, for example, the Organization of Petroleum Exporting Countries [OPEC] attempts to do, with resulting market disruptions as happened in 1973). The authors describe carefully how the NCAA's continued existence as a cartel is based upon price fixing, output controls, low compensation to athletes, and the absence of brand-name and capital asset regulation—all factors in establishing and sustaining a cartel. Understanding the NCAA as a cartel, the authors observe, has important benefits for someone interested in understanding the ethical situation in college athletics.

Francis, Charlie, with Jeff Coplen. **Speed Trap: Inside the Biggest Scandal in Olympic History.** New York: St. Martin's Press, 1990. ISBN 0-3120-4877-7.

Francis was Ben Johnson's track coach for many years before Johnson's stunning performance in the 1988 Olympics, and was also involved in training several other runners. He describes a world where steroids and other drugs are used regularly by track stars to enhance their performance.

Francis seems willing to accept drug use in the Olympics and in sports in general; he is one of a minority who believe that performance-enhancing drugs are the only way that a top competitor can stay even with his or her peers who are also using drugs. Additionally, Francis charges that Olympic officials willingly delude themselves and the public into believing that drug use is not widespread.

This is a disturbing book, not only because of Francis' unwillingness to see the damage that drug use can do to an athlete, but also because, if he is right about the widespread availability of drugs, it is almost impossible to tell if any given athletic performance is truly the best that an athlete can provide, or only an augmented show that depends not on skill and ability, but on the chemicals that flow like water from a variety of laboratories.

Freedman, Warren. **Professional Sports and Antitrust.** New York: Quorum Books, 1987. ISBN 0-89930-191-6.

"A professional sports league requires a certain amount of cooperation among competitor-members for the league to survive, and it is this fact that troubles the antitrust plaintiff."

This book is an attorney's overview of the relationship between professional sports and antitrust legislation. In addition to carefully reviewing each of the important cases involved in sports history, the book also deals with such important legal issues in sport today as the role of sports agents and the relationship of professional sports to First Amendment expression. Freedman's examination occasionally descends into abstruse "legalese," but is relieved by occasional insights and historical perspectives that bring this work within reach of the interested sports-law aficionado.

Giamatti, A. Bartlett. **Take Time For Paradise: Americans and Their Games.** New York: Summit Books, 1989. ISBN 0-671-69130-9.

Take Time for Paradise brought Giamatti the commissionership of baseball; his passion for the game is obvious throughout the work. Yet this extended essay will hardly touch the average reader or sports fan, and, though released to the general public by a trade publisher, the general public cannot be Giamatti's intended audience. The average reader will not be amused by the grandiloquent Ciceronian flourishes with which Giamatti describes his beloved sport of baseball. Nor will the average reader care about Giamatti's far-reaching insights into the American character.

His approach to baseball, an educated amalgam of classicism, sociology, anthropology, and contemporary cultural observation, is difficult to grasp for those of us who do not share his highly educated weltanschauung. Few of us are ready, for example, to consider the truth of Giamatti's assertion that "to know baseball is to continue to aspire to the condition of freedom, individually and as a people, for baseball is grounded in America in a way unique to our games."

Some readers, however, might well find Giamatti's view of baseball and America insightful and stirring; the book sold well when it was published. Others will, with a sigh, put the book aside half unread, overwhelmed with the possibility that baseball is presented here, by a serious academic thinker, as nothing less than the key to our national psyche.

Gregorich, Barbara. **Women at Play: The Story of Women in Baseball.** Orlando: Harcourt Brace Jovanovich, 1993. ISBN 0-15-698297-8.

This is a superb and touching chronicle of the efforts of women to participate in the "national pastime" against stacked odds. While the first professional men's baseball team, the Cincinnati Red Stockings, appeared in 1869, women at Vassar College had already organized two baseball teams by 1866, one year after the school opened. Large numbers of girls and women played hardball, some even competing against men professional players—Jackie Mitchell was celebrated in 1931 as "the girl who struck out Ruth and Gehrig." Though the Babe and the Iron Horse may have been fooling with the young woman for publicity purposes, there's no doubt that Mitchell was a tremendously talented player. Baseball Commissioner Kenesaw Landis voided Mitchell's professional contract in the same year, asserting that baseball was "too strenuous" for women.

Despite Landis' opposition, women continued to play baseball both as amateurs and professionals, barnstorming the country and attracting significant audiences. As made known by the 1992 movie *A League of Their Own*, Phil Wrigley even fielded professional women ballplayers between 1943 and 1953. Women's organized baseball fell victim to the same financial distress that men's professional ball did in the postwar years. While men's sports were able to survive, and are today thriving, women's professional teams never recovered from the financial distress.

Gregorich concludes that the first female major-league baseball player might now be starting her career in Little League or even be on a high-school team, and that "organized baseball can find her . . . if it wants to."

Guttman, Allen. **A Whole New Ball Game: An Interpretation of American Sports.** Chapel Hill: University of North Carolina Press, 1988. ISBN 0-8078-1786-4.

This discussion of the role of sports in American culture is an attempt to merge the two worlds of the academic and the popular. Though not the easiest reading in the world, Guttman does have a knack for clear, interesting interpretations of sport history and culture. Far more accessible to the average reader than many other academic writers, Guttman is concerned with the growth of American sport and the role of the sportsman in the social and economic growth of the country. Sport, in all of its ramifications—from eighteenth-century cockfighting to late-twentieth-century jogging—is used as a mirror of culture.

Along the way, Guttman discusses how racism, drug abuse, and bodily abuse (shown most clearly in professional football) are not aberrations of sport but rather extensions of what we want, at least vicariously. He notes as well a movement away from the culture of pain, which professional football and many other organized sports accept, and towards a desire for individual achievement that does not push us into unhealthy or masochistic environments. This is a well-written, comprehensive work that can both satisfy and challenge a broad audience.

————. **Women's Sports: A History.** New York: Columbia University Press, 1991. ISBN 0-231-06956-1.

Guttman describes in great detail the history of women in sports from antiquity up through the present time, delineating how varied cultural mores affected what women (and older girls) did. Each section of this fact-filled work places the achievements of women in sports against the culture of their time. In recent times, we find that the Baron Pierre de Coubertin, the founder of the Olympic movement, was opposed to women's sports. Even Coubertin, however, gradually was pushed into accepting women in the Olympics, although today's Games still bear the mark of some of the old prejudices (i.e., limited events, especially in track and field).

Most early-twentieth-century opposition to women's participation in sports was based upon two beliefs—that women were physically incapable of participating, and that for women to display themselves in scanty athletic costumes was scandalous and overly stimulating to male onlookers. Time has taken care of both objections. To consider women athletes of today as physically incompetent is clearly absurd. That more than a tinge of voyeurism still remains, however, is more than likely. Guttman notes that Nadia Comanechi, though not the winner in 1977 gymnastics, was still the darling of the world press, quite likely because of her elfin-like appearance.

Compared to other countries, the advance of women in sports was significantly retarded in the United States, in great part because U.S. sports programs operate from colleges, which tend to have conservative attitudes. In European countries, sports and athletic clubs were usually part of everyone's social life, and women's sports were easier to organize and impossible to really hold back.

While what happened three or five or ten years ago may be known to many of us, it does well to be reminded of what happened in the past—the struggles for the right to participate, the stunning achievements of women athletes that time and the media forgot, and the strong personalities that made women's rights an issue long before the more familiar women's liberation movement of the late twentieth century.

Huizinga, Johann. **Homo Ludens: A Study of the Play Element in Culture.** 1950.

This may have been the first book to legitimize the academic study of play and sports as important parts of culture. Huizinga's work is an academic classic in anthropology/sociology because of the recognition that all societies, from the most primitive to the most developed, have sports and games that reflect and reinforce the behavior of the society at large. Although of little practical importance to the average reader today, the work is a classic which has, usually without our knowing it, shaped our understanding of the character and meaning of our leisure activities.

Hyland, Drew. **Philosophy of Sport.** New York: Paragon House, 1990. ISBN 1-55778-189-3.

A professor of philosophy at Trinity College in Hartford, Connecticut, Hyland is a past president of The Philosophical Society for the Study of Sport. As such, he makes clear that the study of sport in society, with some notable exceptions in works by Huizinga and Weiss, has long been a neglected field, especially in the academic world. This book attempts to place the study of sport in the same tradition of study as other cultural activities.

In his discussion of sports ethics (chapter 2, "Ethical Issues in Sport"), Hyland attempts to organize and clarify objectively some of the major issues facing both athletes and spectators in today's world, including the question of drug use. Hyland points out, for example, that drug use (steroids, especially) may not be so different from the use of other techniques, such as weight training, for enhancing performance. Further, Hyland raises the question of whether or not a society has the right (or the need) to prevent people from doing things to themselves that do not particularly harm others.

Elsewhere in the book, Hyland is concerned with a range of other issues, including the role of competitiveness in sports and its relationship to society, sexism and other forms of discrimination, and the relationship of sports values to other activities. Hyland's style is clear and direct; he meets the difficult challenge of making a legitimate academic topic of interest to the nonacademic reader. This book is an impressive achievement. Along with *Jock Culture U.S.A.* by Neil Isaacs and Paul Weiss' *Sport: A Philosophic Inquiry,* it is an essential beginning to any serious study of sports ethics.

Isaacs, Neil D. **Jock Culture U.S.A.** New York: W. W. Norton & Company, 1978. ISBN 0-393-08807-3.

This is one of the most important books ever written about sports. Isaacs, an academic and a sports lover, attempts to define the sociology of the athlete, and to comprehend the roles of athletes and athletics within our society. Despite his love for sports, Isaacs finds that the effect of much of sports is not healthy; the aggressive will to "win-at-all-costs" is far more pervasive than it should be.

Understandably for a groundbreaking work, Isaacs finds so much to comment upon that his presentation is necessarily diffused. Doubtless he would agree that many of the points he touches upon deserve further extensive analysis. But this diffusion also gives his work a great deal of charm and readability—almost any area to which he turns his attention is new ground for interesting and important observation. The role of the athlete as hero, for one example, is traced through historical antiquity and through large portions of literature, and then into modern times.

Jennings, Kenneth M. **Balls and Strikes: The Money Game in Professional Baseball.** New York: Praeger Publishers, 1990. ISBN 0-275-93441-1.

As a professor of industrial relations, Jennings is especially interested in the effect of various historical and economic issues upon groups of people in the baseball world. Wherever possible, Jennings places the information he evaluates in quantifiable and statistical terms. He doesn't hesitate to use whatever tools he can, and some readers may be uncomfortable with such legitimate tools as "chi square" statistical analysis. Jennings begins with a historical review of collective bargaining (going back to 1884) and discusses the effect of collective bargaining up to the present time. He provides the reader with a solid background of such ethics-related issues as racism, alcohol and drug abuse, and the controversy over player salaries, from an industrial-relations point of view. Each area that Jennings reviews is backed by facts, figures, and anecdotes. Though the orientation of this book is somewhat different than many other sports books, it provides a solid grounding in the factual and statistical issues involved in professional baseball.

Jones, Donald G., with Elaine L. Daly. **Sports Ethics in America: A Bibliography, 1970–1990.** Foreword by Thomas H. Kean. Number 21 in Bibliographies and Indexes in American History. New York: Greenwood Press, 1992. ISBN 0-313-27767-2.

With issues in sports ethics being dealt with from a large number of diverse areas (sociology, philosophy, medicine, and anthropology, to name a few), this volume admirably fills a major need; it puts together, as objectively as possible, resources in the sports ethics field over a twenty-year period. The separate subject and author indexes, and the well-drawn individual lists that comprise the body of this work, make it relatively easy for the researcher to locate major works in a variety of fields. Although some of the works are academic, there is a large share of important, nonacademic works. None of the entries are abstracted; apart from some brief, well-thought-out comments in the introduction by Thomas Kean, former governor of New Jersey and now president of Drew University, the reader must go to the works to decide if they are of use.

If only because of the sheer amount of material available, there are undoubtedly some works that an individual reader will expect to find but which will not be represented. In general, however, the work is an essential cornerstone for any study of sports ethics.

Lapchick, Richard. **Five Minutes to Midnight; Race and Sport in the 1990s.** Lanham, MD: Madison Books, 1991. ISBN 9-819-18666-1.

Lapchick is the founder and executive director of the Northeastern University Center for the Study of Sport in Society (CSSS). Growing up in the worlds of both professional and amateur basketball (his father was the renowned coach of the New York Knicks and the St. John's University basketball teams), Lapchick is familiar and comfortable with both sports venues.

The book begins with Lapchick's personal story of being attacked and wounded in 1964 by unknown people who wanted to stop him from organizing a protest against a South African athletic tour of the United States. Living in the South, Lapchick found that the police not only failed to investigate the attack properly, but made an effort to discredit him by claiming that the attack had been a hoax and that he had actually mutilated himself. The balance of the book discusses many of the ethical problems facing professional and college sports, including racial discrimination, positional discrimination ("stacking"), sexual discrimination, academic requirements for college athletes, the use of drugs in sports and professional sports' attempts to deal with the drug problem, and a host of other issues.

Lapchick concludes that, although college and professional sports do have serious ethical problems, they are a clear reflection of society's problems and not merely special cases. Though sports has an important exemplary role to play in society, and may well provide the impetus for eliminating discrimination and other problems, the problems will remain as long as society itself has not addressed them.

Levine, Peter, ed. **American Sport: A Documentary History.** Englewood Cliffs, NJ: Prentice Hall, 1989. ISBN 0-13-031378-5.

A well-respected historian, Levine has assembled a valuable set of documents that is useful in demonstrating to the reader the importance of sport in the American ethos, and how our beliefs about sport have changed through the years. Just as important, the selections in the book are a joy to read.

Levine hits his target in his presentations, beginning with an excerpt from King James' 1618 *Book of Sport,* then moving through the writings of A.G. Spalding, an important figure in the early history of baseball, to the reminiscences of Curt Flood, the baseball player whose lawsuit led to the eventual overthrow of the Reserve Clause in baseball, and more. An excerpt from the writings of Paul Weiss, an excerpt from the autobiography of Billie Jean King, Harry Edwards' discussion of racism in 1979, an excerpt from Robert Lipsyte's *SportsWorld* (1975), and a host of other sources all contribute to making this a superb collection reflecting the full complexity of sport. Intended as a textbook, Levine's interesting and important collection reaches far outside of the classroom.

Lipsyte, Robert. **SportsWorld: An American Dreamland.** New York: The New York Times Book Co., Quadrangle, 1975. ISBN 0-8129-0569-5.

One of the earliest popular books dealing with the relationship of sport to American society, Lipsyte's words still ring true. He describes the American obsession with sports, and especially our focus on the stars and heroes of sport, rather than what sport can ideally be. In his introduction to *SportsWorld*, Lipsyte makes clear that the attitudes he will describe are near universal. Everyone is involved.

The importance of *SportsWorld* is that it provides a filter, albeit a contestable one, with which to view the relationship of sport to society; for Lipsyte, the relationship is, sadly, too close and too pervasive to allow sport to be the emancipating experience of the majority. Instead, sport enslaves both the majority of us who watch, and the minority who play.

Despite the above, Lipsyte is no Malthus announcing eventual doom, and he is certainly no Jeremiah pining for a lost world of innocence. A superb writer and a fine storyteller, Lipsyte brings us face to face with the reality of a world in which we worship the powerful and worthy god of sport, but for the all wrong reasons.

Lorenz, Konrad. **On Aggression.** Translated by Marjorie Kerr Wilson. New York: Hartcourt, Brace, and World, 1966.

Lorenz, an ethnologist, created a small academic revolution with this work, in which he concluded, along with several other concepts, that violent inclinations are worked out both in playing and in watching sports; the player and the observer experience a release of tension which would otherwise be expressed in a less socially acceptable way.

There is little accumulated evidence that Lorenz was correct about this. On the contrary, there is legitimate concern that sports actually encourage antisocial behavior on the part of the players, and there is clear evidence that such unacceptable behaviors as wife-beating actually increase among observers (including television viewers) following major sporting events such as championship boxing matches or major football games. Although no longer considered viable, Lorenz's conception of the positive effect of violence in sport was partly responsible for the acceptance of inappropriate violence on the field in exchange for a theoretical calm elsewhere.

Lucas, John A. **Future of the Olympic Games.** Foreword by Juan Antonio Samaranch. Champaign, IL: Human Kinetics Books, 1992. ISBN 0-87322-357-8.

This is an impressively clear explication of the current and past status of the modern Olympic Movement, and an attempt at foreseeing how, and how well, the Olympics moves into the twenty-first century. Despite the appreciative foreword by Samaranch, Lucas is generally objective and does not hesitate to criticize where criticism is deserved.

Among the many issues that Lucas cites as crying out for resolution are nationalism in the Olympics, drug use, racism, and the role of the Olympics in world politics. Each topic is reviewed with care, and Lucas then proceeds to make several recommendations, many of which make sense though the possibility of implementation may be doubted.

In contradiction to the common perception that the Olympics are a bastion of conservatism, Lucas demonstrates that the games have changed, sometimes creating new problems to replace those the changes ameliorated. The abundance of new sports and athletic contests clamoring for admission, for example, came about because the IOC wanted to keep the events current, and wanted the Olympics to reflect the real world. There are now so many claims to entrance, however, that by 1992 even "demonstration sports" had been eliminated, and Lucas proposes that the number of events be further reduced by eliminating repetitive events in every area (such as the 40 only slightly dissimilar swimming competitions).

Miller, Marvin. **A Whole Different Ballgame: The Sport and Business of Baseball.** Secaucus, NJ: Carol Publishing Group, 1991. 1-55972-067-0.

The first executive director of the Professional Baseball Players' Association provides an amazing story of the conditions of major league player-owner relations when he was first recruited to revivify the players' association cum union in 1974. Miller built the association into a creditable union, and was responsible for many of the achievements in the 1970s and 1980s.

Conditions for ballplayers in the mid-1970s were primitive—there were no collective bargaining, free agency, salary arbitration, or protection against vindictive or wrong-headed owners. Miller saw, correctly, that baseball needed to be brought into the twentieth century. He recognized that the commissioner was not the head of all baseball, despite his public image, but an employee of the owners. He saw clearly that baseball was a business, conducted on the owner's behalf, and not for the benefit of either the players or the fans. He recognized that formalizing the owner-player relationship could, in the long run, benefit both parties.

One expects a representative of labor to be tough on management, and it's difficult to fault Miller for noting that no owner was ever punished for being a partner to collusion during the three-year period when no ball club even tried to bid on a free-agent player. Similarly, Miller may well be on the mark in concluding that George Steinbrenner was outside the "inner circle" of owners and could safely be disciplined for "consorting with a known gambler."

Understandably, Miller is at his best in describing events that he was involved in. His evaluations of owner-commissioner relations, however, though they have the ring of truth to them, push themselves into the realm of opinion. Enhanced by the tale of how poorly ethical considerations have been served by baseball's owners, who piously claim brotherhood with baseball's fans and paying customers while putting the screws to players, Miller's book is a gem as a business case-study, describing how he took advantage of obvious (to him) failings in the system with which he was hired to deal.

Rader, Benjamin G. **In Its Own Image: How Television Has Transformed Sport.** New York: Macmillan and Co., The Free Press, 1984. ISBN 0-02-925700-X.

Rader describes in careful detail the relationship of the American sports world with the media, specifically television. While professional sports have always made an effort to sell themselves to the public through available media, Rader traces the major upheavals in sports and our attitudes toward sports that television has brought (such as rule changes in professional football and the idea of a "sudden death overtime," which Rader asserts was created to satisfy the demands of the television audience for a conclusion to games that otherwise might have ended in ties).

As important as the changes in the way sports are played are those in the public perception of sport. Rader points out that, because professional-quality sports are now so available, our expectations of youth and amateur-level sports have increased:

> Television and the nationalization of sports aroused expectations among fans of seeing only the best.... Consequently, televised sports diminished the significance of, or completely destroyed, sports at the grass-roots level. Hence, the death of minor-league baseball, of semi-pro baseball, and of local fight clubs. Except for a few remote areas such as west Texas, attendance and interest in high-school sports sank to all-time lows.

Though it is arguable that the availability of professional perfection has led directly to the downfall of local sports, Rader is surely correct that we do expect more of our less than top-level athletes, including participants in youth leagues who would prefer to enjoy the challenge of the game they are playing rather than emulate their professional elders.

Reston, James, Jr. **Collision at Home Plate: The Lives of Pete Rose and Bart Giamatti.** New York: HarperCollins, HarperPerennial, 1992. ISBN 0-06-098115-6.

Reston paints convincing portraits of the two men who were involved in what well may be the archetypal clash between an enforcer of ethics and a violator. Giamatti, an eminent academic with a taste for Renaissance ideals, saw baseball as a modern example of an institution where fairness and ethics made for a fascinating contest between equals. Rose, a player who never felt he was a natural athlete, worked long and hard at his success, and believed in harvesting its fruits.

As Rose's career began to ebb, but before he had reached his goal of surpassing Ty Cobb's record of lifetime hits, Rose began to gamble and became, at least tangentially, involved in the drug underworld. That Rose had gone wrong cannot be doubted; he spent time in jail as a result of tax evasion convictions and, by his own confession, had gambled heavily. Reston's account of the investigation that led Giamatti to suspend Rose indefinitely from baseball, and the disorganized way the investigation was followed up, suggests that someone other than the idealistic Giamatti might have handled the Rose affair in a more pragmatic, less torturous way.

Rose's career was tarnished because of his gambling and his drug involvement; he agreed to a suspension that did not accuse him of betting on baseball. Though Giamatti told a press conference that he was certain Rose had bet on baseball, the investigation had not been able to provide proof. Giamatti died of a heart attack shortly after expelling Rose from organized baseball, and Reston is among those who believe the strain of the Rose affair was at least partly responsible. This is a careful examination of an important, reverberating event by an objective and interested observer.

Sparhawk, Ruth, et al. **American Women in Sport, 1887–1987: A 100-Year Chronology.** Metuchen, NJ: Scarecrow Press, 1989. ISBN 0-8108-2205-9.

In this important contribution to the history of women in sports, Sparhawk and her associates demonstrate that, despite prejudices which continue to this day, some women have managed to participate and achieve in organized sports to a degree that the casual observer would not recognize. Though primarily a list of achievers, many of the items presented are amplified with brief facts and quotes that give meaning and color to what could be a bare recital of facts:

> Babe Didrikson Zaharias is the first woman to win over $15,000 in golf. She is selected Woman Golfer of the Year by the LPGA and Woman Athlete of the Year by the Associated Press. Because she also excels at swimming, diving, baseball, basketball, bowling, and track, a sportswriter asks, "Is there anything you don't play?" "Yeah," Babe replies. "Dolls."

Sperber, Murray. **College Sports Inc.: The Athletic Department vs. The University.** New York: Henry Holt and Company, 1990. ISBN 0-8050-1445-4.

Murray Sperber, a former sportswriter, is now a professor of English and American studies with an interest in popular culture. In this heavily researched, well-annotated book, Sperber holds that the prevailing values of college athletics are inimical to the educational missions of the schools that sponsor them. Sperber concludes that, unlike other college activities, sports are meant to provide entertainment to the outside world as well as the college community, and are not an educational experience. In fact, Sperber shows that despite the large amounts of money involved in college sports (especially television contracts), few colleges have athletic programs that operate profitably; most athletic programs are a drain on most colleges' general funds. Sperber observes that both salaries and opportunities for additional gains make athletic directors, coaches, and other members of athletic departments highly overpaid and, not incidentally, more powerful than other members of the college community.

Echoing many in the college sports world who see the National Collegiate Athletic Association (NCAA) as out of control and damaging to college athletics, Sperber views the NCAA as a monopolistic organization functioning in almost the same way as a trade association.

Umphlett, Wiley Lee, ed. **American Sport Culture: The Humanistic Dimension.** Lewisburg, PA: Bucknell University Press, 1985. ISBN 0-8387-5070-2.

This is an impressive collection of academic articles, several of which have been published earlier. The focus of the collection is the relationship, both good and bad, of sports to the rest of society. It is most useful in disclosing the varied and fruitful approaches to sport that the academic world can take, ranging from an analysis of the role of sports in literature to a discussion of the role of women in sports as strenuous as football.

Many of the articles in this anthology are exceptional for their clarity. Allen Sack's "The Amateur Myth: The Rights and Responsibilities of College Athletes," for example, is a crystal-clear exposition of the degree to which college athletes are not amateurs playing genteel games in their spare time (as the college establishment seems to want us to believe). Sack demonstrates that many college athletes are professionals in every sense of the word—hired and paid (albeit poorly) by schools to enhance revenues. Jeffrey H. Goldstein's "Athletic Performance and Spectator Behavior: The Humanistic Concerns of Sports Psychology" will serve the reader as a wide-ranging and intelligent, although somewhat cynical, introduction to the new field of sports psychology.

Voy, Dr. Robert O., with Kirk D. Deeter. **Drugs, Sport, & Politics.** Champaign, IL: Leisure Press, 1991. ISBN 0-88011-409-6.

Voy was appointed the chief medical officer of the USOC in 1984, and a year later also became its director of sports medicine and science. He resigned in 1989, and this book reflects his frustration in those offices with the state of drug testing and enforcement. Voy claims that not only do many top athletes take drugs, but also that the USOC and other national Olympic committees either look the other way or refuse to install adequate drug-testing procedures. The huge amount of money involved in the Olympics (including future athlete endorsements) makes it very difficult, according to Voy, for scandalous conditions to be exposed and corrected; it's just too costly.

In addition to discussing the current (as of 1991) state of drugs and amateur athletics, Voy provides accurate information about specific drugs and their effects, and drug-testing procedures.

In a final two-chapter section, "Prescription for Reform," Voy outlines what he feels is necessary to keep amateur athletics drug-free and restore the public image of the games. Among his recommendations are the establishment of an independent drug-testing organization (separate from amateur sport federations and Olympic committees), and the limiting of sponsorships so that no company can make such a huge investment that it becomes a marketing opportunity that must be protected against scandal. Additionally, Voy concludes that the "gold-medal mentality," both on an individual and national level, leads to a "win-at-any-cost" type of thinking that needs to be done away with in order for amateur athletes to truly function as amateurs.

Wolff, Rick. **Good Sports: A Concerned Parent's Guide to Little League and Other Competitive Youth Sports.** New York: Dell, 1993. ISBN 0-440-50435-X.

Anyone with an interest in organized youth sports should read this book at least once a year. Wolff is a former professional baseball player and college coach who is now a sports psychologist. *Good Sports* sets out in clear, interesting, and incisive language what the challenges, rewards, and drawbacks of youth sports competition are for everyone involved— the child, the parent, and the coach.

Beginning with a challenge to the adult to understand what he or she wants a child to get from youth sports, Wolff makes it clear that organized sports are as important as almost any other activity in which a child can be involved. Wolff is careful to point out repeatedly that adults may have different agendas than children. Some parents might even feel that Wolff is suggesting they abdicate their leadership position in the family, to which Wolff would probably reply that these parents are asking children to spend an inordinate amount of time doing something the parent wants, but that the child feels is a waste of valuable free time. Dealing with gung-ho parents is one of the many problems that he addresses.

Regardless of a parent's knowledge of sport skill, Wolff urges parents to become involved with the organization in one way or the other. Coaches, he points out, don't need to be expert ballplayers; instead, they need to be adults who can understand and work with children, teaching all members of the team how to enjoy sports.

Yaeger, Don. **Undue Process: The NCAA's Injustice for All.** Foreword by Dale Brown. Champaign, IL: Sagamore Publishing, 1991. ISBN 0-915611-34-1.

As the NCAA has become larger and more powerful, especially since the 1950s, the college athletic community has become uncomfortable with the association and its enforcement activities. More than a vocal minority claim that the NCAA has become too powerful, too inefficient, and too bureaucratic to do its job. Worse, NCAA investigative methods are startlingly oppressive. Interviews with those connected with an investigation are reported to the home office only via the investigator's memo; tape recording, stenography, or video recording are simply not allowed. Schools being investigated have little opportunity to disagree with an investigator's recollections, even when it can be proven that his memoranda are incorrect.

Yaeger stresses that the only way to deal with the NCAA is to respond as aggressively as possible to even the hint of an investigation. He is not hopeful, even then, about a school's ability to withstand an NCAA attack: "Universities don't survive NCAA investigations. They endure them." Yaeger paints a picture of a bureaucracy that flatly refuses to correct its own mistakes, and which has overwhelmed its members with enough rules and regulations to make absolute compliance impossible. Yaeger's research depends heavily on interviews with NCAA officials, athletes, and coaches. The story is a fascinating one, and Yaeger's writing is easy to follow. While the list of schools that have been slapped with NCAA violations is a useful appendix to the book, an index, notes, and a bibliography would have been very welcome.

Sports Ethics in Fiction

American sports have long been considered a metaphor for society as a whole; what happens on the field, theoretically, can and does happen in real life. There is a long tradition of sports literature and drama that makes use of this metaphor. In addition, there are many recent works that focus on sports or sports heroes as the centers of attention. As a genre, sports literature occasionally rises to a level of quality that matches the best of other literature; Bernard Malamud's *The Natural* is, perhaps, the best example.

The works listed below are a selected, small portion of the sports-literature genre. Short stories, of which there are many, have been omitted; the reader with interests in short stories is urged to pursue the entries in Grant Burns' *The Sports Pages: A Critical Bibliography of Twentieth-Century American Novels and Stories Featuring Baseball, Basketball, Football, and Other Athletic Pursuits* (Metuchen, NJ: Scarecrow Press, 1987). Burns' work is extensive and informative, and well worth a careful examination by anyone bent on locating the best American literary works dealing with sports. In addition, there are several other worthwhile summaries of sports' role in the arts, including Peter Bjarkman's *The Immortal Diamond*, Don Johnson's *Hummers, Knucklers, and Slow Curves* (1991), Jerome Klinkowitz' *Writing Baseball* (1991), and Andy McCue's *Baseball by the Books* (1990). Although baseball is the one sport about which the most has been written, there is fine material to be found involving almost all sports.

Novels

Deford, Frank. **Everybody's All-American.** New York: Viking, 1981. ISBN 0-670-30035-7.

This is the tale of a college football hero who finds that life in the professional ranks, and life after football, isn't nearly the same world that it had been when he was in school. While our hero is proud of what he has done, he is unable to make the transition from college to living in the present. An excellent and memorable book, this is one of the few novels dealing with the world of football and its tenuous interaction with the world outside the stadium.

DeLillio, Don. **End Zone.** New York: Houghton Mifflin, 1972. ISBN 0-14-008568-8.

A stark, strong work, *End Zone* portrays the attempt of its main character, Gary Harkness, to stave off his obsession with the real threat of nuclear annihilation by engaging in the violence of football. While football seems an escape at the beginning, it eventually merges with the reality of violence everywhere else; there is finally no escape from the danger of destruction. The action takes place in a college town named Logos, suggesting the opening of the Gospel of Matthew, and thus implying that the town is both the beginning and the end of all things: "In the beginning was the Logos . . ."

Foster, Alan S. **Goodbye, Bobby Thomson! Goodbye, John Wayne.** Englewood Cliffs, NJ: Simon and Schuster, 1973.

Baseball and football are seen, at the beginning, as refuges from the violence of the world, emphasized by the death of the narrator's brother in the Korean War. The narrator, Pete, fails to join the army and winds up taking a professional football position with the Cleveland Browns. Following an injury, Pete does join the Army, then resumes his career in football. By the end of the book, sports have become a mirror for the violence in our society, rather than a refuge or a better world.

Gent, Peter. **North Dallas Forty.** New York: Morrow, 1973. ISBN 0-451-169034.

This is a close, careful, and sometimes naturalistic look into the violence and pressures of a professional football player, written by a former offensive end for the Dallas Cowboys. Although the narrator of the novel, Phillip "Phil" Elliott, does gain some insight into his life and the life of the other professionals around him, the book is meant as a fictionalized exposé of a world in which most of the athletes have no concept of what they are doing to themselves, or having done to them. Theirs is a drug-filled world: off the field, players are continually drinking or taking drugs for a variety of reasons, not the least of which is their near-total absence of a sense of reality anywhere but on the football field. And, more importantly, that attitude is fostered by the management— players are kept on regimens of pain-killers and steroids only so they can continue their on-field exploits.

Few sports books have so dramatically pictured the grindingly oppressive world of the professional football player as well as *North Dallas Forty*. Though Gent can be accused of occasional melodrama, some touches of bad writing here and there, and, one hopes, a cynical vision of a drug-filled universe, the book deserves its reputation as a major view of modern professional sports. The book was successfully turned into a motion picture in 1979.

Greenberg, Eric R. **The Celebrant.** New York: Everest House, 1983. ISBN 0-803-27037-2.

Possibly one of the finest sports books ever written. Evocative of the early twentieth century, the book features a well-researched Christy Mathewson, whose observations into the ethical role of baseball and the damage that the "Black Sox" scandal caused transport the reader to another era. Mathewson is resolved to repair the damage caused by the scandal.

Harris, Mark. **Bang the Drum Slowly, by Henry W. Wiggen.** Lincoln: University of Nebraska Press. ISBN 0-8032-7221-9.

Originally published in 1956, this is Harris's most celebrated novel. Baseball catcher Bruce Pearson learns to face death and, in the process, teaches his teammates to live their best at all times with the knowledge that they too, like all men, must die. Supposedly written by Wiggen, another ballplayer who is bound by contract to Pearson, this is a fine book, though its theme makes it more about life and death than specifically about baseball.

Hays, Donald. **The Dixie Association.** New York: Simon & Schuster, 1984. ISBN 0-671-47564-9.

This excellent novel contrasts the freedom of being a baseball player with the confinement of living under state rule. The hero, Hog, leaves a prison where he has served time for armed robbery, and joins the Arkansas Reds, a team in the Dixie Association baseball league. Almost always at odds with the authorities, Hog insists on playing ball, even though society wants him to conform by doing what is prescribed for him; his parole officer had arranged for Hog to drive a library bookmobile, and is not pleased when Hog determines to play ball instead. With exquisite attention to both baseball and the novel's theme, this is an important book that can be enjoyed both by sports fans and by readers with no conception of the pleasures of being in charge of one's own life by participating in the national game.

Kahn, Roger. **The Seventh Game.** New York: New American Library, 1982. ISBN 0-451-12120-1.

A superb baseball story detailing, through flashbacks, the life of aging pitcher Johnny Longboat. A fast-fading superstar, Johnny relives his life during the period of one very, very important game, interspersed with the tales that make him an important and sympathetic character to the reader.

Kinsella, W. P. **Shoeless Joe.** New York: Houghton Mifflin, 1982. ISBN 0-395-32047X

This novel sumptuously reflects the utopian longing for a pure, pristine world dominated by an Eden-like baseball—played according to the rules and filled only with heroes. The book is better than the 1991 movie, *Field of Dreams*. An Iowa farmer, Ray Kinsella hears a mysterious voice telling him to rip out his corn crop and build a ball field: "If you build it they will come." When the field is built, the farmer's favorite legendary players appear, including the disgraced members of the "Black Sox," led by "Shoeless" Joe Jackson. The farmer sees out other frustrated hopes from his past, including a moving reconciliation with his father.

The movie follows the book closely, although some of the subtle humor of the written word is missing. A good part of both is the farmer's successful "kidnapping" and reintegration into society of a famous but reclusive writer now living in the Northeast. In the movie he is nameless; in the book, the writer is J. D. Salinger (who better to pull out of reclusion?). Like Salinger, Kinsella also depicts a romantic quest for a lost, innocent childhood.

————. **The Iowa Baseball Confederacy.** New York: Houghton Mifflin, 1986. ISBN 0-395-389526.

Written after the fabulous *Shoeless Joe,* this book exhibits many of the rich, fantasy-ridden stylistic traits of the earlier book. A league that no one remembers having played in Iowa is discovered by Matthew Clarke and his son, Gideon. Clarke's knowledge comes from almost divine revelation after being struck by lightning; Gideon and his brother, Stan, slip through a crack in time to find a game that has gone on for hundreds of innings, manipulated by an Indian named Drifting Away. Though not quite as well executed as *Shoeless Joe,* this book will be a delight for those who enjoy Kinsella's rich taste for exquisite imagery and extraordinary fantasy. Those who keep returning to the dessert cart of literature will find this novel a rich reward.

Lardner, Ring. **You Know Me Al: A Busher's Letters.** New York: Scribner's, 1925.

An American classic, *You Know Me Al* is a humorous, epistolary novel that combines a realistic view of the baseball world of the early twentieth century with an exaggerated main character, Jack Keefe. Keefe's letters to his hometown friend/business manager, Al, reveal an incredible egotism and an ability to always blame others for failure and difficulties in life. Keefe's inability to see himself as anything but the center of the universe leads to the destruction of his baseball career, leaving his life in shambles.

Lardner was one of sports writing's nobility. Though the baseball world he described has changed in certain aspects, his picture of the overweeningly confident athlete will be familiar to even casual readers of the sports pages.

Malamud, Bernard. **The Natural.** New York: Farrar Straus Giroux, 1952. ISBN 0-38-0506092.

A superb book; with baseball as the background, Malamud tells the story of Roy Hobbs (i.e., "hobbled king") who begins his career attempting to be the best. His impressive talents land him and his team in the World Series. Agreeing to throw a game, Hobbs has second thoughts at the last moment, and heroically continues to do his best. Unable to recover the lost game, and destroying his favorite bat in the process, Hobbs finds redemption in his noble actions. A clear recapitulation of the Arthurian grail legend, this was Malamud's first book, and gave him immediate status as a serious novelist.

The book was made into an excellent movie in 1984, starring Robert Redford, although the ending was changed—Hobbs wins the ball game.

Nemerov, Howard. **The Homecoming Game.** Columbia: University of Missouri Press, 1992. ISBN 0-826-20870-3.

Originally published in 1957, this is an interesting novel, if only because of the author's prestige as one of America's finest poets. *The Homecoming Game* tells the story of a college professor, Charles Osman, who flunks a star player on the football team. When Osman agrees to let the student, Raymond Bient, take the test again, he finds out that Bient has purposely failed the test the first time to avoid a commitment he has made to throw the big game. Sport is as real, and as threatening, as life.

Shainberg, Lawrence. **One on One.** New York: Holt, Rinehart & Winston, 1979.

A complicated and marvelous book about a character named Elwood Baskin, a former NBA star, who comes to seek a Zen-like perfection both in his game and in a new type of shot, which changes not only his way of playing but also himself. In seeking perfection, Baskin withdraws from all around him; he focuses solely on the relationship between himself and the ball, the one thing that matters to him. Grant Burns asserts that *One on One* "is . . . perhaps, the best piece of fiction about basketball ever written."

Stein, Harry. **Hoopla.** New York: Knopf, 1983.

Focusing on the "Black Sox" scandal of 1919, this novel weaves a story from the special problems and dilemmas faced by those who played for White Sox owner Charles Comiskey. The players, including "Shoeless" Joe Jackson, are made into fully realized, generally sympathetic characters. The "Black Sox" herein are not just a bunch of evil-doing ballplayers—they are real people, struggling with real problems, and trying to make the best decisions on their way through real life.

Wallop, Douglas. **The Year The Yankees Lost the Pennant.** New York: W. W. Norton, 1954.

A lighthearted, affectionate version of the Faust legend, set against the backdrop of baseball. Joe Boyd becomes the youthful superstar, Joe Hardy, and, like the original Faust, learns that there are some trade-offs in life that shouldn't be made. This is easy reading in the best sense of the phrase. As a significant retelling of the classic Faust story, it doesn't have a chance. As a pleasant baseball tale making use of a literary vehicle, it's a pleasure. It was even more enjoyable and popular as the Broadway musical *Damn Yankees,* and as a movie of the same name.

Williams, John A. **The Junior Bachelor Society.** Garden City, NY: Doubleday, 1976.

This is the excellent story of Chappie Davis, an aging former coach of high-school and college athletes. His former students have formed an alumni society, and plan to throw a testimonial dinner for Davis' seventieth birthday.

By tracing the careers of his former athletes through Davis' mind, the postgraduate lives of black high-school and college stars are disclosed. A well-written, appealing, and ultimately sad story, this is an excellent novel with broad appeal.

Movies and Plays

Amazing Grace and Chuck

Type:	VHS, Beta
Length:	115 mins.
Date:	1987
Cost:	$19.99
Source:	HBO Home Video

Directed by Mike Newell. Starring Jamie Lee Curtis, Alex English, Gregory Peck, William L. Petersen, Joshua Zuehlke, Dennis Lipscomb, and Lee Richardson.

A 12 year-old little league star decides to stop playing baseball until the nations of the world agree to do without nuclear weapons. This novel idea is so persuasive that soon adult, professional sports figures join in the sports boycott. Enough people were able to "suspend disbelief" to make this movie a reasonable success in 1987.

The Babe

Type:	VHS
Length:	115 mins.

Date: 1992
Cost: $19.98
Source: MCA/Universal Home Video

Is it possible to be accurate when retelling a legend? This movie seems to do just that. Like Babe Ruth in real life, actor John Goodman is always the center of attention when he's on screen. Ruth was a complicated jumble of contradictory urges and actions— irascible, impulsive, lovable, loud, crude, demanding, voracious, and charming. Goodman's insightful characterization is nearly as great as the original Babe had to be.

Bad News Bears

Type: VHS, Beta
Length: 102 mins.
Date: 1976
Cost: $14.95
Source: Paramount Home Video

Directed by Michael Ritchie. Starring Walter Matthau, Tatum O'Neal, Vic Morrow, and others.

An enjoyable though lightweight comedy that has remained popular among video renters, the film tells the story of the boys on a youth baseball team who consistently lose. Their luck changes when they acquire a new coach, played by Walter Matthau, and a girl pitcher with a powerful arm. Matthau's characterization of the gruff coach, and O'Neal's interpretation of the pitcher, Amanda, are effective. Twelve-year olds are capable of being both cute and funny, and the young players here are no exception. The cute and funny push out any sincerity about whether the boys can follow a girl as team leader, or how they relate to a decidedly unchildish coach.

This film is a passable entertainment if it comes your way in a video store, library, or rerun television. It may not be worth going out of your way to find.

Bang the Drum Slowly

Type: VHS, Beta
Length: 97 mins.
Date: 1973
Cost: $14.95
Source: Paramount Home Video, Facets Multimedia

Directed by John Hancock. Starring Robert DeNiro, Michael Moriarty, and Vincent Gardenia. (See Harris, Mark, page 184 for annotation.)

The Bear

Type: not available on video
Date: 1984

Cost: n.a.
Source: n.a.

Starring Gary Busey and Harry Dean Stanton.

An idealized biography of University of Alabama football coach Paul "Bear" Bryant. This is a "regional" movie (one made specifically to be shown outside of New York and Los Angeles). Allen Barra believes that the movie "may not have been seen by a single ticket buyer north of the Mason Dixon line." As of mid-1994, it was not available on video.

Bingo Long Traveling All-Stars and Motor Kings
Type: VHS, Beta
Length: 111 mins.
Date: 1976
Cost: $49.95
Source: MCA/Universal Home Video, Facets Multimedia

Directed by John Badham. Starring James Earl Jones, Billy Dee Williams and Richard Pryor.

The story of barnstorming baseball veterans of the 1930's Negro League.

Blue Chips
Type: not available on video
Date: 1994
Cost: n.a.
Source: n.a.

Directed by William Friedkin, this film stars Nick Nolte as Pete Bell, a college basketball coach who, despite his efforts to win with the talent he has available, eventually decides that he has to recruit heavily among high-school players. In his odyssey, Bell finds that the corrupt recruiting practices that the NCAA has banned are very much alive; high-school players expect a serious recruiter to consider buying a house for the recruit's mother, or paying several thousand dollars in cash as a "signing bonus." The film is filled with fast-moving, realistic basketball action, generated by actual college athletes and by Nolte's costar, basketball superstar Shaquille O'Neal.

Bull Durham
Type: VHS, Beta
Length: 107 mins.
Date: 1988
Cost: $19.98
Source: Orion Home Video, Home Vision Cinema

Directed by Ron Shelton. Starring Kevin Kostner, Susan Sarandon, and Tim Robbins.

A well-drawn 1988 movie, stolen by Susan Sarandon as Annie Savoy, an aging baseball groupie. She's everything a ballplayer could want in a fan, and more. "I believe in the Church of Baseball," she says at the beginning of the movie, "the only church that truly feeds the soul, day in, day out, is the Church of Baseball." Each year, Annie chooses another minor-league baseball player to sleep with, and everyone that she has ever chosen has gone on to the big leagues. Problems develop when she takes up with an aging player on his way down, Crash Davis, played by Kevin Kostner.

Janet Maslin's comments about the movie in the *New York Times* are accurate; the movie is about

> the roguishness of the players, the overripe poetry in their souls (and in their conversations), the specialness that lets them live outside life's usual rules. This last conceit is an awfully lucky one, since the Susan Sarandon character—the baseball angel who lives for the game, is a big help at batting practice, and obligingly works sex into her training program for new players—would undoubtedly be stoned to death if she ever interacted with anyone other than ballplayers. (11 September 1988)

Chariots of Fire
Type: VHS, Beta
Length: 123 mins.
Date: 1981
Cost: $19.98
Source: Warner Home Video, Facets Multimedia,
             Baker & Taylor Video

Directed by Hugh Hudson. Starring Ben Cross, Ian Charleson, Nigel Havers, Nicholas Farrell, and Ian Holm.

This is a richly textured, poetic film, based on a true story, which is far better seen than read about. The two protagonists, Harold Abrahams and Eric Liddell, train for and conquer the difficulties of Olympic track running in 1924. On their hard-won way to success, the viewer sees the force of ambition and hunger for success, fame, and social recognition handled carefully and with aplomb by the protagonists. Perhaps because the subject is track, a sport in which the challenge is so much a matter of contesting one's own abilities as well as contesting the skills of an opponent, success depends greatly upon bending one's personality to the achievement of a physical goal.

Damn Yankees
Type: VHS, Beta
Length: 110 mins.
Date: 1958

Cost: $19.98
Source: Warner Home Video, Facets Multimedia,
            Home Vision Cinema

Directed by George Abbott. Starring Stanley Donen, Gwen Verdon, Ray Walston, and Tab Hunter. (See Wallop, Douglas, page 187 for annotation.)

Eight Men Out

Type: VHS, Beta
Length: 121 mins.
Date: 1988
Cost: $9.98
Source: Orion Home Video, Facets Multimedia

Directed by John Sayles. Starring Charlie Sheen, D.B. Sweeney, Christopher Lloyd, John Cusack, Clifton James, and Michael Lerner.

A fascinating look at the world of early-twentieth-century baseball, this drama recounts the "Black Sox" scandal of 1919.

Fear Strikes Out

Type: VHS, Beta
Length: 100 mins.
Date: 1957
Cost: $14.95
Source: Paramount Home Video

Directed by Robert Mulligan. Starring Anthony Perkins, Karl Malden, Norma Moore, and Adam Williams.

A fictionalized biography which describes how the pressures of big-league play contributed to the nervous breakdown of Boston Red Sox pitcher Jim Piersall.

Freshman

Type: VHS, Beta
Length: 75 mins.
Date: 1925
Cost: n.a.
Source: Time-Life Video and Television

Directed by Harold Lloyd. Starring Harold Lloyd, Jobyna Ralston, and Brooks Benedict.

A Harold Lloyd comedy about football that might have been the decade's highest grossing comedy. The ending football game is used in the opening of Preston Sturges's *The Sin of Harold Diddlebock* (1946), a paean to Lloyd.

Hoosiers

Type: VHS, Beta
Length: 115 mins.
Date: 1986
Cost: $14.95
Source: Live Home Video

Directed by David Anspaugh. Starring Gene Hackman, Barbara Hershey, and Dennis Hopper.

A solid basketball story as well as an inspiring one. A failing college coach gets his last chance to win by leading a high-school team to victory.

Horse Feathers

Type: VHS, Beta
Length: 67 mins.
Date: 1932
Cost: $14.98
Source: MCA/Universal Home Video

Directed by Norman McLeod. Starring the Marx brothers, Thelma Todd, David Landau, and Robert Greig.

The film concludes with a hilarious football game, Darwin v. Huxley, with Chico Marx as a quarterback. It opens with Groucho Marx as college dean John Quincy Wagstaff asking, "Do we have a university? Do we have a football stadium? Well, we can't afford both. Tomorrow we start tearing down the university."

Knute Rockne, All American

Type: VHS, Beta
Length: 96 mins.
Date: 1940
Cost: $19.98
Source: MGM/UA Home Video, Family Home Entertainment

Directed by Lloyd Bacon. With Pat O'Brien as the Notre Dame coach, Ronald Reagan as George Gipp, Gale Page, and Donald Crisp.

This is the most famous of a group of films espousing the unity of family, teamwork, loyalty to the college, and football. It presents a world in which football builds character, or brings out the best in its players.

A League of Their Own

Type: VHS, Beta
Length: 127 mins.
Date: 1992

Cost: $19.95
Source: Columbia Tristar Home Video

Directed by Penny Marshall. Starring Tom Hanks, Geena Davis, Madonna, Lori Petty, Jon Lovitz, David Strathairn, Garry Marshall, and Bill Pullman.

A superb fictionalized account of the Women's Professional Baseball League that flourished during 1943–1953. With many men baseball players away during World War II, an entrepreneur forms a "girls' league." What begins as an exhibition that comes close to being a carnival sideshow turns into serious baseball as the women demonstrate that they can play quality baseball.

The relationships between the players, and especially between two sisters, show the difference in the way these ballplayers approached the game. They are as competitive as men, but much more caring about each other.

Major League
Type: VHS, Beta
Length: 107 mins.
Date: 1989
Cost: $14.95
Source: Paramount Home Video

Directed by David S. Ward. Starring Tom Berenger, Charlie Sheen, Corbin Bernsen, and Margaret Whitton.

A baseball comedy. What has to be the world's worst professional team finally pulls itself together in order to prevent the owner from moving the team to Florida. It reinforces the concept that winning games is much more a matter of trying hard and believing in yourself than in innate skill. All the cliché characters are here: the aging, cranky manager, the aging players desperate to stay in the game, the superstitious home-run hitter, the juvenile-delinquent pitcher with a heart of gold, and more. The movie doesn't take itself too seriously, which is all for the best. This is unpretentious, pleasant entertainment that succeeds.

The Natural
Type: VHS, Beta
Length: 134 mins.
Date: 1984
Cost: $14.95
Source: Columbia Tristar Home Video

Directed by Barry Levinson. Starring Robert Redford, Robert Duvall, Glenn Close, Kim Basinger, and Barbara Hershey. (See Malamud, Bernard, page 186 for annotation.)

The Pride of the Yankees

Type: VHS, Beta
Length: 128 mins.
Date: 1942
Cost: $19.98
Source: CBS/Fox Video

Directed by Sam Wood. Starring Gary Cooper, Teresa Wright, Babe Ruth, and Walter Brennan.

With Gary Cooper miscast as Lou Gehrig, the baseball great known as "The Iron Horse," this is a melodramatic, overdone, sentimental charmer that's loved almost as much for its faults as for its subject. The kicker is that Gehrig may well have been the charmer this movie makes him out to be.

Best seen in the company of a preadolescent the night before Little League practice begins, this is the story of the American sports hero as we want him to be, and as, perhaps, he can be.

Requiem for a Heavyweight

Type: not available on video
Date: 1962
Cost: n.a.
Source: n.a.

Directed by Ralph Nelson. Starring Anthony Quinn, Jackie Gleason, Mickey Rooney, Julie Harris, Nancy Cushman, Madame Spivy, and Cassius Clay (now Muhammad Ali).

A classic film, adapted by Rod Serling from a play originally produced on television. The hero is able to maintain his integrity in the dirty world of professional boxing while he is active. After retirement he simply doesn't have the resources to fight back.

Whether seen as a metaphor for an inevitable grinding down administered by life, the ultimate opponent, or seen as a parable of only the fight business, this is a superb story that brings out the best in the actors and challenges the minds of its viewers.

Rocky (series)

Type: VHS, Beta
Length: 125 mins.
Date: 1976
Cost: $14.95
Source: MGM/UA Home Video, CBS/Fox Video, Baker & Taylor Video

Directed by Sylvester Stallone. Starring Sylvester Stallone and Talia Shire. 1976–1990.

The first of five "Rocky" movies, detailing the career of Rocky Balboa, a salt-of-the-earth, not-too-smart man with iron fists, a heart of gold, and a girlfriend (later wife) who learns that Rocky was born to bleed. There's lots of fight action and some insightful characterizations; Stallone's Rocky is a romantic who, despite his many rough edges and ability to function in a cold, heartless environment, never loses his warm and fuzzy inner self. But the message that all it takes for the average Joe to win is lots of heart gets weary by the end of the first movie; by the fourth sequel, Stallone's sincerity is more than tiresome.

Written by Stallone (the hero dies in the ring in the original writing), Stallone's and Shire's acting is generally acceptable, and even reaches some quality moments from time to time. The series is a good excuse to settle in with a couple of barrels of popcorn and feel that, no matter what, good conquers evil, and Rousseau's noble savage can still appear on the silver screen.

Rollerball
Type: VHS, Beta
Length: 123 mins.
Date: 1975
Cost: $14.95
Source: MGM/UA Home Video

Directed by Norman Jewison. Starring James Caan, John Hoseman, Maud Adams, John Beck, Moses Gunn, and Ralph Richardson.

In the twenty-first century, violence has been outlawed everywhere but in this hybrid sport of skating cum hockey sans a puck.

Jewison may not have known that he was exploring the ideas of Konrad Lorenz to a logical extreme; make sport violent enough, and society should be able to have zero violence outside the arena. As noted elsewhere, Lorenz was incorrect, and this film illustrates, among other things, that violence is not easily restricted to athletic events. After that realization becomes obvious, there is little to interest the viewer besides the technical merits of the direction and photography, and on-screen violence that's much better acted than the average professional wrestling match.

White Men Can't Jump
Type: VHS
Length: 115 mins.
Date: 1992
Cost: $19.98
Source: FoxVideo

Directed by Ron Shelton. Starring Woody Harrelson and Wesley Snipes.

A comedy that makes fun of racist conceptions that white men can't possibly play basketball as well as black men. A white con man teams with a black man to hustle pick-up basketball games in Los Angeles. This movie is not particularly challenging, but it's good fun to watch, and a reminder that racist attitudes can backlash.

Index